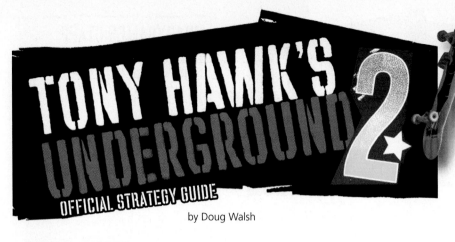

TONY HAWK'S UNDERGROUND 2

OFFICIAL STRATEGY GUIDE

by Doug Walsh

TABLE OF CONTENTS

INTRO

It's been one year since you climbed the ranks from local skate punk to world-renowned professional skater and, surprisingly, not much has changed. You're still skating the dumpster ramps in Jersey, still hanging out with your old friends, and it's actually quite relaxing. That whole "Pro Tour" thing wasn't all it's cracked up to be. Sure, the fame was nice, but living out of a suitcase, dealing with the endless tournaments, and putting up with the crazed fans got old in a hurry. Fortunately for you, Tony Hawk, Bam Margera, and a bunch of the other pros feel your pain and they have a plan for making tours fun again. It's called vandalism!

Tony Hawk's Underground 2 is not about skating in tournaments and pleasing sponsors. It's about traveling the world with a bunch of friends and partaking in a malicious contest to see who can prank the most people from Boston to Berlin and Barcelona to New Orleans. There will be plenty of skating, loads of partying, and some good-natured competition to sweeten the experience. The World Destruction Tour is going to take professional skating back underground and you get to witness it first-hand.

Back from the trip already? *Tony Hawk's Underground 2* isn't just about embarking on a crazy adventure with a bunch of skaters; there's also Classic Mode. Challenge yourself with 140 old-school goals from back in the days of *Tony Hawk's Pro Skater® 3*. The friendly two-minute timer is making a comeback, as are all the old standbys like Collect S-K-A-T-E, Get the Secret Tape, Get the Pro Score, and many more. Veterans of the series will no doubt welcome the chance to tackle today's enormous courses with the timer and newcomers will get a chance to experience the foundation of the series.

There's a ton of gameplay packed into *Tony Hawk's Underground 2* and this strategy guide is your blueprint for completing every goal, on every difficulty setting, for both modes of play. Additionally, tips and maps show how to find all of the 600+ gaps that have been crammed into the game's many courses. If you want to unlock all there is to get in this game, you need those maps! Whether you're new to the series looking for a step-by-step walkthrough or a seasoned veteran looking to learn how to perform the new tricks like the Natas Spin and Sticker Slap, you are covered. Enjoy the game, and keep on skating!

Intro

Skater Basics

Trick Lists

Story Mode

Gaps

Classic Mode

Multiskater

Secrets

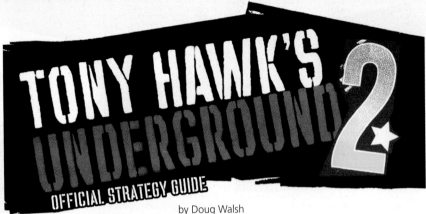

OFFICIAL STRATEGY GUIDE

by Doug Walsh

BradyGAMES® Publishing
An Imprint of Pearson Education
800 E. 96th Street
3rd Floor
Indianapolis, Indiana 46240

ISBN: 0-7440-0445-4
Library of Congress Catalog No.: 2004113349
Printing Code: *The rightmost double-digit number is the year of the book's printing; the rightmost single-digit number is the number of the book's printing. For example, 04-1 shows that the first printing of the book occurred in 2004.*

07 06 05 04   4 3 2 1
Manufactured in the United States of America.

AUTHOR ACKNOWLEDGMENTS

I'm very happy to be concluding my fourth strategy guide in this venerable series. Not just because of the great fun I've had exploring the intricacies of these games, but also because of the great people I get to work with each and every fall. Like the books that have come before this one, a lot of what they are is because of the hard work and dedication put forth by Ken Schmidt, my editor at BradyGames. It was great having you out here in the Pacific Northwest in August, I look forward to getting together with you again soon. I'd also like to acknowledge Leigh Davis and Mike Degler of BradyGames for having trusted me with this series for so long. I also want to thank our talented designers, Brent Gann and Bob Klunder, for making my pile of maps and text come together as a great looking book. Last but definitely not least, I owe tremendous thanks to Kevin Mulhall of Neversoft. He and his team can not only be counted on for making great games year in and year out, but for consistently going out of their way to accommodate me during the process of writing these guides. Your level of cooperation is astounding and I appreciate it a great deal. Till next year…

BradyGAMES would like to extend a big fat thanks to everyone at NEVERSOFT.

BRADYGAMES STAFF

Publisher
David Waybright

Editor-In-Chief
H. Leigh Davis

Director of Marketing
Steve Escalante

Marketing Manager
Janet Eshenour

Creative Director
Robin Lasek

Licensing Manager
Mike Degler

Assistant Marketing Manager
Susie Nieman

Team Coordinator
Stacey Beheler

CREDITS

Senior Development Editor
Ken Schmidt

Book Designer
Brent Gann

Production Designer
Bob Klunder

Screenshot Editor
Michael Owen

ACTIVISION CREDITS

Snr. Manager, Licensing & Bus. Dev. -
Justin Berenbaum

Executive Producer - Brian Bright

Producer - Stacey Drellishak

Production Coordinator - Doug Heder

Vice President, Global Brand Management
- Will Kassoy

Global Brand Manager - Gary Pfeiffer

Associate Brand Manager - Joanne Wong

Director, Business & Legal Affairs -
Greg Deutsch

Quality Assurance- Josh Chandler, Lee Cheramie, Joe Favazza, Randy Guillote, David Kabelitz, Kris Kauthen, Ian Moreno, John Rosser

Additional thanks to Dani Kim, and Stefan Makhoul

SKATER BASICS

GAMEPLAY MODES

HIGH SCORE/FREE SKATE

Free Skate mode allows skaters to session any of the courses unlocked in Story mode (or designed in the Create-A-Park mode) for as long as they see fit. There are no goals or timer involved and the score received for one combo is instantly replaced by the next. This is the perfect mode to come to when learning how to navigate a newly unlocked course, for practicing the ultimate combination, and for searching for gaps (remember to load your Story Mode or Classic Mode first).

STORY MODE

Story mode picks up in New Jersey some time after the events of *Tony Hawk's Underground.* This time around, however, players partake in a hilarious World Destruction Tour while skating alongside Tony Hawk, Bam Margera, and other well-known skaters and celebrities. Story Mode takes place throughout a total of 8 different locations and tests your abilities in nearly 20 goals per course. Fortunately, you have plenty of help from Pro Teammates, Guest Skaters, and even some Secret Skaters too. A large portion of this strategy guide is devoted to helping you tackle every goal in Story Mode.

CLASSIC MODE

Classic Mode is your chance to experience the timer-based gameplay of the original *Tony Hawk's Pro Skater* games. There's no story to follow and no cutscenes to take you out of the action; it's just you, a 2:00 timer, and 140 of the goals that helped build this franchise's popularity. Classic Mode features tons of gameplay with many of the courses from the first three games in the series making a return. Be sure to flip ahead to Chapter 6 for detailed tips and maps for all 14 courses in Classic Mode. But be warned, the old-school way can be tougher than you remember.

Difficulty Modes

Tony Hawk's Underground 2 features three different difficulty settings for Story Mode and two different settings for Classic Mode. This guide was written for the Normal difficulty levels for both Modes. The main Story Mode does not differ between difficulties—they each contain the exact same challenges and scripted events—but the physics and the winning conditions for some of the individual goals do vary. For example, one particular challenge may require a score of 20,000 points on Easy mode, but that same challenge may require 80,000 and 140,000 points on the Normal and Sick modes, respectively. Additionally, the requirements to earn increased Stats also become harder on each progressive difficulty option. Classic Mode does not contain an Easy Mode.

Easy	**Less difficult goals for those fairly new to the Hawk series.**
Normal	**Challenging goals for the average to good Tony Hawk player.**
Sick	**For hardcore veterans who have mastered the Hawk games.**

STATS

Whether you play Story Mode or Classic Mode, increasing stats is of vital importance. In Classic Mode, each level has 5 Stat Point icons floating around for you to grab and assign to any of the ten different abilities. In Story Mode, you earn them by accomplishing various tasks that show your increased skill in that area. The tables that follow contain the requirements for each and every Stat Point for all three difficulty settings.

GAMECUBE ONLY!

If you're playing on the GameCube, there are two substituions you must keep in mind when you encounter commands involving the Rotate Buttons. If you're asked to walk somewhere, use the Z Button to get off the skateboard. If the instructions talk about hanging on an object, use the R Button.

Intro

Skater Basics

Trick Lists

Story Mode

Gaps

Classic Mode

Multiskater

Secrets

EASY MODE

AIR
Your jump height out of a half pipe.
Air transfer 15 feet.
Air transfer 20 feet.
Land 1 Backflip grab.
Land 1 BS Roll grab.
Land a 500 point air.
Land a 1,000 point air.
Land a 2,000 point air.

SPIN
How fast you spin in the air.
Land a 360 grab or flip trick in a half pipe.
Land a 540 grab or flip trick in a half pipe.
Land a 720 grab or flip trick in a half pipe.
Do 2 grabs in one combo.
Do 3 grabs in one combo.
Do 4 grabs in one combo.
Do 5 grabs in one combo.

LIP
How well you balance during lip trick stalls.
Hold a lip trick for 1 second.
Hold a lip trick for 3 seconds.
Hold a lip trick for 4 seconds.
Hold a lip trick for 6 seconds.
Hold a lip trick for 7 seconds.
Nose Stall 1 time in a combo.
Nose Stall on a lip 2 times in a combo.

OLLIE
How high you jump on flat ground.
Ollie 15 feet.
Ollie up 5 feet.
Ollie up 10 feet.
Ollie down 10 feet.
Ollie down 15 feet.
Sticker Slap 1 time in a combo.
Sticker Slap 2 times in one combo.

RUN
How long your run timer will last.
Caveman 1 time in a combo.
Caveman 2 times in one combo.
Throw something at 1 pedestrian in one combo.
Throw something at 2 pedestrians in one combo.
Graffiti Tag 1 time in a combo.
Graffiti Tag 2 times in one combo.
Get mad and freak out.

SPEED
Your top speed on the ground.
Land a 1,000 point combo.
Land a 7,500 point combo.
Land a 10,000 point combo.
Land a 20,000 point combo.
Land a 30,000 point combo.
Spine Transfer 1 time in one combo.
Spine Transfer 2 times in a combo.

FLIP
How fast your flip tricks will turn.
Do 2 flip tricks in one combo.
Do 3 flip tricks in one combo.
Do 4 flip tricks in one combo.
Do 5 flip tricks in one combo.
Do 6 flip tricks in one combo.
Double Kickflip 1 time in one combo.
Double Kickflip 2 times in one combo.

SWITCH
When maxed, skate equally well switched and regular.
Acid Drop 1 time in a combo.
Air 20 feet high.
Air 30 feet high.
Land a 3 trick combo.
Land a 5 trick combo.
Land a 7 trick combo.
Land a 9 trick combo.

RAIL
How well you balance on rails.
Grind for 2 seconds.
Grind for 4 seconds.
Grind for 8 seconds.
Grind for 10 seconds.
Natas Spin 1 time in a combo.
50-50 2 times in one combo.
50-50 4 times in one combo.

MANUAL
How well you balance during manuals.
Manual for 2 seconds.
Manual for 4 seconds.
Manual for 6 seconds.
Manual for 8 seconds.
Manual 1 time in one combo.
Manual 2 times in one combo.
Manual 3 times in one combo.

NORMAL MODE

AIR
Your jump height out of a half pipe.
Air transfer 30 feet.
Air transfer 40 feet.
Land 1 Backflip grab.
Land 1 BS Roll grab.
Land a 5,000 point air.
Land a 10,000 point air.
Land a 15,000 point air.

SPIN
How fast you spin in the air.
Land a 540 grab or flip trick in a half pipe.
Land a 720 grab or flip trick in a half pipe.
Land a 900 grab or flip trick in a half pipe.
Do 3 grabs in one combo.
Do 4 grabs in one combo.
Do 6 grabs in one combo.
Do 8 grabs in one combo.

LIP
How well you balance during lip trick stalls.
Hold a lip trick for 2 seconds.
Hold a lip trick for 4 seconds.
Hold a lip trick for 5 seconds.
Hold a lip trick for 7 seconds.
Hold a lip trick for 8 seconds.
Nose Stall on a lip 2 times in one combo.
FS Noseblunt on a lip 2 times in one combo

OLLIE
How high you jump on flat ground.
Ollie 20 feet.
Ollie up 10 feet.
Ollie up 20 feet.
Ollie down 15 feet.
Ollie down 20 feet.
Sticker Slap 2 times in one combo.
Sticker Slap 4 times in one combo.

RUN
How long your run timer will last.
Caveman 2 times in one combo.
Caveman 3 times in one combo.
Throw something at 2 pedestrians in one combo.
Throw something at 4 pedestrians in one combo.
Graffiti Tag 2 times in one combo.
Graffiti Tag 3 times in one combo.
Get mad and freak out.

SPEED
Your top speed on the ground.

Land a 10,000 point combo.
Land a 30,000 point combo.
Land a 50,000 point combo.
Land a 100,000 point combo.
Land a 250,000 point combo.
Spine Transfer 2 times in one combo.
Spine Transfer 4 times in one combo.

FLIP
How fast your flip tricks will turn.

Do 3 flip tricks in one combo.
Do 4 flip tricks in one combo.
Do 5 flip tricks in one combo.
Do 8 flip tricks in one combo.
Do 10 flip tricks in one combo.
Double Kickflip 2 times in one combo.
Triple Kickflip 2 times in one combo.

SWITCH
When maxed, skate equally well switched and regular.

Acid Drop 2 times in one combo.
Air 40 feet high.
Air 70 feet high.
Land a 4 trick combo.
Land a 6 trick combo.
Land a 10 trick combo.
Land a 20 trick combo.

RAIL
How well you balance on rails.

Grind for 5 seconds.
Grind for 10 seconds.
Grind for 15 seconds.
Grind for 20 seconds.
Natas Spin 3 times in one combo.
50-50 3 times in one combo.
Crooked 3 times in one combo.

MANUAL
How well you balance during manuals.

Manual for 4 seconds.
Manual for 6 seconds.
Manual for 8 seconds.
Manual for 10 seconds.
Manual 3 times in one combo.
Manual 5 times in one combo.
Pogo 2 times in one combo.

AIR
Your jump height out of a half pipe.

Air transfer 40 feet.
Air transfer 60 feet.
Land 2 Backflip grabs in one combo.
Land 3 BS Roll grabs in one combo.
Land a 10,000 point air.
Land a 20,000 point air.
Land a 40,000 point air.

SPIN
How fast you spin in the air.

Land a 720 grab or flip trick in a half pipe.
Land a 900 grab or flip trick in a half pipe.
Land a 1080 grab or flip trick in a half pipe.
Do 5 grabs in one combo.
Do 10 grabs in one combo.
Do 20 grabs in one combo.
Do 30 grabs in one combo.

LIP
How well you balance during lip trick stalls.

Hold a lip trick for 3 seconds.
Hold a lip trick for 5 seconds.
Hold a lip trick for 8 seconds.
Hold a lip trick for 10 seconds.
Hold a lip trick for 13 seconds.
BS Boneless on a lip 3 times in a combo.
Gymnast Plant on a lip 3 times in a combo.

OLLIE
How high you jump on flat ground.

Ollie 30 feet.
Ollie up 20 feet.
Ollie up 25 feet.
Ollie down 25 feet.
Ollie down 35 feet.
Sticker Slap 4 times in a combo.
Sticker Slap 6 times in one combo.

RUN
How long your run timer will last.

Caveman 3 times in one combo.
Caveman 4 times in one combo.
Throw something at 4 pedestrians in one combo.
Throw something at 7 pedestrians in one combo.
Graffiti Tag 2 times in one combo.
Graffiti Tag 3 times in one combo.
Get mad and freak out.

SPEED
Your top speed on the ground.

Land a 100,000 point combo.
Land a 400,000 point combo.
Land a 750,000 point combo.
Land a 1,500,000 point combo.
Land a 3,000,000 point combo.
Spine Transfer 3 times in a combo.
Spine Transfer 6 times in a combo.

FLIP
How fast your flip tricks will turn.

Do 5 flip tricks in one combo.
Do 10 flip tricks in one combo.
Do 20 flip tricks in one combo.
Do 30 flip tricks in one combo.
Do 50 flip tricks in one combo.
Double Heelflip 4 times in one combo.
Triple Kickflip 3 times in one combo.

SWITCH
When maxed, skate equally well switched and regular.

Acid Drop 4 times in a combo.
Air 60 feet high.
Air 100 feet high.
Land a 25 trick combo.
Land a 50 trick combo.
Land a 75 trick combo.
Land a 100 trick combo.

RAIL
How well you balance on rails.

Grind for 10 seconds.
Grind for 15 seconds.
Grind for 20 seconds.
Grind for 25 seconds.
Natas Spin 5 times in one combo.
Crooked 5 times in one combo.
Darkslide 5 times in one combo.

MANUAL
How well you balance during manuals.

Manual for 6 seconds.
Manual for 10 seconds.
Manual for 14 seconds.
Manual for 17 seconds.
Pogo 5 times in one combo.
Casper 6 times in one combo.
Half Cab Impossible 6 times in one combo.

The following tables outline all of the tricks in each trick category, including the number of points that are earned for performing them successfully. Many tricks can be linked directly to another trick via a second or third press of a button, or via a combination of button presses. The point values represent both the number awarded for "tapping" a trick for the first time in the Normal and Switch stances. The Scoring section explains the point scoring system in greater detail.

OLLIE TRICKS

An Ollie is the most fundamental trick in skateboarding. Simply put, it all begins with the Ollie. The following variations of the Ollie add style to a scoring line and, in the cases of the Fastplant and Boneless, help add extra height to a jump.

All skaters have the entire assortment of Ollie Tricks. The only difference to some moves is the name assigned to the trick in the case of the Beanplant, Boneless, and Fastplant. These names are used interchangeably throughout the book and are synonymous with one another.

GROUND TRICKS

Name	Command	Points (Normal/Switch)
Ollie	Jump	0/0
Nollie	Jump (Nollie stance)	200/NA
Fakie Ollie	Jump (Switch stance)	NA/200
Pressure	Jump (Pressure stance)	200/240
No Comply	Up + Jump	100/120
Beanplant	Up, Up + Jump	250/300
Boneless	Up, Up + Jump	250/300
Fastplant	Up, Up + Jump	250/300

PRESSURE TRICKS

Pressure tricks are similar to ollies, but require different foot movements by skaters. Use Pressure tricks to perform several specific "pressure flips". Tap the Switch Stance Button once to move into a Pressure stance, then perform an ollie. Use the following button combinations to perform the following pressure tricks.

PRESSURE TRICKS

Name	Command	Points (N/S)
BS 180 Flip	Flip, Right	100/120
BS Toe Flip	Flip, Left	100/120
BS 360 Flip	Flip, Up	200/240
FS 360 Flip	Flip, Down	200/240

THE CAVEMAN

Press the Rotate Left and Rotate Right Buttons simultaneously to have the skater get on or off the skateboard. This not only allows for greater exploration (climbing ladders, scaling rooftops, shimmying on wires, etc.,) but it also makes it possible to perform unique combos.

Skaters in the midst of a combo can perform a Combo Run Out by ollieing into the air and stepping off the board. The Combo Run Out is worth 50 points and increases the multiplier. There are roughly 5 seconds to run or climb somewhere and Caveman into a grind, manual, Graffiti Tag or Acid Drop. The Caveman is essentially the act of transitioning directly from running on foot directly into a trick before all four wheels touch down on the ground. Performing a Caveman increases the multiplier, earns 750 points and keeps the combo alive. The five seconds of running allowed is per combo, not per Combo Run Out. Increase the skater's Run stats to extend this timer.

NEW TRICK! GRAFFITI TAG

Run up to any wall or surface and press the Grind Button to Graffiti Tag it. Visit the Create-A-Graphic mode and design your own multi-layered graffiti tag and spray it all over town. Use Graffiti Tag to increase the multiplier during a Combo Run Out.

WALL TRICKS

Perform a Wallride by riding parallel to a wall, then ollieing into it and press the Grind Button. During the Wallride, it's possible to transition to a grind on a rail or ledge as well as to ollie out of the Wallride for additional height.

NEW TRICK! STICKER SLAP

Ollie out of a rail or manual into a wall (approach perpendicular to it) and press the Jump Button just as the skater is about to hit the wall. Use this move to go back and forth across the same rails and ledges, regardless of the walls that may surround the area.

NEW TRICK! VERT WALLPLANT

Leap out of a ramp as normal, then quickly tap the Jump Button to push off the wall and gain extra height.

WALL TRICKS		
Name	Command	Points (N/S)
FS Wallride	Jump, Grind (facing wall)	200/240
BS Wallride	Jump, Grind (back to wall)	200/240
Wallie	Jump (during Wallride)	250/300
WalliePlant	Up, Jump (during Wallride)	500/600
Wallplant	Down, Jump (airing to wall)	750/900
Wallpush	Push away from wall	10/12
Sticker Slap	Jump (airing to wall)	750/900
Vert Wallplant	Jump (airing up wall)	750/900

SKITCHIN'

To hitch a ride on any passing vehicle, skate up to the rear of it and press Up. Next, switch your attention to the Balance Meter that appears. Tap Left and Right to keep the needle centered. Tap Rotate Right or Rotate Left to slide to the right or left side of the vehicle if necessary.

Skitchin' is a good way to earn points (initial score of 500 points just for grabbing on), and it's a fast way to get around town. Tap Down on the controls during a Skitch to release the Skitch and gain a speed boost. Since the skater takes off past the vehicle, this is best done when Skitchin' on the corner of the vehicle so as to not plow into it!

MANUALS

Tapping Up, then Down as the skater is about to land from a jump executes a Manual. Tap Down, then Up to Nose Manual. Both the Manual and the Nose Manual have initial point values of 100 points, but points continue to accrue throughout the duration of the manual. While in a manual, press the Revert Button to Pivot or Nose Pivot. Pivots are worth 250 points and increase the multiplier.

NEW TRICK! GOTCHA

Each course in *Tony Hawk's Underground 2* has a box of items that can be used as ammunition. These may range from cans of spray paint to tomatoes. Stock up on the items, then skate around and press the Flip Button to chuck them at pedestrians. Hitting a pedestrian with an item scores 500 points (600 in Switch), and it adds to the multiplier.

Pay attention to the Balance Meter that appears as it indicates whether the skater is leaning too far in one direction. Tap Up and Down on the controls to keep the needle in the center.

There are numerous Special Manual tricks that help link tricks and earn huge points. Use manuals between jumps and grinds as a way of chaining lengthy combinations together.

Intro

Skater Basics

Trick Lists

Story Mode

Gaps

Classic Mode

Multiskater

Secrets

FLATLAND TRICKS

Flatland tricks are extensions of the Manual and Nose Manual. These impressive maneuvers can best be described as dancing. Flatland tricks require a great deal of balance and skill, but once mastered can drastically improve anyone's scoring ability.

Flatland Tricks bear a similar Balance Meter to Manuals. Although the points they award are high, be sure to watch the meter and ollie out of the trick before bailing.

NOT SO FAST!

Flatland Tricks are best performed while the skater is as close to stationary as possible. Try tacking a quick succession of flatland tricks onto the end of a lengthy chain right when the skater appears to be losing steam. Avoid trying to ride it up a ramp or over a funbox. The resulting drop in speed and balance will likely ruin what could have been a valuable scoring line.

All modifiers are performed by double-tapping the Flip Button, Grab Button and Grind Button. Rotations are performed by pressing the Revert Button. Points accrue during the entire time in which the flatland trick is held. The scores represent the base score awarded for beginning the trick. By pressing the same button combination twice, the skater goes from a manual to a flatland trick, then back to a manual.

FLATLAND TRICKS

Trick	Command	Points	Modifier	Points	Rotation
Anti Casper	Flip, Grab	1100	Anti Casper Flip	500	Anti Casper Spin
Casper	Flip, Grind	1100	Casper Flip	500	Casper Spin
To Rail	Grab, Flip	1050	Rail Flip	500	N/A
One Foot Manual	Grab, Grind (Manual)	1050	360 Fingerflip	450	Pivot
One Foot Nose Manual	Grab, Grind (Nose Manual)	1050	Half Cab Impossible	450	Nose Pivot
Spacewalk	Left, Right, Flip	1200	360 Fingerflip	450	Nose Pivot
Pogo	Grind, Grind	750	Wrap Around	500	Pogo Spin
Switch Foot Pogo	Grind, Grab	800	Half Wrap Truck Transfer	500	Pogo Spin
Truckstand	Grind, Flip	800	Truckstand Flip	500	Truckspin
Handstand	Grab, Grab	1100	Handflip	500	N/A
Half Cab Impossible	Flip, Flip (Nose Manual)	750	360 Fingerflip	450	Nose Pivot
360 Fingerflip	Flip, Flip (Manual)	750	Half Cab Impossible	450	Pivot

GRINDS

Grinds make for a good source of points, and they enable skaters to cover distance during a trick. A grind requires a mastery of balance to pull off over significant distances. Pay attention to the Balance Meter and aim to keep the needle in the center.

The points earned for Grind tricks are based on the distance the grind is performed. Grinding a ledge from one side of a building to another earns more points than simply grinding the length of a park bench.

END THAT GRIND

A long, fast, grind on a curving ledge can be difficult to ollie out of safely, especially if there's water nearby! Well, you're in luck. A press of the Left or Right Revert Button drops a grind at a moment's notice. Doing so awards 100 points.

HOLD-GRIND

Every now and then, you encounter objects that are closely spaced. It's possible to continue a grind across objects under these circumstances without ollieing. Continue to hold down the Grind Button to continue the grind without interruption. Use the directional buttons to switch up the grind while going across the small gap to boost the multiplier!

NEW TRICK! NATAS SPIN

Natas Kaupas had a style all his own back in the day and the time has come for you to learn his signature trick. Skate towards any post-like object such as a fire hydrant or pole and ollie onto it while pressing the Grind and Rotate Right Buttons. The skater balances on the center of the deck and spin in circles over and over. The initial instance of the Natas Spin is only worth 50 points, but it quickly increases with each revolution.

GRIND COMBOS

It's possible to transition from one grind directly to another with two quick button presses. Input the commands in the following table to transfer to the specified grind. It becomes harder to maintain balance with each successive grind combo. Return to the previous grind trick by repeating the same button presses.

Each of the grinds listed in the table may be performed frontside (FS) or backside (BS).

BASIC GRIND TRICKS

Trick	Command	Points
50-50	Grind	100
Boardslide	Grind (perpendicular to ledge)	200
Lipslide	Grind (perpendicular to ledge)	200
Tailslide	Left or Right + Grind	150
Noseslide	Left or Right + Grind	150
Nosegrind	Up + Grind	100
5-0	Down + Grind	100
Crooked	Up/Right or Up/Left + Grind	125
Overcrook	Up/Right or Up/Left + Grind	125
Smith	Down/Right or Down/Left + Grind	125
Feeble	Down/Right or Down/Left + Grind	125
Bluntslide	Down, Down + Grind	250
Nosebluntslide	Up, Up + Grind	250

Trick	Combo Command
50-50	Grind, Grind
Noseslide	Grind, Flip
Nosegrind	Grind, Grab
Crooked	Grab, Grab
Bluntslide	Grab, Flip
Nosebluntslide	Grab, Grind
Smith	Flip, Flip
5-0	Flip, Grab
Tailslide	Flip, Grind

KISS AND TELL

If the skater attempts to grind on an object that is too short, or if the grind is initiated too close to the end of the rail, the points awarded are for having 'Kissed the Rail'. Kissing the rail awards 50 points while in the normal stance and 60 for a switch stance.

DOUBLE-TAP GRINDS

In addition to the basic grinds, there are eight other tricks that, although being a bit harder to balance, earn more points. Ollie to a rail or ledge and give one of these double-tap grind tricks a try.

DOUBLE-TAP GRIND TRICKS

Trick	Command	Points
Nosegrind to Pivot	Up + Grind, Grind	400
5-0 Overturn	Down + Grind, Grind	400
Hurricane	Left + Grind, Grind	400
Salad	Right + Grind, Grind	400
Hang Ten Nosegrind	Up/Left + Grind, Grind	400
Crail Slide	Up/Right + Grind, Grind	400
Double Blunt Slide	Down/Left + Grind, Grind	400
Darkslide	Down/Right + Grind, Grind	400

SHUFFLE BONUS!

'Shuffling' involves taking advantage of a particularly wide ledge or curb to quickly trick in and out of grinds from one edge to the other. This is an experts-only type of maneuver and requires the player to alternate taps of the Grind and Jump Buttons very quickly while simultaneously tapping Left and Right on the controls. Although this skill is not required at any time in either Story or Classic mode, those wishing to do more than hold their own online may want to practice it. In addition to rapidly increasing the multiplier, a "Shuffle Bonus" of 100 points is awarded.

LIP TRICKS

Lip Tricks require approaching the rail at a 90-degree angle (from below, typically), and they demand incredible balance and strength on the part of the skater. Monitor the Balance Meter and tap Up or Down as necessary to keep from falling.

COMMAND CUSTOMIZATION!

The commands for lip tricks, flips and grabs, and Special Tricks can all be customized to fit the player's preference. Because of this, there are no command inputs listed for the individual tricks.

As was the case with grinds and flatland tricks, it's possible to seamlessly transfer into and out of different lip tricks, provided they are the same style. For example, all tricks that are performed on the lip of the ramp or on the rail with the board touching the surface can be linked together through the commands listed in the Lip Extras table. Similarly, all tricks that are performed upside-down can be linked together via the commands in the Invert Extras table. The one exception to this is the Andrecht Invert, which has its own special link to The Switcheroo. Once the transfer is made to The Switcheroo, however, all of the available Invert Extras are open for comboing.

LIP TRICKS

Trick	Points	Combos To
Nose Stall	300+	Lip Extras
Andrecht Invert	550+	Andrecht Extra
Axle Stall	400+	Lip Extras
Blunt to Fakie	500+	Lip Extras
BS Boneless	550+	Lip Extras
Disaster	600+	Lip Extras
Eggplant	550+	Invert Extras
Gymnast Plant	575+	Invert Extras
Varial Invert to Fakie	450+	Invert Extras
Invert	500+	Invert Extras
FS Noseblunt	550+	Lip Extras
FS Nosepick	550+	Lip Extras
One Foot Invert	500+	Invert Extras
Rock to Fakie	500+	Lip Extras
The Switcheroo	600+	Invert Extras

LIP EXTRAS

Trick	Combo Command
Axle Stall	Grab, Grab
BS Boneless	Grab, Flip
Disaster	Flip, Flip
Rock to Fakie	Flip, Grab
FS Noseblunt	Grind, Grind
FS Nosepick	Grind, Flip
Blunt to Fakie	Grind, Grab

INVERT EXTRAS

Trick	Combo Command
Gymnast Plant	Grab, Grab
Varial Invert to Fakie	Grab, Flip
One Foot Invert	Flip, Flip
Eggplant	Flip, Grab
Invert	Grind, Grind
Andrecht Invert	Grind, Grab

ANDRECHT EXTRA

Trick	Combo Command
The Switcheroo	Grind, Grind

AIR TRICKS

FLIP TRICKS

Some flip tricks, like the Kickflip and Heelflip, can be done so quickly that their use is pervasive throughout nearly every scoring line. Other, more intricate, tricks such as the Sal Flip or Varial, require much greater height than a simple Ollie affords.

Thanks to the relative simplicity of the Kickflip and Heelflip, there is seldom a reason for a plain ollie. While the 'Variety Enforcing Points System' may reduce the Kickflip's value to near nothing over the course of a run, Kickflipping into a grind boosts the Multiplier. On big, 7-figure scoring lines, each extra Kickflip or Shove-It could be worth over 50,000 points!

Study the trick slot assignments and the tables below to know which tricks are the most valuable and what their double-tap combos are.

TRIPLE-TAP?

While the Flip Tricks screen in the game does contain the Double Tap tricks, the screen doesn't show the available triple tap tricks. Each of the five basic flip tricks (Kickflip, Heelflip, Impossible, Pop Shove-It, and Shove-It) can each be performed three times in one leap by tapping the Flip Button 3x after the initial directional press.

THE SAME, BUT DIFFERENT

When it comes to 'Variety Enforcing Point System' each of these tricks are tracked separately. This means that even once a Double Kickflip is only netting 25% its original value, a Triple Kickflip performed for the first time earns the full 1,000 points!

CONFIGURABLE FLIP TRICKS

Trick	Points (N/S)	Double-Tap Trick	Points (N/S)	Triple-Tap Trick	Points (N/S)
Kickflip	100/120	Double Kickflip	500/600	Triple Kickflip	1000/1200
Heelflip	100/120	Double Heelflip	500/600	Triple Heelflip	1000/1200
Impossible	100/120	Double Impossible	500/600	Triple Impossible	1000/1200
Pop Shove-It	100/120	360 Shove-It	500/600	540 Shove-It	1000/1200
FS Shove-It	100/120	360 FS Shove-It	500/600	540 FS Shove-It	1000/1200
Back Foot Kickflip	150/180	Double Back Foot Flip	550/660	N/A	N/A
Backfoot Heelflip	150/180	Double Back Foot Heelflip	500/600	N/A	N/A
Back Foot Shove-It	150/180	360 Back Foot Shove-It	500/600	N/A	N/A
Old Skool Kickflip	300/360	N/A	N/A	N/A	N/A
Varial Kickflip	300/360	360 Flip	550/660	N/A	N/A
Varial Heelflip	300/360	360 Heelflip	500/600	N/A	N/A
Hardflip	300/360	360 Hardflip	500/600	N/A	N/A
Inward Heelflip	350/420	360 Inward Heelflip	500/600	N/A	N/A
Front Foot Impossible	525/630	Double Front Foot Impossible	1075/1290	N/A	N/A
Ollie Airwalk	500/600	Ollie Airwalk Late Shove-It	1050/1260	N/A	N/A
Ollie North	169/203	Ollie North Back Foot Flip	1050/1260	N/A	N/A
Bigspin Flip	500/600	N/A	N/A	N/A	N/A
FS Bigspin	500/600	N/A	N/A	N/A	N/A
BS Bigspin	500/600	N/A	N/A	N/A	N/A
FS Flip	500/600	N/A	N/A	N/A	N/A
BS Flip	500/600	N/A	N/A	N/A	N/A
Fingerflip	700/840	Double Fingerflip	1000/1200	N/A	N/A
180 Varial	700/840	360 Varial	900/1080	N/A	N/A
Heelflip Varial Lien	800/960	N/A	N/A	N/A	N/A
Sal Flip	900/1080	360 Sal Flip	1150/1380	N/A	N/A

GRAB TRICKS

The great thing about grab tricks is that they can be held for additional points, but use this feature with restraint. Although it's safe to hold on to the board to squeeze some extra points out of an Airwalk or Method, be sure to let go before the skater begins to land. Holding onto the Grab Button for even a split-second too long can send the skater headfirst into the pavement!

CONFIGURABLE GRAB TRICKS

Trick	Points (N/S)	Double-Tap Trick	Points (N/S)
Japan	350/420	One Foot Japan	800
Crail Grab	350/420	Tuck Knee	400/480
Wrap Around	450/420	Body Wrap	600/720
Cannonball	250/420	Fingerflip Cannonball	500/600
Stalefish	350/420	Stalefish Tweak	400/480
Benihana	300/420	Sacktap	1500
Crossbone	425/510	Crooked Cop	550/660
Airwalk	450/540	Christ Air	550/660
Indy Nosebone	350/420	Del Mar Indy	400/480
Tailgrab	300/360	One Foot Tailgrab	500/600
Madonna	750/900	Judo	1150/1380
FS Shifty	500/600	BS Shifty	800/960
Melon	300/360	Method	400/480
Nosegrab	300/360	Rocket Air	400/480
Mute	350/420	Seatbelt Air	500/600
Indy	300/360	Stiffy	500/600
Barrel Roll	800/960	N/A	N/A

Intro

Skater Basics

Trick Lists

Story Mode

Gaps

Classic Mode

Multiskater

Secrets

ROLLS AND FLIPS

One of the new features introduced in *Tony Hawk's Underground 2* is the ability to perform a Roll, Frontflip, or Backflip at will. Hold the Grab Button and double-tap in one of the four directions to flip or roll. Best of all, other tricks can be performed during these maneuvers to help add even more value to your scoring lines!

AERIAL FLIPS

Trick	Command	Points
Frontflip	Grab + Up, Up	1000
Backflip	Grab + Down, Down	1000
Roll	Grab + Left, Left	1000
Roll	Grab + Right, Right	1000

SPINE TRANSFER

By tapping the Spine Transfer Button while lifting off the top of a spine or vert ramp, skaters transfer to the other side of the ramp or to a ledge or rail beyond the lip of the ramp.

Use Spine Transfers to transfer up and down ramps that aren't even adjacent, so long as they're lined up with one another. Additionally, Hip Transfers are possible between two quarter pipes that are at a right angle to one another. Ultimately, when combined with the manual and the Revert, the Spine Transfer makes it possible to extend a scoring string through most any situation.

It's possible to perform a maneuver known as the Acid Drop when there is a quarter pipe directly below the skater. Ollie out over the ramp, then tap the Spine Transfer Button to straighten out and drop into it from above. This is a great way to avoid landing on flat ground and helps the skater maintain speed.

REVERT

Tap the Revert Button as the skater touches down on a vert ramp to buy enough time to transition into a manual or another vert trick! Keep the controller's vibration function active since the controller rumbles during the 'window' in which to perform the follow up trick.

Every time the Revert is used, there is a significant drop in speed. No speed equals no height. This isn't to say that one or two hits in the half pipe can't be linked together, but you may need to mix in a grind to regain the speed that was lost.

In addition to the 100/120 points earned by landing a FS/BS Revert, it serves as a convenient Multiplier to end scoring lines. Consider beginning and ending lengthy scoring chains with big jumps off of vert ramps followed by a Revert. Sandwich lengthy grinds and manuals with these jump-to-Revert combos to really milk the courses for all the points they're worth.

SPECIAL TRICKS

When it comes to scoring big points with a single trick, look no further than the collection of Special Tricks. Assign any of these multiple-command tricks, then bust them out when the Special Meter is full. Additional Special Trick slots are unlocked throughout Story Mode. Use the additional slots to assign any of these highly technical tricks to use at a later time.

SPECIAL AIR TRICKS

Trick	Points (N/S)
360 Varial McTwist	5750/6900
540 Tailwhip	2500/3000
360 Varial Heelflip Lien	3500/4200
Back Spin Air	3500/4200
FS 540	5500/6600
Gazelle Underflip	3500/4200
360 Ghetto Bird	3500/4200
Indy 900	11000/13200
Kickflip Backflip	3750/4500
McTwist	5000/6000
The 900	9000/10800
Double Kickflip Madonna	2250/2700
Casper Flip 360 Flip	2500/3000
BigSpin Shifty	2000/2400
Flamingo	2000/2400
360 Flip Tail Grab	1750/2100
Samba Flip	1850/2220
Shifty Shifty	2500/3000
Sit Down Air	1200/1440
Beaver Blast	1000/1200

HIGH SPEED SPECIAL AIR TRICKS

Trick	Points (N/S)
1-2-3-4	2500/3000
540 Flip	2250/2700
Double Kickflip Varial Indy	2500/3000
Fingerflip Airwalk	2750/3300
Hardflip Late Flip	2500/3000
Kickflip Underflip	1750/2100
Quad Heelflip	3250/3900
Semi Flip	2500/3000
Bam Bend Air	1300/1560
Head Kick Backflip	2550/3060
Half Cab Underflip	3500/4200
Endless Kickflip	1200/1440
No Problem 900	1750/2100
Darkside Japan	1200/1440
Endless Handflip	1200/1440
Double Fistin'	1450/1740
Don't Feed Phil	1800/2160
Sheckler Grab	2000/2400
Rotisserie	2500/3000
Board Snap	2750/3300
Salute	1000/1200

SPECIAL LIP TRICKS

Trick	Points (N/S)
Heelflip FS Invert	6500+/7800+
Ho Ho Sad Plant	6750+/8100+
Around the World	7250+/8700+
BAM	6750+/8100+
Russian Boneless	6500+/7800+

SPECIAL GRIND TRICKS

Trick	Points
360 Shove-It Nosegrind	800+
5-0 Fingerflip Nosegrind	500+
Big Hitter II	500+
Coffin	500+
Crook BigSpinFlip Crook	500+
Elbow Smash	500+
Fandangle	500+
5050 Switcheroo	400+
Nollie 360 Flip Crook	800+
Crooks Darkslide	800+
Moonwalk Five-0	800+
One Foot Darkslide	800+
One Foot Smith	500+
Primo Handstand	800+
Rodney Primo	400+
Darkslide Handstand	800+
Tailblock Slide	500+
Grind N Barf	500+
Stupid Grind	500+
Muska 5-0 Flames	600+
Worm Grind	600+
The Bird	600+
Espana Sword Slide	600+
Bite Board	600+
Chainsaw Rocker Grind	600+
Boardslide Body Varial	600+
Shark	600+
Waxslide	600+
Hero Grind	600+
Franklin Grind!!!	600+

SPECIAL MANUAL TRICKS

Trick	Points
Ahhh Yeahh!	4000+
Casper Handstand	4500+
Ho Ho Street Plant	4500+
Flip 2 Switch	4500+
Mix it Up	4500+
No Comply 360 Shove-It	4500+
One Wheel Nose Manual	4100+
Primo	4000+
Rusty Slide Manual	4500+
Slam Spinner	3500+
Sproing	4500+
Primo Spin	4500+
Paulie Butt Manual	4000+
Manual Entertainer	4500+
Hot Rod	4250+
Surfer	4500+
Running Manual	4500+
Boomerang	4500+
Yeah Right	3100+

SCORING

The ability to score large quantities of points is an integral part in succeeding in *Tony Hawk's Underground 2*. However, completing the various scoring goals requires more than repeating a Kickflip Underflip over and over. Tricks are worth progressively less each time they are performed, and other factors such as riding "Switch", linking tricks for multipliers, spinning, etc. all affect the amount of points that are earned. This section breaks down each of the different factors that control how many points are earned.

RIDING SWITCH

Although riders are always stronger in their "Normal" stance, whether it be Regular-footed (left foot forward) or Goofy-footed (right foot forward), expert riders can perform nearly all of the tricks in their repertoire in a Switch stance. The word "Switch" appears in the upper left-hand corner of the screen whenever the skater is in the Switch stance. Performing tricks while in the Switch stance is worth an additional 20% in terms of points.

MULTIPLIERS

For every trick that is done without the board touching down, an additional multiplier is added. Every time another trick is done or another gap is hit, the multiplier grows by one. Should the skater eventually touch down without bailing, the total points (base score) for the string of tricks will be multiplied by the number of tricks and gaps completed.

Being able to link tricks with manuals, Reverts, and grinds is of extreme importance in building up a huge multiplier. Practice incorporating a couple of gaps into each combination and scoring hundreds of thousands, if not millions, of points per chain will be a common occurrence.

Intro

Skater Basics

Trick Lists

Story Mode

Gaps

Classic Mode

Multiskater

Secrets

SPINNING

One of the easiest ways to ramp up the points earned for completing tricks is to add rotation. Granted, a 720 Rocket Air is significantly more difficult to land than a straight Rocket Air, but the opportunity to raise the points earned by a factor of four is hard to ignore. Although the bonus increases for every 180 degrees of rotation, remember to come out of the spin before striking the ground.

Adding rotation to a trick isn't the only way to milk some extra points out of an aerial. If after performing at least 180 degrees of rotation the skater lands on the ramp at a perfect right angle, a 1,000-point "Perfect Landing" bonus is awarded. On the other hand, a really ugly landing is deemed "Sloppy" and 500 points are deducted from the base score.

SPINNING MULTIPLIERS

Rotation	Bonus
180	1.5x Trick Score
360	2x Trick Score
540	3x Trick Score
720	4x Trick Score
900	6x Trick Score

SPINNING IN CIRCLES

There are two ways to rotate while in the air. Spin to the left or right by pressing in the chosen direction on the controller. Another option is to use the Rotate Right and Rotate Left Buttons. Using the specified Rotate Buttons is the preferred method, as there is less chance of the spin interfering with the trick inputs.

GAPS

Each of the courses in *Tony Hawk's Underground 2* has between 20 and 70 gaps. Gaps are bonuses that are awarded for completing a specific type of trick involving a piece of the environment. Many gaps require the skater to transfer between two ramps, grind a particular series of rails, or manual along a set ledge. Gaps add points to the score and are used to build the multiplier as well. Complete each course's gaps checklist to unlock a special prize!

VARIETY-ENFORCING POINTS SYSTEM

The percentages in the following table are based on the original point value for the trick. All tricks performed more than five times are worth 10% of the original score. The points for tricks decline independently between those performed in a Normal stance versus thus done while riding Switch.

POINTS DEPRECIATION FOR TRICK REPETITION

Trick Instance	Percent of Base Score
First time you land a trick	100%
Second time	75%
Third time	50%
Fourth time	25%
Fifth time	10%

FREAK OUT

As much fun as playing *Tony Hawk's Underground 2* can be, there is no denying the overwhelming frustration one feels when bailing during a lengthy combo. Fortunately, now there's a way to let that anger loose in the game environment and actually get some points back in the process! It sure beats throwing controllers!

Immediately after bailing, a Freak Out meter appears on the screen. Quickly start hammering on the Grind Button to fill the meter as high as possible. The skater reacts in a number of different ways, depending on how high the meter was filled. Best of all, you receive a fraction of the points lost from the previous combo to help get you started on the next combo. You have several seconds to hop into a grind or manual to get the next line underway.

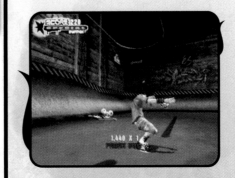

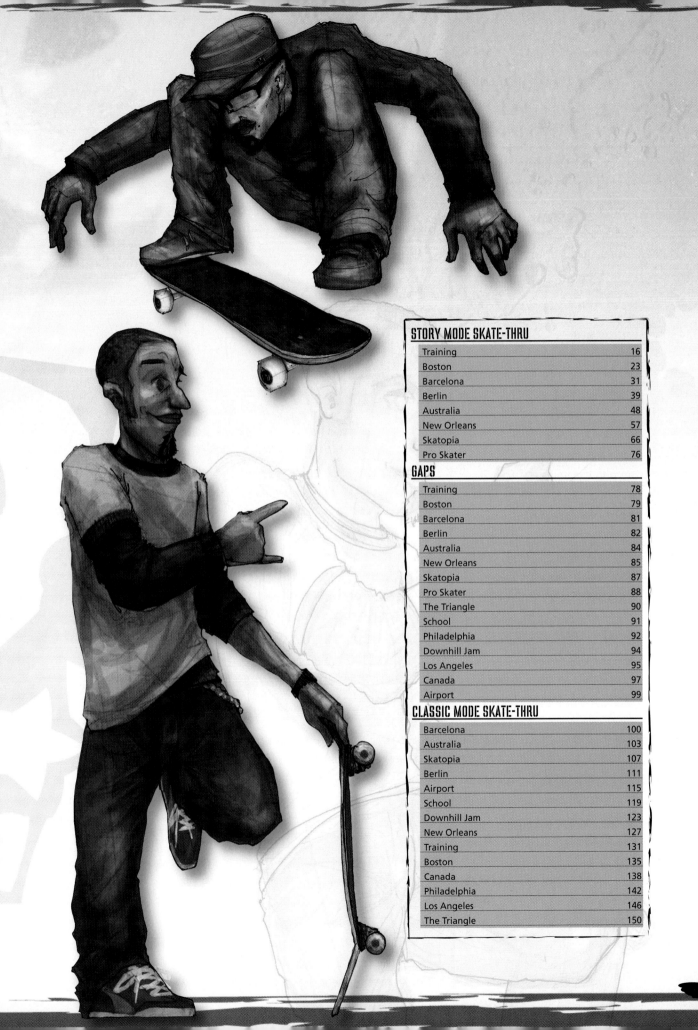

YOUR GOALS

- Learn to Ollie
- Learn to Manual
- No Comply Over the Taxi
- Boneless Over the Taxi
- Kickflip Over the Gap
- Grind the Rail
- Lip the QP
- QP Grind
- Melon off a Vert
- Learn to Spin
- Get out of a Half Pipe
- QP Transfer
- Sticker Slap the Walls
- Tear down the Wall
- Open the Door
- Wallie and Grind the Rail
- Fun with Tomatoes
- Spine Transfer the Fun Box
- Hip Transfer
- My First Combo
- Side Jumping Combo
- Caveman Time
- Jump on the Crates
- Jump and Hang
- Climb the Ladder
- Shimmy to the Opening
- Acid Drop
- Tag the Place
- Do a McTwist
- Do a Backflip
- Do a Roll
- Vert Wallplant Session
- Do a Real Combo
- Keep the Focus
- Hang'n Tag
- Skitch the Forklift
- Find an Arcade Machine and Set the High Score

TRAINING

0 Goal Points are required to unlock this location.

0 Goal Points are available.

There are no teammates available to choose from.

Breakable Wall

Arcade Machine

Tony Hawk

Breakable Walls

YOUR GOALS

YOU CAN GO HOME AGAIN!

Welcome to the spot that started it all. Tony's training grounds are known as the Warehouse; the first level in the original *Tony Hawk's Pro Skater*. Soak up the nostalgia while skating around and start boosting those Stats. A new pool has been installed, but aside from that all of the gaps, rails, and ramps are right where Neversoft left them back in 1999. Loosen up the fingers, then skate over to Rodney Mullen to get this show on the road.

LEARN FROM THE PROS

Each of the professional skaters has some lessons they want to share, starting with Rodney Mullen. Unsure of what to do next? Skate up to the lone skater standing still and press the Grab Button to acquire the next goal. None of the goals earn you Goal Points, nor are they mandatory (except "Keep the Focus"), but they provide a good refresher on the basics and also introduce some new skating techniques.

Rodney Mullen's Lessons

Learn to Ollie

Press the Jump Button to ollie 3 times. The ollie is the most basic skateboarding maneuver. Hold the Jump Button down longer to ollie higher and farther.

Learn to Manual

Manual from one set of cones to the other. Skate slowly towards the first set of cones and press Up, then Down on the controls to initiate a manual. Maintain balance until passing the other set of cones. It's possible to hold the Jump Button while manualing to skate faster.

No Comply Over the Taxi

Skate towards the kicker ramp near the taxi and quickly press Up, then the Jump Button to perform the No Comply over the taxi for the **Car Hop** gap bonus.

Boneless Over the Taxi

Now it's time to do the same thing as before, but now you must press Up on the controls twice before pressing the Jump Button. The Boneless is the ultimate ollie as it allows the skater to gain maximum height with a simple jump. One can always tell when a Boneless has been done by the scraping noise the tail of the board makes against the ground.

Kickflip Over the Gap

Skate towards the ramps near the puddle on the floor and ollie off the ramp over the gap. While in the air, press Left and the Flip Button to perform a Kickflip and to score the **Ramp Hop** gap.

Chad Muska's Lessons

TRAINING

Training
Boston
Barcelona
Berlin
Australia
New Orleans
Skatopia
Pro Skater

Grind the Rail

Ollie onto the rail and press the Grind Button just as the skater is about to smack the metal. Tap Left and Right on the controls to maintain balance while grinding across the length of the rail on the skateboard's trucks. Grind all the way to the opposite end of the rail for the **Big Rail** gap.

Sticker Slap the Walls

Ride towards the wall near the half pipe and ollie into it. Press the Jump Button just as the skater is about to hit the wall to perform the Sticker Slap. The Sticker Slap is a stylish way of performing a wall plant while simultaneously leaving your mark on the terrain.

Intro

Skater Basics

Trick Lists

Story Mode

Gaps

Classic Mode

Multiskater

Secrets

My First Combo

The key to scoring points in *Tony Hawk's Underground 2* is to build up lengthy scoring combos by linking tricks together without interruption. To perform this first combo, roll up the quarter pipe into a left-hand grind, then ollie out of the grind into another grind on the raised rail in the center of the funbox. Finish the combo by ollieing off the rail into another grind on the coping of the quarter pipe on the other side. Mix in some quick flip tricks during the ollies to increase the score and, more importantly, the multiplier.

Side Jumping Combo

This combo is almost identical to the previous one, but the skater must now ollie to the side in order to reach the desired rail for the middle grind. Use the kinked portion of the quarter pipe to get some extra pop and hold to the Left on the controls when ollieing over to the rail in the middle of the funbox. Land in a grind and then ollie back to the right to land in a final grind back on the quarter pipe.

Tag the Place

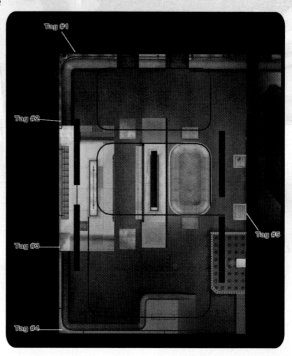

There are five blank posters scattered throughout the skatepark. Skate up to each of them (or climb) and get off the board and press the Grind Button to Tag them.

Head to the corner of the room and climb the yellow ductwork to the ledge near the ceiling. Jump onto the ledge and Tag the poster on the right.

Drop back to the ground and begin a counter-clockwise loop around the room to find the next poster. It's located on the wall above the funbox where you performed your first combo.

Continue to the left from the second poster and drop down onto the next ledge. The third poster is near the quarter pipe.

The fourth poster is right in the corner of the room, to the left of the third poster. Jump off the board and leap onto the edge of the quarter pipe to Tag it.

The final poster is on the wall above the stacked crates. Leap onto the wooden crates and press the Grind Button to Tag the poster.

Hang N' Tag

Run and jump from the wooden crates to the ledge near the ladder and climb up to the alcove above. Drop into a hanging position and shimmy towards the "Bladerz Rule" poster to the right.

Skitch the Forklift

Roll up behind the forklift truck and press Up on the controls to grab it. The forklift cruises around the skatepark and it's up you to maintain balance for 10 seconds. Watch the Balance Meter carefully and tap Left and Right to keep from falling off.

Find an Arcade Machine and Set the High Score

Approach the arcade cabinet and press the Grab Button to take a shot at setting a new High Score. You have 1:00 to score at least 30,000 total points. Hop into a grind on the quarter pipe near the hole in the wall and trick across the gaps in the ramp while grinding counterclockwise around the skatepark. Transition into snack room and build speed on the ramp and then Spine Transfer into the pool and link up several aerials by Reverting into a Manual on the flatbottom of the pool.

Bob Burnquist's Lessons

Lip the QP

The majority of the ramps encountered have a lip to them. Sometimes it's metal coping, other times it is a concrete ledge or some other material. Either way, it's possible to skate straight up a ramp and pause at the top. This is known as a lip trick. Skate up the ramp perpendicular to the upper edge and press the Grind Button at the top. So long as the skater isn't on an angle, he or she automatically transitions into a lip trick. Tap to the Left and Right to maintain balance while paused at the lip. Press the Jump Button to ollie out of the lip trick.

QP Grind

Skate up the ramp on an angle instead of perpendicular to the lip and press the Grind Button to transition into a grind trick on the edge of the ramp. Tap to the Left and Right to maintain balance during the grind and ollie out of the grind to end the trick.

Melon off a Vert

Hold the Jump Button down while skating on the ramp to build speed, then release the button just as the skater is about to reach the top of the ramp. While airborne, tap to the Left and hit the Grab Button to perform the trick called the Melon.

Learn to Spin

Jump from the top of the ramp and use the controls and either the Flip Button or Grab Button to quickly perform a trick. Spin the skater a full rotation to the left or right by either holding down the Left or Right controls or by holding either of the other Rotate buttons (if applicable).

Get Out of a Half Pipe

Although it's possible to skate up a ramp and hold Up on the controls to force the skater out of the ramp, it's much easier to perform a Spine Transfer. Ride up the ramp and leap into the air. Once airborne, press the Spine Transfer Button to exit the ramp and to level out so that the skater lands on all four wheels.

Intro

Skater Basics

Trick Lists

Story Mode

Gaps

Classic Mode

Multiskater

Secrets

QP Transfer

Few things are more exciting than transferring between two ramps that aren't connected. This is known as "gapping" and requires having enough speed to clear the distance, approaching at the right angle, and jumping at the right time. Skate towards the ramp on the right while angling roughly 45-degrees to the left. Hold the Jump Button during the approach and release it at the top of the ramp to propel the skater across the channel to the other ramp. Completing this goal earns the **QP Transfer** gap bonus.

Vert Wallplant Session

The Vert Wallplant is a maneuver that allows skaters to get extra height when launching from a quarter pipe that is flush against a wall. Skate up the ramp and press the Jump Button below the edge of the ramp as if performing a normal aerial. Tap the Jump Button again when in the air alongside the wall to boost off the wall for extra height. This trick requires some practice in order to perfect the timing of, so keep at it!

Mike Vallely's Lessons

Tear Down the Wall

Use a Sticker Slap to break through weakened structures, like the wall to the left. Grind the lip of the quarter pipe towards the wall and perform a Sticker Slap near the large crack.

Open the Door

The other skaters don't want to squeeze through a hole in the wall, so you must open the door for them. Ride towards the wall with the large red button on it and then ollie towards it on an angle. Hold the Grind Button to perform the Wallride and roll across the face of the button to press it. Doing so earns the **Red Button Wallride** gap bonus.

Caveman Time

Press the Rotate Right and Rotate Left Buttons simultaneously to leap off the board and run around on foot. Jump into the air and press the two buttons again to Caveman back onto the board. A timer appears when skaters are off their boards, so Caveman back into a grind or manual before the timer expires to keep the combo alive.

Jump on the Crates

Get off the board and walk up to the crate. Jump up while pressing Up on the controls to climb onto it. Jump back down and approach the taller stack of crates. It's possible to "double jump" onto the upper crate by pressing the Jump Button twice while holding Up on the controls.

Jump and Hang

Now it's time to run and leap for the ledge surrounded by water. Hold the Jump Button down while sprinting to the edge and then leap for the ledge. Press and hold the Rotate Right Button to grab onto the edge in a hanging position. Press Up on the controls to climb up.

Climb the Ladder

Being on foot makes it possible to climb ladders and other scalable objects. Simply walk towards the ladder and press Up on the controls to begin climbing.

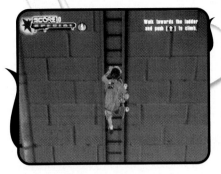

Shimmy to the Opening

Approach ledges slowly to turn around and drop into a hanging position. It's possible to shimmy along the edge by pressing either Right or Left on the controls when hanging. Shimmy past the "Bladerz Rule" poster to the alcove to the far right.

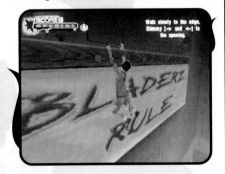

Acid Drop

Jumping off a platform into a quarter pipe or half pipe is called an Acid Drop and it is performed by pressing the Spine Transfer Button. Skate past the rail in the alcove and ollie through the grate and press the Spine Transfer Button to Acid Drop into the pool below.

Bam Margera's Lessons

Wallie and Grind the Rail

It's possible to reach greater heights by ollieing during a Wallride, a move known as a Wallie. Skate alongside the wall with the graffiti on it and ollie into a Wallride. Quickly press the Jump Button again to ollie up towards the rail on top of the wall and press the Grind Button to grind on it.

Spine Transfer the Funbox

Find Bam Margera in the snack room under the large funbox and use the ramp to get enough speed to break through the flimsy wall. Hit the quarter pipe outside the snack area and leap high into the air and press the Spine Transfer Button to transfer up and over the **Funbox Spine** and into the pool on the other side.

Hip Transfer

Ride up the quarter pipe on an angle and leap into the air as if going for a normal aerial. Press the Spine Transfer Button to make the skater straighten out in line with quarter pipe perpendicular to the one he took off from for the **Hippin** gap bonus. Transferring between two ramps that are on an angle with one another is known as a Hip Transfer.

Do a Real Combo

Launch off the quarter pipe in the alley and perform a grab trick while in the air. Tap the Revert Button while landing on the ramp, then immediately tap into a Manual to complete the combo. Although this is all Bam wants to see right now, normally you would be able to trick out of the Manual and continue building on the trick combo.

Do a McTwist

Use the ramps near the wall and in the center of the skatepark to light the Special Meter by performing several tricks and landing them cleanly. Skate towards the ramp against the far wall and launch into the air and quickly tap into the McTwist Special Trick (Right, Down + Grab Button).

Intro

Skater Basics

Trick Lists

Story Mode

Gaps

Classic Mode

Multiskater

Secrets

Do a Backflip

Skating has evolved to the point where flips and rolls aren't all that out of the ordinary anymore. Now it's possible to perform these inverted stunts anytime by just holding the Grab Button and double tapping a direction on the controls. A Backflip can be performed in the air by holding the Grab Button and pressing Down on the controls twice.

Do a Roll

Rolls are similar to flips, except they are performed by tapping to the left or right instead of up or down. Launch off the ramp into the air and press and hold the Circle Button while tapping Left or Right on the controls twice.

Fun With Tomatoes

Skate over to the large crate of tomatoes and pres the Grab Button to pick 10 of them up. Now skate around and press the Flip Button to throw the tomatoes at Phil as he waddles back and forth across the skatepark in his mighty whiteys. Use the controls to aim while throwing and hit him 5 times to complete the lesson. Hitting a pedestrian with an item is a fun way to gain some extra points and to also increase the multiplier if you're in the midst of a combo.

Tony Hawk's Lesson

Keep the Focus

Focus is a new feature that makes it possible to slow down the tricks as they are performed so that landing them becomes easier. Trick out the Special Meter and begin a combo. While in the combo, press the Focus Button and watch in awe as the skater's actions are slowed. Keep the combo alive to maintain Focus and touch down cleanly to end the combo. Not only does Focus make it easier to land complex combos, but it also causes the camera to zoom in on the action—this looks especially cool when performing flatland tricks.

YOUR GOALS

Find the Special Guest (25 pts)
Find Ben Franklin (25 pts)
Mark Your Territory (50 pts)
Hospital Duty (50 pts)
Arcade Machine High Score (50 pts)
Dance, Sucka (50 pts)
Decapitate the Statues (50 pts)
Combo on the RV Ramp (75 pts)

PRO GOALS

Combo the 4 Benches (25 pts)
Ye Olde Cannon Grind (25 pts)
Skitch a Seaworthy Vehicle (25 pts)
Salute the General (25 pts)
Great Balls of Fire (25 pts)
Slap the Signs (25 pts)
Tag a Big Billboard (50 pts)
Finest Rails in Boston (50 pts)

GUEST GOALS

All About the Benjamins (50 pts)
Combo on the High Seas (50 pts)
Skate the Liberty Trail (50 pts)
Team Challenge (50 pts)

SECRET GOALS

Kill the Grind Blockers (25 pts)
Jump the Cars (50 pts)
Scooter Vs. Wheelchair (50 pts)
Spine Transfer Tour (50 pts)

BOSTON

Training
Boston
Barcelona
Berlin
Australia
New Orleans
Skatopia
Pro Skater

BOSTON

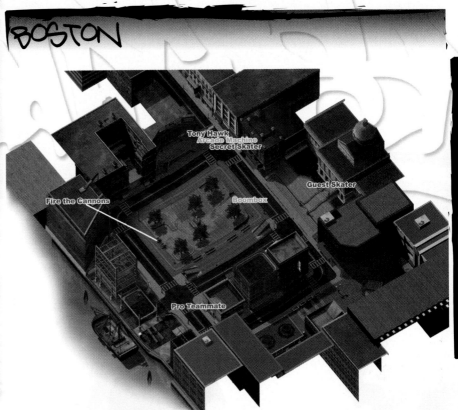

Tony Hawk
Arcade Machine
Secret Skater

Guest Skater

Boombox

Fire the Cannons

Pro Teammate

0 Goal Points are required to unlock this location.

1000 Goal Points are up for grabs.

Bob Burnquist is your teammate.

YOUR GOALS

Find the Special Guest

Locate the special guest and he will help you complete some more goals.

Jesse James of West Coast Choppers is hanging out at a bar where everyone knows his name. Locate the "Jeers" bar to the left of the Statehouse and walk down the ramp to its basement entrance. Approach the door to find Jesse James and to unlock the Secret Goals.

Intro

Skater Basics

Trick Lists

Story Mode

Gaps

Classic Mode

Multiskater

Secrets

Find Ben Franklin

A Ben Franklin impersonator is located somewhere around Boston. He will help you out if you can find him.

Ben Franklin is hiding out in the historical building up the hill from the statue of George Washington. Locate the half pipe on the right-hand side of the building (as viewed while facing it) and use it to air up and through the windows into the secret hallway above. Follow Ben Franklin through the doorway to complete the goal and to unlock the Guest Goals.

Mark Your Territory

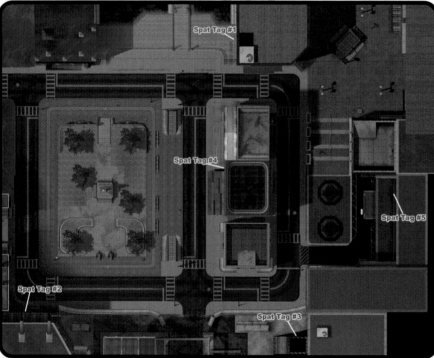

A graffiti punk named Spat has been leaving his tag all over the city. Make sure you tag over all of the Spat tags.

The first Spat tag is on the right-hand wall near the Statehouse. Walk across the lawn and Graffiti Tag over the Spat on the wall beside the quarter pipe.

Head down the street towards the construction site and locate the Spat tag on the blue wall to the right. It's right across the street from the cannons.

Spat tagged the side of the enormous vert ramps to the left of the construction area, near the ship. The tag is on the other side of the chain link fence from the corner near the hospital.

The fourth Spat tag is between the steps of the church and the raised mini-pipe above the scaffolding. It's easy to miss since it's written vertically.

The final Spat tag is atop the hospital. Use the banked walls to air up to the roof above the hospital entrance and Graffiti Tag over that Spat tag.

Hospital Duty

You need to steal a gurney from the local hospital and take the injured kid to meet his idol, Tony Hawk.

Taking the sick kid to meet Tony Hawk wouldn't be a problem if not for the numerous nurses who want to stop you. In order to complete this task, you must zigzag past the nurses while avoiding traffic.

Sprint across the street and cut through the alley between the church and the library. Loop around the park in a clockwise direction past the construction area and townhouses and be ready to swerve onto the grass to avoid one of the nurses. Cut across the street towards the road barricade to bring the boy to Tony.

Arcade Machine High Score

Find an arcade machine and set a high score.

The arcade machine is located across the street from the children's museum and the high score to beat is 50,000 points and you have 1:00 to do it.

There's a myriad of places to score points in Boston, but a nice scoring line exists right near the arcade machine. Grind the rail in front of Jeers and link it to a couple of grinds near the Statehouse building for the **Rail Hop** gap. Continue past the Statehouse building to the bus stop and then towards the plaza near the bank.

Wallie into a grind atop the ledge near the government building and Sticker Slap the wall above the ATM for the **Wall Slap** gap and land back in another grind on the ledge. Link it up with a manual towards the large ramps near the hospital.

Sick Mode: 100,000 points in 1:00.

Dance, Sucka

Locate the boombox and complete the tricks to the beat.

The boombox repeats a beat and it's up to the skater to perform the requested flip trick during the fourth note in the beat. The trick name and the boombox flash red when it's supposed to be performed. Listen to the music for a few moments, then ollie and perform the trick in time with the beat. Press Down on the controls to keep from skating away from the boombox. Only Kickflips and Heelflips are called for here.

Sick Mode: Look for an occasional Pop Shove-It and Impossible.

BOSTON

Training
Boston
Barcelona
Berlin
Australia
New Orleans
Skatopia
Pro Skater

Decapitate the Statues

Find a way to remove the heads of the 3 statues.

Skate down the hill towards the George Washington statue in the center courtyard and Spine Transfer over it in a lengthwise direction. Tap the Grind Button while soaring over it to knock off George's head. Spine Transferring over this statue also nets the **Washington Air** gap bonus.

The other two statues are posing as immobile sentries near the steps of the Statehouse building. Use the small ramps on either side of the stairs to leap into a lip trick atop each statue. Balance the stall long enough to hear the statue crack and ollie off as the head begins to fall.

Intro

Skater Basics

Trick Lists

Story Mode

Gaps

Classic Mode

Multiskater

Secrets

Combo on the RV Ramp

Start and land a 5,000 point combo while skating on the RV ramp.

JUMP THE CARS FIRST!

You must first help Jesse James complete the "Jump the Cars" goal in order to gain access to his special RV Ramp. The ramp is visible in the alley, but remains out of bounds until the cars are jumped while riding the scooter.

The RV Ramp cruises around the park at a rather modest speed, but staying on the ramp as it rounds each corner can prove to be difficult. Wait near one of the corners and skate up to the ramp and ollie onto it just as it turns the corner. Quickly launch into the air and link up several tricks and land it for the 5,000 point combo.

Sick Mode: Start and land a 25,000 point combo on the RV Ramp.

TRY THIS!

Having trouble landing a big aerial on the ramp while it's moving? If so, then try a combination of lip tricks. Roll up the ramp into an Invert. Double tap the control buttons to switch into other lip tricks. This is also a great time to initiate Focus, which should help with the tricky landing.

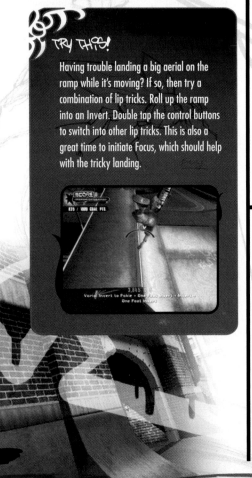

PRO GOALS

Combo the 4 Benches

Grind all four park benches in the same combo.

Locate the four benches near the park, across from the library. The benches are split into two pairs with a small gap between them. Although it's possible to hold-grind across each of the paired benches, an ollie is required between the second and third bench to keep the combo alive.

Ye Olde Cannon Grind

Locate and grind a cannon.

Two cannons are located directly across the street from the large construction site. Skate up to one of the cannons and ollie into a grind on it to complete the goal.

BRINGING DOWN THE BIG DIG

Grind both of the cannons while the skateboard is on fire to light the wicks on each of them, then stand back. Each cannon fires a cannonball at the construction site, thus causing it collapse into a new configuration—one perfect for skating! Use a Spine Transfer to reach the upper levels of the construction.

Skitch a Seaworthy Vehicle

Find a seaworthy vehicle and skitch on it for 20 seconds straight.

Boston is famous for its amphibious vehicles and although they are no good to skaters when they are on sea, these combination cars and boats are perfect for skitching behind while they're on the streets. Roll up behind the large sightseeing vessel and press Up on the controls to begin Skitching. Tap to the Left and Right on the controls to maintain balance as it cruises around town. Tap Down on the controls to release the skitch safely after 20 seconds.

Salute the General

Bust out a Benihana over the statue of Washington.

Leap off the banked base of the George Washington statue in the center of the park and tap the Spine Transfer Button to hit the **Washington Air** gap. Tap Down/Left + Grab Button to perform a Benihana while airing over the statue.

Great Balls of Fire

Start and land a 20,000 point combo while your board is on fire.

There is a garbage can with a fire burning in it on the corner in front of the construction site. Ollie through the flames to light the board on fire and launch into a combo.

Air off the ramp in front of the townhouse, Revert to a manual and steer back across the street to the wall that encircles the park. Trick into a grind on the wall and double-tap the various buttons to transition to other grind types to build the multiplier. Trick across the gap in the wall for the **Ledge Hop** gap, then ollie down to safety.

Sick Mode: Land a 50,000 point combo while your board is on fire.

Slap the Signs

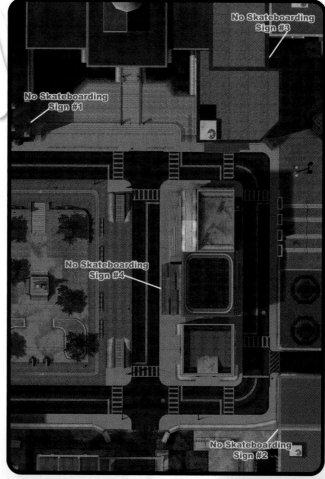

BOSTON

Training
Boston
Barcelona
Berlin
Australia
New Orleans
Skatopia
Pro Skater

Place a sticker on all 4 "No Skateboarding Signs" by performing the Sticker Slap trick.

Grind the upper fence in front of the Statehouse building towards the wall to the left. Ollie out of the grind and press the Jump Button when the skater is hitting the wall to Sticker Slap the sign.

Grind the fence in front of the construction site towards the hospital. Ollie off the fence just before it curves towards the hospital and Sticker Slap the sign on the wall.

*The next sign is on the side of the Riboff Bank. Grind the ledge atop the brick wall and ollie off the edge to Sticker Slap the sign above the ATM in the corner of the plaza. This also scores the **Wall Slap** gap bonus.*

The fourth sign is the easiest to hit, but is arguably the hardest to spot. It's right on the side of the blue scaffolding under the mini-ramp. Ollie up and Sticker Slap at your leisure.

Intro

Skater Basics

Trick Lists

Story Mode

Gaps

Classic Mode

Multiskater

Secrets

Tag a Big Billboard

Find a way up to this big billboard and spray it with your Graffiti Tag.

Head over to the construction site, then jump up and grab the large yellow chute with the ladder on it. Climb up the ladder and leap over to the hanging materials on the right. Hold the Jump Button down to sprint and run and leap for the second batch of suspended construction materials. Climb up and approach the large white sign and press the Grind Button to Graffiti Tag it.

Finest Rails in Boston

First grind the metal sculpture. Then, grind the rail in front of Jeers. Finally, grind the kid's museum rail.

Skate to the plaza up the steps from the hospital and grind the wavy metal sculpture to start the run at this goal. Head down the street to the right, past the Statehouse building, then ollie into a grind on the railing above the entrance to Jeers. Quickly ollie out of the grind and cross the street on an angle to the left. Grind any of the rails on the children's museum.

BEN FRANKLIN'S STATS

Category	Rating
Air	10
Spin	10
Lip	10
Ollie	1
Run	1
Speed	5
Flip	10
Switch	10
Rail	10
Manual	10

THE FRANKLIN GRIND

Switching off to Ben Franklin unlocks a new Special Trick called the Franklin Grind. Feel free to switch out the controls for the trick or to use the new Special Trick Slot to assign a different trick after switching back to your custom skater.

All About the Benjamins

See if you can get inside the Riboff Bank.

Continue in a counter-clockwise direction past the hospital to the large plaza up the steps to locate the Riboff Bank. Gain speed off the subway entrance in front of the Tony Hawk portrait and then skate past the metal sculpture towards the banked wall. Launch off the wall on an angle and rotate through the air to crash through the metal grate to land inside the bank for the **Bank Transfer** gap.

Combo on the High Seas

Start and land a 10,000 point combo while skating on the Tea Party Boat.

BOMBS AWAY!

This goal can easily be completed immediately following the "Skate the Liberty Trail" goal by using the momentum gained from the Acid Drop off the crow's nest to launch extremely high into the air off the quarter pipe at the ship's bow. Link up several grab and flip tricks while rotating to score a very fast 10,000 points.

The bow of the ship on the lower deck is rimmed with a lengthy quarter pipe that is perfect for launching into a quick five-figure combo. Use plenty of rotation to increase the score and link up several quick flip tricks and grabs with a Revert on the landing to get the requisite score to complete the goal.

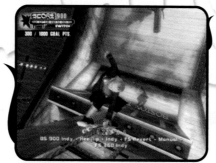

Sick Mode: Start and land a 25,000 point combo on the Tea Party Boat.

Skate the Liberty Trail

First do a Pop Shove-It down the Statehouse stairs, then vert transfer over a library mural. Finally, Acid Drop from the crow's nest of the Tea Party Boat.

Start atop the steps where Ben Franklin goes after being found and ollie down the steps while tapping Down + Flip Button to perform a Pop Shove-It while nabbing the **Statehouse Stairs** gap bonus.

Head down the street to the left of the courtyard and use the vert ramps on either side of library to vert transfer up and over the mural. Approach at a relatively steep angle and ollie off the edge of the ramp to clear the mural without hitting the ledge for the **Library Mural** gap.

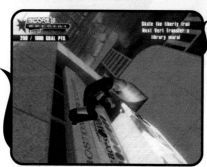

Turn to the left and Spine Transfer into the Tea Party Boat. Quickly leap off the board and climb the ladder to the crow's nest. Approach the edge and jump into the air and press the Revert Button to Acid Drop onto the deck below for the **Tea Bomb** gap bonus.

Team Challenge

3 of your team members must do a flip trick over an inline skater.

There's a shirtless inline skater doing laps around the park and he needs to be reminded that this is territory is strictly for skateboarding. Skate towards him and perform a flip trick while ollieing into his head for the **Blader Hop** bonus. The flip trick only counts if you knock him to the ground, hence the blow to his noggin. Heelflips, Kickflips, and Hardflips are most suitable for this goal. Perform the flip trick over the inline skater with Ben Franklin, Custom Skater, and your chosen Pro Skater to earn the Goal Points.

JESSE JAMES'S STATS

Category	Rating
Air	1
Spin	10
Lip	10
Ollie	1
Run	1
Speed	5
Flip	10
Switch	10
Rail	10

BOSTON

Training
Boston
Barcelona
Berlin
Australia
New Orleans
Skatopia
Pro Skater

JESSE JAMES RIDES AGAIN!

Jesse James isn't about to start hoofing it on a skateboard; he doesn't touch anything that doesn't have an engine. Enjoy cruising around on his scooter. He can grind, jump, and do amazing spins. The one thing he can't do, however, is bail.

Kill the Grind Blockers

Remove all 4 of the grind blockers from the vent rail.

Ride over to the hospital on Jesse James' scooter and hop into a grind on the ledge alongside the ventilation unit. Hold the grind for a complete lap to knock off all four of the grind blockers. This ledge is underneath the portion of the hospital that sticks out on the second floor.

Jump the cars

Jump over 3 vehicles while driving around on Jesse James' scooter.

Cruise over to the park and watch the cars drive around the town in endless loops. Inch out onto the sidewalk and wait for a car to pass. Hold the Jump Button down for speed, then rush forward and jump over the car as it passes. Score the **Car Hop** bonus with Jesse James three times to complete the goal.

Scooter Vs. Wheelchair

Race Paulie around the block and back on Jesse James' scooter. Ride past the church, library, and hospital and get back here before Paulie does.

Head over to the plaza up the steps from the hospital and talk to Paulie to challenge him to a race. The racecourse is a quick loop around the block in front of the hospital. Start by speeding past the Riboff Bank to the church steps. Continue down the street to the library and turn to the left. Hold the Jump Button down to race past the hospital entrance. Jump into a grind on the ledge near the stairs to quickly ascend the steps towards the plaza where the race began. Manage to complete the lap before Paulie does to claim victory.

Spine Transfer Tour

Start with a Spine Transfer over a subway entrance. Next, Spine Transfer over a hospital volcano. Finally, Spine Transfer over the water into the Tea Party Boat.

Ride up to the subway entrance in front of the church and Spine Transfer over it for the **Subway Spine** gap. Cruise around the side of the church towards the hospital and slowly hop the curb towards either of the brick cylinders. Spine Transfer over either of these objects for the **Hospital Volcano Spine**. Speed off towards the Tea Party Boat and Spine Transfer from the ramp at the edge of the construction site into the boat for the **Tea Party Transfer** gap.

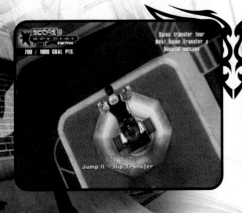

The Power of the Hawk Side

Skate over to the apartment building to the right of the construction site and enter the front plaza area. Use the quarter pipes to air up to the window on the left-hand side (as viewed while facing the street) and crash through the window. Quickly dismount and approach the boy on the couch and press the Grab Button. The force is strong with this one. Press the Grab Button a second time to make him stop before he hurts someone.

Dances with Livestock

Break through the right-hand apartment window and hop off the board to stop and watch as this crazy Bostonian cuts a rug for his favorite goat.

BARCELONA

Training
Boston
Barcelona
Berlin
Australia
New Orleans
Skatopia
Pro Skater

YOUR GOALS

Free the Bull Fighter (25 pts)

Find the Special Guest (25 pts)

Hit 5 Peds with Tomatoes (25 pts)

Spine the Guell Planters (25 pts)

Help Peg Leg (25 pts)

Mark Your Territory (25 pts)

Take Out the Trash (25 pts)

Arcade Machine High Score (50 pts)

PRO GOALS

Combo the Sants Benches (25 pts)

Catapult 720 Grab (25 pts)

Tag the Big Billboard (25 pts)

Focus Combos (50 pts)

Rail Rated Challenge (50 pts)

Transfer Over the
Guell Entrance (50 pts)

Acid Drop Off a Tram (50 pts)

Team Challenge (100 pts)

GUEST GOALS

La Perdrera Spiral Rail (25 pts)

Smells Like Bull Dung (50 pts)

Make Your Own Phoenix (50 pts)

Don't Touch the Ground (50 pts)

SECRET GOALS

Steve-O Vs. the Bull (25 pts)

Parc Guell Combo (50 pts)

Yee Haw! Fan Boost (50 pts)

Flip Barcelona's Finest (100 pts)

BARCELONA

500 Goal Points are required to unlock this location.

1000 Goal Points are up for grabs.

Select Mike Vallely or Rodney Mullen as a teammate.

Map labels: To Tram · To Tram · Guest Skater · Secret Skater · To Tram · Pro Teammate · To Catapults · Tony Hawk · Arcade Machine · To AC Vent · To Tram

YOUR GOALS

Free the Bull Fighter

The Bull Fighter needs your help! Find a way to safely get him down from there.

Grab some tomatoes from the crate on the busy street in front of the bridge and skate back to the alley between the Parc Guell and the museum. Walk up next to the guy throwing tomatoes at the bull and press the Flip Button to lob a tomato at the bull. A direct hit angers the bull and sends him crashing out of his enclosure. The bull goes on a rampage throughout the city, but more importantly, the Bull Fighter and his corresponding Secret Goals become available.

Intro

Skater Basics

Trick Lists

Story Mode

Gaps

Classic Mode

Multiskater

Secrets

Find the Special Guest

That crazy man Steve-O is hiding some place. If you find him, he'll help you complete more goals.

Enter the open doors directly across from the "Farmacia" sign to be whisked to the upper floor of the office building. Steve-O is sitting atop his mechanical bull just steps ahead! It's also possible to use the quarter pipes below the office building to air up and crash through the windows onto the floor with the skybridge.

Hit 5 Peds with Tomatoes

Try to hit 5 different pedestrians with a tomato.

There are people walking around all over the place. Why not hit them with tomatoes? Load up on ammunition from the crate of tomatoes near the bridge or from the one near the Parc Guell entrance and skate around, hitting people with them. Press the Flip Button to throw the tomatoes when facing in the general direction of a pedestrian. Although hitting the same pedestrian over and over is quite funny, you must hit five different people to complete this goal.

Spine the Guell Planters

Spine Transfer over all 3 of the planters in Parc Guell.

There are several quarter pipes that can be used to Spine Transfer in this area, but there are only three planters. Approach the Parc Guell and Spine Transfer up and over the planter in the middle area to the left for the **Guell Planter Spine Transfer** gap. Cross over the entryway to the large treed area on the right and Spine Transfer up and over both of the planters in the center there.

Help Peg Leg

Peg Leg has got his boat stuck in the netting. You should find a way to free his boat.

There's a single rope entangling Peg Leg's boat and it's up to you to grind across it to free him. Ollie over the police barricades near the bridge and grind the right-hand railing near the edge of the bridge. Transfer the grind to the net line on the right and balance the grind across the rear of the boat for the **Arghhh** gap. Ollie off the rope into the water once the boat is free.

THE OTHER SIDE OF BARCELONA

Freeing Peg Leg's boat from the ropes allows the drawbridge to close, granting access to the other side of the city. Cross the bridge to explore some of the other sights by the water.

Mark Your Territory

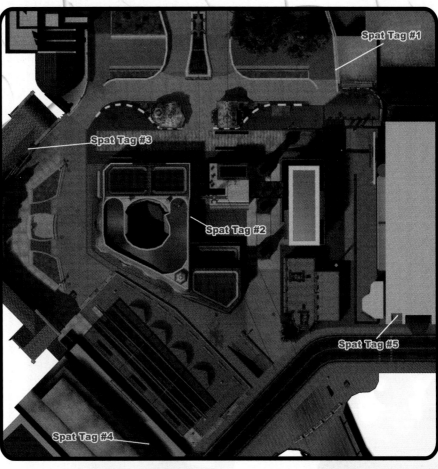

Spat Tag #1

Spat Tag #3

Spat Tag #2

Spat Tag #5

Spat Tag #4

Spat has made his way to Barcelona and is at it again. Locate his 5 tags and spray your Graffiti Tag over them.

The first of the Spat tags is located on the wall near the Guell Planters. Pass by the Parc Guell entrance in a clockwise direction as if headed towards the trapped Bull Fighter. The tag is near the street corner.

There is another Spat tag on the side of the La Perdrera building. Enter the alley directly across from the fountain at the entrance to the Parc Guell and Graffiti Tag the wall on the right.

Spat somehow tagged a wall of a building high off the ground. Travel in a counter-clockwise direction from the entrance to Parc Guell and double jump onto the building with the brick lattice. Drop into a hanging position on the edge and shimmy across the wire to the blue building to Graffiti Tag over the large Spat.

The fourth Spat tag is on the wall above the Estacion Sants. Leap into a grind on the upper rail and the ollie out of the grind and Graffiti Tag over Spat's work.

The final Spat tag is next to the glass wall of the museum, near the busy street. Run and leap over the ledge to get close enough to it to make the tag.

Intro

Skater Basics

Trick Lists

Story Mode

Gaps

Classic Mode

Multiskater

Secrets

Take Out the Trash

Locate and empty out 4 different trash cans.

There are over a half dozen trash cans scattered throughout the city. Find four different trash cans and ollie into a grind on top of them. They're so narrow that you'll likely only score a "Kissed the Rail" grind, but that's all that is necessary. Grinding a trash to score the **Taking Out the Trash** gap.

Arcade Machine High Score

Find an arcade machine and set a high sore.

The arcade machine is located right near the busy street, down the road from the museum and the bridge. A score of 65,000 points is required to gain the high score on the machine.

Those with good grind balance can lay claim to the high score in seconds by skating over to the bridge. Light the Special Meter by tricking into a grind on the left-hand rail in the center of the bridge. Switch up the grind to increase the multiplier and then trick into a Special Grind. Ollie into another Special Grind on the upper rail to the left on the far side of the bridge for the **Bridge Rail Transfer** gap and finish off the combo with a quick grind on the side of the building before throwing a Double Kickflip into the mix while dropping back to the ground below.

Sick Mode: 250,000 points in 1:00.

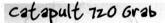

PRO GOALS

Combo the Sants Benches

In front of the Estacion Sants station are 8 benches. Grind all of these benches in one combo.

There are eight benches lined up in a row between the Estacion Sants station and the La Perdrera building. Ollie into a grind on the bench at either end of the row and hold the Grind Button down to hold-grind across all of them. The score will likely show numerous "Kissed the Rail" tricks, but that's all it takes to complete the goal and to nab the **Sants Benches** gap bonus.

Catapult 720 Grab

Perform a 720 grab trick after getting launched from a catapult.

Skate out onto the busy street and line up with the arched entrance to the castle. Skate into the building to immediately get launched from one of two catapults on the roof. Start rotating to the left or right while performing a grab trick. Depending on how fast the skater is able to spin, there shouldn't be much trouble landing a 720 or 900 rotation during the **Catapult Launch**.

Tag the Big Billboard

Find a way up to this big billboard and leave your Graffiti Tag.

The best way up to the big billboard is to Spine Transfer down off the rooftop of the building near the La Perdrera building, across from the catapults. Use the rooftop pools to Spine Transfer up onto the roof and line up with the building with the large billboard tower on it. Spine Transfer down to ground level and use the quarter pipe at the base of the building with the billboard to launch high into the air and onto the roof.

Once atop the roof of the office building, hop off the board and carefully climb the ladder to the billboard. Jump over to the ledge in front of the sign and press the Grind Button to Graffiti Tag it.

Focus Combos

Get Focus, and then perform 3 different 2,500 point combos.

The trick to completing this goal is to remember that you must be in Focus before beginning the combo. Trick out the Special Meter and roll to an area where you'd like to begin the brief combo. Initiate Focus, then go about starting and landing a 2,500 point combo.

The best way to rack up the points for the Focus Combo is to flip trick into a manual and link a few quick flatland tricks together. The Focus makes it easier to balance and a multiplier of 3 or 4 should be all it takes, especially with a Kickflip into a Special Manual. Repeat this tactic two more times to complete the goal.

Rail Rated Challenge

First grind the three chain rails in front of the Estacion Sants station. Next, Sticker Slap the Jeep sign on the hospital. Finally, grind the rail that is on top of the station roof.

Start in the street near the arcade machine and wait for the pedestrian traffic to disperse a bit. Ollie into a grind on the chain rail nearest the street. It's important to be quick, so be ready to transfer the grind across all three of the chain rails with two quick ollies. The skater pops upwards off the third chain rail. Sticker Slap the large Jeep sign to gain extra height and to reverse direction. Land in a grind on the yellow rail above the Barcelona-Sants sign.

Transfer Over the Guell Entrance

Perform a ramp-to-ramp transfer from one side of Guell park to the other.

Approach the Parc Guell area and skate up to the upper terrace on the right-hand side. Trick off the quarter pipe for speed and then Spine Transfer up and over the two planters for the **Guell Planter Spine Transfer** gap. Hit the quarter-pipe near the entrance at a pretty shallow angle to launch up and over the fountain and the entrance. Rotate to the right to help pull the skater through the air to the quarter pipe on the other side for the **Guell Planter Dragon Transfer** gap.

Acid Drop Off a Tram

Take a ride on a tram and then jump off and Acid Drop into a ramp.

ALL ABOARD!

There are three places where you can be teleported directly to the top of a tram tower. For starters, enter either of the stations at the two tram towers (one above Parc Guell and the other near the pier). There is also a tunnel underneath the fountain at Parc Guell that also leads directly to the top of the tram tower.

Skate across the bridge to the pier area and enter the tram tower at the edge of the course. The skater is automatically teleported to the roof of the tower. Stand still and wait for a tram to approach on the right-hand cable and carefully jump onto its roof. Stand on the top of the tram and wait for it to begin passing over the building directly across from the castle with the catapults on it. Jump off the tram and press the Spine Transfer Button to Acid Drop into the quarter pipe atop the roof. There are many other ramps that can be used to complete this goal, but this is the safest bet.

BARCELONA

Training
Boston
Barcelona
Berlin
Australia
New Orleans
Skatopia
Pro Skater

Intro

Skater Basics

Trick Lists

Story Mode

Gaps

Classic Mode

Multiskater

Secrets

Team Challenge

4 of your team members must get thrown into the air by the bull and perform a 5,000 point combo.

A BUNCH OF BULL

This goal cannot be completed until after the bull has busted out of his pen. Complete the "Free the Bull Fighter" goal in order to get the requisite stampede.

Once on the loose, the bull endlessly speeds through the alleyways of Barcelona, knocking over everything and everyone it contacts. Fortunately, the bull won't cause the skater to bail. Instead, it actually boosts the skater into the air for the **Bull Air** bonus. Track down the bull (follow the dust cloud and steaming piles of digested bull food) and skate into him to pop into the air. Let Bull Air be the starting point for a combo worth 5,000 points with each team member to complete the goal.

This goal can be a bit tricky when skating as Steve-O on his mechanical bull, but just remember to land in a manual (Wheelie for Steve-O) and quickly hop into a grind for extra points. If you're having trouble, get in front of the bull as the skaters fly higher into the air when hit by the bull's horns. It's possible to link up a Bull Air with a **Fan Boost** by soaring over the dragon fountain and also over the fans atop the building.

GUEST GOALS

BULL FIGHTER'S STATS

Category	Rating
Air	10
Spin	10
Lip	10
Ollie	10
Run	10
Speed	10
Flip	10
Switch	10
Rail	10
Manual	10

THE ESPANA SWORD SLIDE

Switching to the Bull Fighter unlocks a Special Trick slot, as well as the ability to use this matador-inspired Special Grind called the Espana Sword Slide. One part 50-50 grind plus one part fencing equals two parts of high scoring coolness.

La Perdrera Spiral Rail

Start at the top of the building and grind down the entire La Perdrera spiral rail.

Spine Transfer onto the roof of the building adjacent the La Perdrera building and hop off the board. Run and leap onto the roof near the top of the spiral and ollie or Caveman into a grind on the spiral. Carefully maintain balance all the way to the ground without popping out of that initial grind. It's important that the skater maintain a single grind from top to bottom to complete the goal and to gain the **La Perdrera Spiral** gap.

Smells Like Bull Dung

Launch off a pile of bull dung and perform a grab trick.

There are dozens of piles of bull dung littering the ground around the castle and Estacion Sants areas. Hold the Jump Button down for speed and steer into one of the piles to pop into the air. Grab a handful of board while airborne to complete the goal. Pulling a quick Nosegrab or Melon is a quick and easy way to meet the objective with little risk.

Make Your Own Phoenix

Find a way to light your board on fire, then find a bird to make a phoenix.

Locate the burning car across the busy street from the castle and ollie over it to light the skateboard on fire. Cross the street and enter the arched doorway to the castle to be catapulted into the flock of birds high above. Use this particular doorway as the other catapult is not in line with the flock of birds.

STEVE-O'S STATS

Category	Rating
Air	10
Spin	10
Lip	10
Ollie	1
Run	1
Speed	5
Flip	10
Switch	10
Rail	10
Manual	10

GIDDY UP STEVE-O!

Steve-O may be riding a mechanical bull, but that doesn't mean he can't do some tricks. He can do grabs (Yee Haw!), spins (Bull Flip), and he can even do a manual (Wheelie). Unfortunately, Steve-O can also fall off his trusty mechanical steed.

BARCELONA

Training
Boston
Barcelona
Berlin
Australia
New Orleans
Skatopia
Pro Skater

Don't Touch the Ground

Make it from one end of the bridge to the other without touching the ground.

Skate over to the street in front of the castle and face the left-hand side of the bridge Grind off the angled sign to get the height needed to reach the wavy red rail on the side of the bridge for the **Rambla del Agua** gap. Grind this upper rail and drop off the end into another grind on the handrail near the bridge's surface for the **Bridge Rail Transfer** gap. Hold the grind until another wavy red rail on the left dips down within reach. Hop into a grind on this final rail in order to reach the end of the bridge without ever touching the ground for the **Rambla no Terrano** gap.

Steve-O Vs. the Bull

Have Steve-O play chicken with the bull on the loose. Go head-to-head and see who backs down first.

The bull is a fast moving creature and Steve-O needs to charge him head on in order to complete this goal. Consider waiting for the bull in front of the museum, right where the bull was originally penned up. Watch for the bull to round the corner and then hold the Jump Button and speed off directly at him for the **Bull Vs Bull** bonus.

Parc Guell Combo

Start and land a 35,000 point combo while skating in the Parc Guell area.

Ride the bull over to the Parc Guell area and head up to the top of the park to where the tram tower is. Grind the back ledge in a clockwise direction and link up the grind with a few quick Spine Transfers up and over the planters. There won't be any time to Wheelie between the Spine Transfers so concentrate on getting off the Revert in time. Rotate as much as possible while airborne and throw down as many Bull Flips and Yee Haws! as possible. Keep the combo alive until the 35,000 points have been obtained.

Sick Mode: Start and land a 60,000 point combo while skating the Parc Guell area.

Link up multiple **Guell Planter Spine Transfers** with the **Guell Planter Dragon Transfer** for extra points and hop into a grind if necessary.

Intro

Skater Basics

Trick Lists

Story Mode

Gaps

Classic Mode

Multiskater

Secrets

Yee Haw! Fan Boost

Use the fans on the building to get a boost. Do a Yee Haw! grab and then Acid Drop into a QP.

Spine Transfer onto the buildings near the castle, then turn and Spine Transfer back down to the street to gain speed. Quickly angle Steve-O to right and Spine Transfer up onto the roof of the office building to catch the **Fan Boost**. Snag a quick Yee Haw! grab in while airborne and tap the Spine Transfer Button again to Acid Drop back onto one of the ramps below.

Flip Barcelona's Finest

Barcelona is famous for some great skate spots. Land a flip trick at each of the following spots: Land a flip trick off a table by the Estacion Sants station. Land a flip trick off the ledge in front of the museum. Land a flip trick over the rail from the Besos waves.

Ride over to the Estacion Sants station and slowly roll up to one of the tables and jump onto it. Hold the Jump Button down to get a short burst of speed and perform the Bull Flip trick while leaping from the table for the **Sants Bench Flip** gap.

The next spot is the museum near the castle. Grind the long ledge in front of the glass wall and perform a Bull Flip out of the grind for the **MAMO Flip** gap.

The final spot is the Besos waves across the bridge. Slowly roll through the waves away from the subway entrance and then leap up and over the railing while pulling off another Bull Flip for the **Besos Flip** gap.

BERLIN

Training
Boston
Barcelona
Berlin
Australia
New Orleans
Skatopia
Pro Skater

YOUR GOALS

Inliners Rule (25 pts)	
Free the Spirits (25 pts)	
Find the Special Guest (25 pts)	
Help Wee-Man (25 pts)	
Stop the Kids From Smoking (25 pts)	
Arcade Machine High Score (50 pts)	
Find the Graffiti Tagger (50 pts)	
Berlin Gets Owned (50 pts)	

PRO GOALS

Grind N' Barf (25 pts)	
Almighty Combo (25 pts)	
Learn the Natas Spin (25 pts)	
Hats on Fire (50 pts)	
So Focused, So Clean (50 pts)	
Tourist Time (50 pts)	
Disrupt Communication (50 pts)	
Pro Tour Line (75 pts)	

GUEST GOALS

Paint Bomber (50 pts)	
Mark Your Territory (50 pts)	
Tag the Big Billboard (50 pts)	
Tagger Skillz (50 pts)	

SECRET GOALS

Berlin Tour (25 pts)	
Wheelin' Combo (50 pts)	
Skills on Wheels (50 pts)	
Team Challenge (100 pts)	

BERLIN

1000 Goal Points are required to unlock this location.

1000 Goal Points are up for grabs.

Bam Margera is your teammate in Berlin.

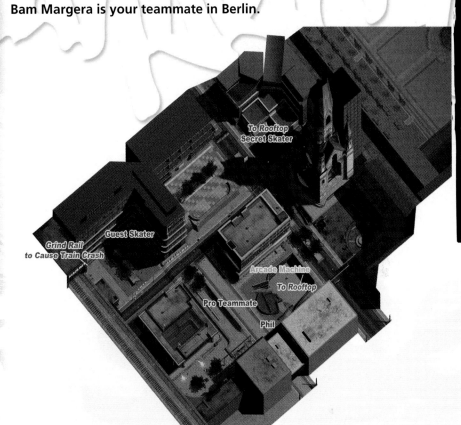

To Rooftop Secret Skater

Guest Skater

Grind Rail to Cause Train Crash

Arcade Machine To Rooftop

Pro Teammate

Phil

YOUR GOALS

Inliners Rule

The inliners think they own this city. Smash the 2 "Inliners Rule" signs, and show them who really rules.

The first of the two signs is to the right of Gretchen's Bar, in the Oktoberfest area. Air up from the quarter pipe in the plaza and grind across the top of the sign to smash it.

The second sign is in the plaza across from the "Berlin Platz" sign). Head down the street past the Gallerie building from the first sign and use the quarter pipe near the floor of the plaza to air up and either lip trick or grind atop the sign.

Intro

Skater Basics

Trick Lists

Story Mode

Gaps

Classic Mode

Multiskater

Secrets

Free the Spirits

There are spirits trapped inside the bombed-out church. Find a way to set those spirits free.

Skate over to the large church and roll around to the right-hand side where the graffiti artist is spray painting his "Toy" tag. Spine Transfer up and over the wall for the **Into Church** gap. Between all of the quarter pipes is a large stone door with several cracks in it. Gain some speed off the ramps and Sticker Slap this cracked door two times to break it down, thereby freeing the spirits.

Find the Special Guest

The special guest in this city is your own teammate, Paulie. Find out where he is and have him give you a hand with some goals.

Paulie is on the roof of the ornate yellow building, across the street from the bombed-out church. Ride up the small wooden ramp near the curved steps and simply skate through the gray doors in the corner to be teleported to the rooftop to find him.

Help Wee-Man

Help Wee-Man release his favorite fish from the aquarium.

Wee-Man is standing in front of the fish tank by the aquarium near the church. Skate towards the glass tank and Sticker Slap it twice to break the glass and release the fish.

WEE-MAN CAN WAIT

Hold off on completing this goal until after you've helped Bam Margera light the Berlin cops' hats on fire. The water from the fish tank submerges much of the walkway where the cops patrol, making it harder to keep the skateboard aflame.

Stop the Kids From Smoking

Prevent kids from buying cigarettes. Smash the 3 tobacco dispensers.

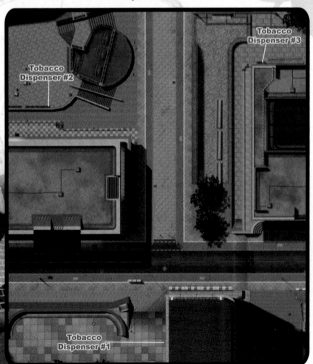
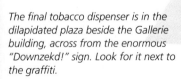

The first tobacco dispenser is in the plaza across from the "Berlin Platz" sign. It's the plaza with the pink, yellow, and gray floor tiles. Skate up to it and Sticker Slap it.

The second tobacco dispenser is right next to the arcade machine, down the steps at the Ausfarht Center.

The final tobacco dispenser is in the dilapidated plaza beside the Gallerie building, across from the enormous "Downzekd!" sign. Look for it next to the graffiti.

Arcade Machine High Score

Find an arcade machine and set a high score.

The arcade machine is down the steps near the Ausfarht Center and you must score 85,000 points or higher to take over the top score. There are great places to score points right near the arcade machine.

Bust a few quick grab tricks while airing up and over the **AusFarht Transfer** gap, then quickly Revert into a manual and ollie into a Special Grind on the rail going up the steps. Expect to lose speed and start to descend that same rail. Manual across the ground back to the ramps and leap into a lip trick above the sign for the **AusFarht** Lip.

Sick Mode: 350,000 points in 1:00.

Link up the following Spine Transfer gaps by traveling from the aquarium around the block in a counter-clockwise direction: **Into Church**, **Out of Church**, **Sonata Spine**, **Sonata Hip**, and another final **Sonata Spine** on the way back down to the street.

Find the Graffiti Tagger

Find a local graffiti tagger and have him join your team.

There are several graffiti taggers in Berlin, but only one who is willing to join your merry band of skating delinquents. Return to the plaza with the pink and yellow floor tiles and use the quarter pipe to air up to the second ledge. Hop off the board and climb the ladder in the corner to the uppermost ledge. Carefully run along the ledge in a clockwise direction around the yellow portion of the building. The tagger is standing on this ledge near a box of paint cans, up above the Oktoberfest party.

Berlin Gets Owned

Remove some letters from this sign so that it says "Owned!"

Three letters must be removed from the large sign in order to spell out "Owned!" The way to do this is to use the curved yellow rails on the awning below it to leap up and lip trick atop the letters that need to be removed.

Wallie into a grind on the large wall alongside the street and ollie into a grind on the leftmost yellow rail. Ollie out of this grind straight into a lip trick atop the "D".

Remove the "Z" and "K" in a similar fashion. Grind the wall surrounding the walkway of the building across the plaza and use the kinked edge of the wall to pop into a grind on the yellow rail under the desired letter (push left or right in the air to reach the correct rail). Grind up the banked rail and leap into a lip trick atop the letters to make them drop.

ONE GRIND TO OWN THEM ALL

It's possible to grind up the left-hand awning rail near the "D" and transition into a grind towards the right and knock down all three of the necessary letters at once. Don't worry, the other letters won't fall.

PRO GOALS

Grind N Barf

Find the 2 Rent-A-Cops and perform the Grind N Barf trick on the ledges right above them.

The first of the two Rent-A-Cops is standing right near the wall where Bam was hanging out with his fans. Trick out the Special Meter and charge the end of the wall on the far right. Use the quarter pipe at the base of the ramp to pop straight into the air, then tap the Spine Transfer Button to level out while airborne. This makes it possible to land in the Grind N Barf Special Grind without passing the copper.

The other Rent-A-Cop is standing by the entrance to the AusFarht Center. Head up onto the busy road above the center and ollie into a Grind N Barf on the railing above the Rent-A-Cop. Hold the grind past the cop to make sure he gets good and showered.

BERLIN

Training
Boston
Barcelona
Berlin
Australia
New Orleans
Skatopia
Pro Skater

41

Intro

Skater Basics

Trick Lists

Story Mode

Gaps

Classic Mode

Multiskater

Secrets

Almighty Combo

Score a 35,000 point combo while skating in the bombed-out church.

Spine Transfer over the wall and into the church and string an aerial-rich combo together off the numerous quarter pipes at the base of the walls. Go back and forth across the church floor connecting tricks together with timely Reverts and manuals. Don't worry about busting huge, exotic, tricks off the ramps. Add rotation to standard tricks and work on increasing the multiplier.

Sick Mode: 45,000 point combo while skating in the bombed-out church.

Learn the Natas Spin

Find Natas Kaupas and have him teach you how to perform the Natas Spin trick.

Those who skated in the late 1980's and early 1990's will certainly remember the name Natas Kaupas. This old school skater still has some tricks to teach the current generation, so pay close attention to what he has to say. Natas is chilling out on the median in front of the church. Roll up to him and press the Grab Button to learn how to do the Natas Spin.

The Natas Spin can only be performed on posts and fire hydrants and other similar shaped objects. Ollie onto the post and simultaneously press the Rotate Right + Grind Button. Tap to the Left and Right on the controls to maintain balance while the skater spins like a top, er, atop the pole. Use the nearby poles to perform 3 Natas Spins to complete this goal.

Hats on Fire

Locate 3 Berlin cops and see if you can set their hats on fire all at once.

There are three Berlin cops patrolling the area near the zoo and the AusFahrt Center. Grind across the flaming gas pipe in the trench near the street to light the skateboard on fire and ollie over each of the three cops to ignite their hats. Each of the Berlin cops are dressed in brown uniforms and have large, highly combustible hats on their heads. Spend a few moments pinpointing each of the cops' whereabouts before lighting the skateboard on fire. The fire on the skateboard goes out after roughly 15 seconds, but it's possible to re-light the fire and finish the job. All three Berlin cops must have their hats on fire simultaneously to complete the goal.

So Focused, So Clean

Land 3 clean 10,000 point combos while you are focused.

It's not enough to just get Focus and bust out a 10,000 point combo. In order to complete this goal, you must end each combo by cleanly landing a trick with at least 180 degrees of rotation. Although this certainly makes the task more difficult, skaters are awarded a 1,000 point bonus for clean landings so it's actually easier to reach the requisite score. In order to get credit for a clean landing, the landing must be done without any crookedness or wobble.

The interior of the bombed-out church is a great place to complete this goal, as the quarter pipes provide plenty of place to score points and the hallway between the main area of the church and the area where the spirits were is a great place to punctuate each combo with a quick 180 flip trick. Use the quarter pipes to trick out the Special Meter and then land cleanly and get Focused.

Start at the back of the church, under the suspended ladder, and launch into a aerial combo. Revert to a manual upon landing and carefully end the line with a 180-degree Kickflip or Pop Shove-It. Repeat this line two more times to complete the goal.

Sick Mode: Land 3 clean 15,000 point combos while focused.

Tourist Line

First grind the zoo ledge. Next, grind the blue pipe. Next, grind the barriers. Next, grind the stairs. Next, grind the ledge. Next, Sticker Slap the blue sign. Next, grind the ledge again. Finally, Acid Drop into the wall ramp.

Skate over to where Wee-Man was staring at the fish and hop into a clockwise grind on the ledge of the zoo. Cross the street, grind the pipe, then link up quick grinds across the barriers and the steps that curve to the right for the **Ledge Hop** gap. Cross the plaza, ride up the wooden ramp on an angle to the left and grind the top of the ledge. Ollie off the end of the ledge, Sticker Slap the blue-lit sign, and land back in a grind on the ledge. Use the kinked end of the ledge to pop high into the air and press the Spine Transfer Button to make a blind Acid Drop onto the ramp on the other side of the wall near the street for the **Wall Drop** gap.

Disrupt Communication

First, get a jump boost from this vent. Then Acid Drop on to the Gallerie QP. Perform a Rocket Air over the satellites from one ramp to the other.

The first step in performing this stunt is to get to the top of the building with the vent. Although it's possible to grind across the cable from the building with the yellow ledges, it's much easier to enter the doors of the AusFarht Center and be teleported to the rooftop. Once on the roof, skate across to the vents and ollie off the roof while directly above the vent. The gush of air sends the skater soaring into the air. Press the Spine Transfer Button while in the air to Acid Drop onto the roof of the Gallerie. Speed across the roof on an angle to the left and transfer up and over the glass roof and the two satellite dishes to the ramp on the far left. Tap into a Rocket Air during the vert transfer (Up, Grab, Grab) to complete the goal.

Pro Tour Line

First, skate up this quarter-pipe. Next, grind the lower ledge. Next, grind the middle ledge. Next, grind the upper ledge. Next, grind the lower ledge of the Gallerie. Next, grind the awning rails towards the letters. Finally, lip the letters.

Head over to Gretchen's Bar and use the quarter pipe below the yellow ledges to leap into a grind on the lower ledge. Grind to the right and pop off the kink in the ledge to reach the middle ledge for the **Second Tier** gap. Continue to the right and leap off the next kinked portion to reach a grind on the upper ledge to score the **Third Tier** gap. Ollie off the end of the ledge and land in a grind on the ledge near the Gallerie building across the street. Pop off the kink at the end of the ledge and grind up one of the yellow awning rails into a lip trick atop the lettered sign.

Intro

Skater Basics

Trick Lists

Story Mode

Gaps

Classic Mode

Multiskater

Secrets

GUEST GOALS

GRAFFITI TAGGER'S STATS

Category	Rating
Air	10
Spin	10
Lip	10
Ollie	10
Run	10
Speed	10
Flip	10
Switch	10
Rail	10
Manual	10

DOUBLE FISTIN'

The Graffiti Tagger has some awesome skating abilities, but finding him unlocks an extra Special Trick slot and access to his patented Double Fistin' trick. Double Fistin' is a very quick Special Air trick that showcases the Graffiti Tagger's fondness for aerosol. The trick occurs so fast that it's possible to land a Double Fistin' out of a simple ollie.

Paint Bomber

Grab some spray paint cans and throw them at 5 rival taggers.

PAINT CAN SUPPLIES

There are several boxes full of spray paint cans in the area. There's a box of cans on the ledge where the Graffiti Tagger was originally found. There's a box near the arcade machine. There's also a box behind the Gallerie building, near the chatting girls.

The first rival tagger is spray painting the side of the church, near the aquarium. You've probably Spine Transferred right over him several times.

Climb the ladder in the corner of the building where the pink and yellow ledges come together. The next tagger is on the uppermost level, to the right.

Ollie off the roof of the Gallerie building into a grind on the ledge that wraps around towards the "Downzked!" sign. The next tagger is in the corner, on the ledge under the train tracks.

Another rival tagger is on the ledge near the large blue pipe that goes up and over the street above the AusFarht Center. It's possible to stand in the street and hit him with can from afar.

The final tagger is on the ledge next to the Berlin Platz sign. Either drop down from the roof or grind the ledge near the "Afropick" sign, then hop off and throw the can at him.

Mark Your Territory

Tag the Big Billboard

BERLIN

Training
Boston
Barcelona
Berlin
Australia
New Orleans
Skatopia
Pro Skater

This billboard looks like the perfect place to leave your mark. Find a way up here and tag it.

Skate over to the plaza across the street from the Berlin Platz building and climb the ladder in the left-hand corner, where the pink ledges meet the yellow ones. Climb all the way to the top of the ladder and carefully walk around the upper yellow ledge to the front of the building. Double Jump onto the narrow concrete ledge under the large billboard. From there, Double Jump into a hanging position on the upper edge of the billboard and hit the Grind Button to tag it.

Spat is always one step ahead of you. Make sure you tag over all 5 Spat tags.

The first Spat tag is on the wall right where the Graffiti Tagger was hanging out waiting for you to switch to him. Follow the steps clockwise around the plaza from Gretchen's Bar to find it.

Skate around to the rear of the Gallerie building to find the next Spat tag. It's on the wall between the large yellow arrows.

The third Spat tag is on the side of the large piece of wall facing the Gallerie building. It's on the opposite side of the wall from where Bam was standing.

Spat made his way onto the middle roof of the fancy gold building. His tag is near the inside corner of where the building makes an "L" shape, under the arched portion of the roof where Paulie was hiding.

The final Spat tag is on the exterior wall of the church, right near the flaming gas pipe.

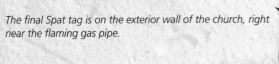

Intro

Skater Basics

Trick Lists

Story Mode

Gaps

Classic Mode

Multiskater

Secrets

Tagger Skillz

Graffiti Tagger, break in and mark up the mural in the ruined church. Be sure to tag the whole wall.

Spine Transfer up and over the wall to get **Into Church** and Sticker Slap the cracked wall to gain access to the secret portion. Grind the ladder on the ground for speed and launch straight off the quarter pipe into the air. Press the Rotate Right and Rotate Left Buttons while in the air to hop off the board, then press the Rotate Right Button to grab onto the ladder high above the floor for the **Ladder Skillz** gap. Climb the ladder to the ledge above.

The guy standing off to the right will talk about the beautiful mural that was once on this wall. Walk up to each panel of the wall and press the Grind Button to Graffiti Tag it. Not only does the Graffiti Tagger bring the old mural back to life, but he also takes a little artistic license and splashes his own "Thug" tag across it. Tag the entire mural from one side of the wall to the other to complete the goal.

GALLERIE IS OPEN FOR SKATING!

Completing the "Tagger Skillz" goal unlocks the indoor skatepark-turned discothèque at the Gallerie. Head on over to the Gallerie and talk to the disc jockey to have him crank up the bass. Once the windows have all been cracked by the music, you're free to smash through each and every windowpane in the place. Use the pool to air up and through the glass in the ceiling.

SECRET GOALS

PAULIE'S STATS

Category	Rating
Air	10
Spin	10
Lip	10
Ollie	1
Run	1
Speed	5
Flip	10
Switch	10
Rail	10
Manual	10

WHEELS OF FURY

Paulie may be down, but don't count him out. Paulie has modified his normal repertoire of tricks to accommodate his new ride. Watch him bust One Handers, Sit Flips, and other tricks all from the safety of his wheel chair. He can also manual, grind, and Revert too!

Berlin Tour

First, grind the stairs. Next, grind the planter in the courtyard. Next, grind the middle ledge on the gold building. Next, grind the ledge on the sign building. Finally, grind the top of the fountain.

Hop into a counter-clockwise grind on the stairs of the building where Paulie was hanging out. Cross the street and grind the planter in the center of the plaza and use the quarter pipe to leap into a grind on the middle ledge of the building. Grind all the way off the end of the ledge to pop across the street on an angle to grind the ledge under the "Afropick" sign. Chair Hop off the ledge into a grind on the fountain below to complete this brief tour of Berlin.

Wheelin' Combo

Score a 15,000 point combo with Paulie in the wheel chair.

Take Paulie out onto the main street and Sit Flip into a Chair Grind on the median. Hop into a Wheelie and link up a couple more Chair Grinds before pulling another Wheelie en route to a One Hander off the ramp at the police barricade. Stick the landing with Paulie still in the wheel chair to complete this goal.

Sick Mode: Score a 25,000 point combo with Paulie.

Skills on Wheels

Launch from the ramp with Paulie and perform a Sit Flip and then Acid Drop into the ramp.

Go through the doors of the AusFarht Center to reach the roof of the Berlin Platz building. Slowly roll off the edge of the building between the two kicker ramps to drop onto the awning below. Use the quarter pipe against the wall to gain a little speed and then jump from the kicker-like edge of the sign to cross the street towards the plaza. Perform a quick Sit Flip while in the air (Right + Flip Button), then hit the Spine Transfer Button to Acid Drop into the ramp on the plaza.

Team Challenge

Bam must manual from one set of cones to the other set. Paulie must grind in a circle for 10 seconds. You must get a 5,000 point air combo while skating inside the bombed-out church.

Bring Bam over to the golden building near the church and trick off the quarter pipe near the cones to get some speed. Tap into a manual and maintain balance through the cones, down the road, and then through the set of cones in the plaza on the right.

Steer Paulie's wheel chair over to the aquarium and zoo and hop into a Chair Grind on the circular planter in front of the entrance. Tap to the Left and Right on the controls to maintain balance while Paulie grinds around in circles for 10 seconds.

Head back to the church and air up to the suspended ladder for the **Ladder Skillz** bonus, as if going to paint the mural. Once on the ledge in front of the mural, take a step or two to the side and Acid Drop back into the quarter pipe below. Steer the skater straight across the floor to the ramp directly in front of it and watch in amazement as the skater soars into the air. Grab the rail and start spinning. An Indy 900 yields more than enough points to complete the goal.

LOCAL FLAVOR

Street Musician

Across the street from the Berlin Platz building is a large plaza with pink and yellow floor tiles. Approach the old man near the planter and press the Grab Button to make him play a song. He'll play a catchy little ditty on his clarinet, perfect background music for a nice flatland combo.

Train Wreck

Tipping over garbage cans and rearranging the letters of signs is fine, but if this World Destruction Tour is really going to live up to its billing, you need to up the ante. What better way to show you mean business than by causing a train wreck?

Skate over to the Oktoberfest area and leap into a counter-clockwise grind on the yellow ledge above the quarter pipe. Use the kinked end of the ledge to pop up to the middle ledge and Wallie off the Quiksilver

sign in the corner to land in a grind on the yellow and black striped rail above Gretchen's Bar. The weight of the skater on that rail is all it takes to cause a large sign to fall and block the tunnel. The oncoming train has no choice but to slam on the brakes and derail right into the nearby plaza. Causing this little dose of mayhem earns a 10,000 point bonus!

BERLIN

Training
Boston
Barcelona
Berlin
Australia
New Orleans
Skatopia
Pro Skater

YOUR GOALS

Arcade Machine High Score (25 pts)

Boardwalk Grind Combo (25 pts)

Lipping the Mini (25 pts)

Find the Special Guest (25 pts)

Drain the Tide Pool (25 pts)

Interrupt a Meal or Six (25 pts)

Find the Shrimp Vendor (25 pts)

Wake Up Sleeping Beauty (75 pts)

PRO GOALS

Jumping Without a Parachute (25 pts)

Tag the Big Billboard (25 pts)

Treasure Huntin' Hank (25 pts)

Focusing on a Clean Double Flip (50 pts)

Kenny's Real Feelings (50 pts)

Team Challenge (50 pts)

Everybody Loves Bigguns (75 pts)

Balance Up and Over (75 pts)

GUEST GOALS

Shrimp Slap (25 pts)

Rollin' Rollin' Rollin' (50 pts)

Seagull Scatter (75 pts)

Real Men Flip Stairs (75 pts)

SECRET GOALS

Handicap Havoc (25 pts)

Paradise Combo (25 pts)

Mini Go-Kart Blast Off (25 pts)

Help Local Skate Rats (75 pts)

SHRIMP SLAPPED!

It's possible to increase the multiplier while grinding by tossing shrimp at the pedestrians. This is especially easy to pull off while grinding the base of the circular fountain as one needn't concentrate on jumping and tricking. Hop into a grind, tap Left or Right on the controls to keep balanced, then tap the Flip Button to lob shrimp at people for extra points.

AUSTRALIA

1500 Goal Points are required to unlock this location.

1000 Goal Points are up for grabs.

Select Mike Vallely or Rodney Mullen as a teammate.

Arcade Machine
Guest Skater
To Paradise
Tony Hawk
Secret Skater

YOUR GOALS

Arcade Machine High Score

Find an arcade machine and set a high score.

The arcade machine is on the sidewalk underneath the balcony of the restaurant. You must score at least 125,000 points in 1:00 to claim the high score on this machine.

With the dozens and dozens of rails and ledges to grind in Sydney, there's virtually no end to the number of places one can string together lengthy combos. Start by grinding down the hill on the ledges and steps, then transferring the grind to the yellow rail. Grind and trick across the street towards the apartments and wrap back around via the ledges on the other side, above the boardwalk. Use the quarter pipe on the boardwalk to cap off the first combo.

Another good combo starts by grinding the brick wall near the street. Those with fast fingers may wish to try for a Shuffle Bonus on this ledge, then transfer the grind past the footbridge and onto the circular fountain near the headless statue. Finish off the combo with a Spine Transfer down onto the boardwalk.

Sick Mode: 500,000 points in 1:00.

Use the lengthy wires over the beach and the circular fountain to link up high scoring grind combos. Tap into numerous grinds to up the multiplier while grinding the fountain and go big off the quarter pipes to up the base score.

Boardwalk Grind Combo

Grind all 3 of the boardwalk railings and score 50,000 points in one combo.

Skate past the three boardwalk railings to scope out the sight, then head to the end of the boardwalk near the tide pool. Get some speed off the quarter pipe and ollie into a Special Grind on the first rail. Trick across the gap in the rail to the second railing and grind it off the far end of it. The kink in the rail pops the skater up into the air. Land in a grind on the circular rooftop for the **Life Guard Roof Tap** gap, grind partly around the roof in a counter-clockwise direction, then quickly trick down into one final Special Grind on the third railing. Trick out of the grind to complete the combo with the requisite points.

Sick Mode: Score 75,000 points in one single combo while grinding all 3 of the boardwalk railings. Get the extra points by manualing out of the final grind and going big off the quarter pipe at either end of the boardwalk.

Lipping the Mini

Perform a 15,000 point combo on the mini ramp. The combo must include a lip trick.

Linking aerial combos together on a mini ramp can be done without even requiring a manual between jumps due to the speed one gets, but pausing to add a lip trick mid-combo can be tough. For this reason, it's best to begin the combo with the lip trick. Ride up the ramp into a lip trick and tap into other lip tricks by pressing various combinations of the Grind, Flip, and Grab Buttons to build the multiplier. Ollie out of the combo and Revert the landing to tack on one more trick for good measure.

Sick Mode: Score a 20,000 point combo on the mini ramp while including at least one lip trick.

Find the Special Guest

The native likes to ride around in a mini go-kart! Find him and see if he will give you a ride.

Skate over to the wall that the crane operator destroyed with the koala statue's head and ollie over the rubble to the walkway behind it. Skate through the door under the "Outback Tours" sign to enter the secret paradise alcove. The Aborigine is sitting in his go-kart on the edge of the pool near the waterfall.

BRINGING DOWN THE WALL

The Special Guest can't be found until after the "Wake Up Sleeping Beauty" goal has been completed. Jar the crane operator out of his slumber and watch as he creates a secret passage.

Drain the Tide Pool

Find a way to drain the tide pool so that you and your team can skate it.

The tide pool is located at the end of the boardwalk, near the cliffs by the beach. Skate around the edge of the pool to the large generator with the yellow sticker on it, then ollie into it and perform a Sticker Slap to break it. With the generator out of commission, the pool empties and becomes completely skateable for the team.

Interrupt a Meal or Six

Find a place where people are eating and see to it that the food starts flying.

Head to the main road up the hill from the beach and use the kicker ramps near the bus stop to air into a grind on the ledges above. Ollie onto the balcony café and steer straight through the six dinner tables. It's not necessary to crash through all six tables in a single combo, but doing so makes for good practice!

Find the Shrimp Vendor

Find the wandering Shrimp Vendor and get him to join your team.

Hop off the board and run down onto the beach near the lifeguard station. Face away from the ocean, then approach the locker room under the boardwalk, to the left of the lifeguard station. Walk through the blue-lit tunnel to find the Shrimp Vendor. The Shrimp Vendor has some amazing skills and waits on the street outside the lockers for whenever you want to make the switch.

AUSTRALIA

Training
Boston
Barcelona
Berlin
Australia
New Orleans
Skatopia
Pro Skater

Intro

Skater Basics

Trick Lists

Story Mode

Gaps

Classic Mode

Multiskater

Secrets

Wake Up Sleeping Beauty

Find a way to startle and wake up the crane operator.

A quick chat with the construction worker near the fountain reveals that the crane operator is dozing off on the job. Grinding on the crane doesn't seem to be loud enough to wake him, but that fire hydrant across the street may be of some use. Ollie into a Natas Spin on the fire hydrant to unscrew the bolt on top. Balance atop the fire hydrant while spinning for five seconds to totally unscrew the bolt. The water shoots the cap across the street at the crane.

Tag the Big Billboard

The local vegetarians are upset about this emu burger advertisement, and it just happens to be placed in a prime location. Find a way up to the billboard and spray your tag over the ad.

The apartment building to the left of the Kenny statue has a tall fire escape on it that stretches from the ground all the way to the uppermost ledge. Climb the ladders to the upper ledge, then carefully run and jump to the ledge to the right and continue across to the large emu burger billboard. Although it's possible to run and leap from ledge to ledge, grinding and ollieing is another viable option.

Once on the ledge above the billboard, carefully walk to the edge to drop into a hanging position and press the Grind Button to tag it. Don't jump down after completing this goal, as the "Jumping Without a Parachute" goal can be completed just a few steps from here.

PRO GOALS

Jumping Without a Parachute

Climb up to the highest balcony in the city and perform an Acid Drop into the tide pool down below.

There is a tall ladder that stretches up from the ground in an alcove near the boardwalk and extends all the way to the uppermost balcony in Sydney. Either climb the ladder from the ground or run and leap to it from the emu burger billboard. Climb to the top of the ladder and continue to the right once on top of the balcony.

ADD-ON GOAL

Consider following the tips outlined below for the "Tag the Big Billboard" goal, then running and jumping to the ladder in the alcove that leads up from the boardwalks. It's an efficient way of knocking off both goals quickly.

Leap off the corner of the ledge nearest the beach and press the Spine Transfer Button to Acid Drop into the tide pool below. Landing the Acid Drop completes the goal scores the **Check Your Pants** gap bonus. Link this amazing stunt with an out-of-this-world aerial to earn some additional Stat Points in the Air and Spin categories.

Treasure Huntin' Hank

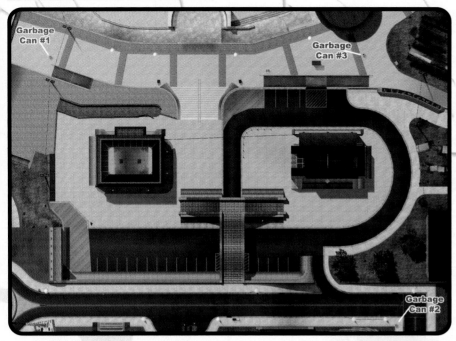

Garbage Can #1

Garbage Can #3

Garbage Can #2

Treasure Huntin' Hank needs some help. The poor metal detecting fella is out here every weekend hoping to find anything that will make his little device go 'beep'. See if you can find a few soda cans for him.

Completing this goal requires a Natas Spin on all three metal recycling cans around the area. Once three soda cans have been collected, head out onto the beach and find Treasure Huntin' Hank.

The first garbage can is near the blue wall with all of the graffiti by the boardwalk and tide pool.

Head back up to the city streets and find the metal garbage can on the corner at the opposite end of the street from the Kenny statue.

The final metal garbage can is on the sidewalk near the mini ramp. It's in front of the yellow wall with all the graffiti on it.

Once all three cans have been found, jump the railing and head out onto the beach. Hank is likely walking around not too far from the lifeguard station.

AUSTRALIA

Training
Boston
Barcelona
Berlin
Australia
New Orleans
Skatopia
Pro Skater

Focusing On a Clean Double Flip

Get focused and then land a clean 180 Double Kickflip over two parked cars.

Skate up to the parking lot near the footbridge and trick out the Special Meter on the quarter pipes. Line up with the pair of parked cars and hit the Focus Button. Skate towards the cars and ollie up and over them while performing a Double Kickflip (Left + Flip, Flip) and rotate 180 degrees while in the air. Land perfectly straight for the Clean Landing bonus that is required for this goal.

Kenny's Real Feelings

After years of dedicated service as a mascot at the zoo, Kenny was awarded a statue. Natas Spin on Kenny's fingers to see how he really feels.

Roll over to the large fountain where the headless statue of Kenny is and come to a stop across the street near the brown staircase. Wait for traffic to pass, then skate towards the statue and pop off the banked edge of the fountain to soar up and over Kenny's decapitated body into a Natas Spin on his raised fingers. Landing in a Natas Spin scores the **Peace Off** gap and safely ollieing down to the street earns the **Peace Out** gap. Hold the Natas Spin on his fingers long enough to get credit for completing the goal, then hop on down.

Intro

Skater Basics

Trick Lists

Story Mode

Gaps

Classic Mode

Multiskater

Secrets

Team Challenge

3 skaters... 1 high awning. You, your pro teammate, and the Shrimp Vendor, have to each grind TC's Awning. It's a bit trickier to catch than it looks.

Use the kicker ramp near the front porch of the brick building to pop up into the air and grind across the roof of the awning for the **TC Awning** gap. Repeat this trick with all three of the specified team members.

Everybody Loves Bigguns

Find and hit the Biggun's ramp 2 ramp transfer.

In order to complete this goal, transfer from the quarter pipe in front of the flagpole near the red brick building all the way to the lower quarter pipe down by the tide pool. Grind the logs in front of the brick building to gain speed, then hit the quarter pipe on a hard angle to the right. The skater should exit the ramp at the upper right-hand corner of the ramp. Rotate hard to the right while in the air to pull the skater over the brick ramp on the middle level and down onto the concrete ramp near the tide pool. Completing this transfer earns the **Biggun's Ramp 2 Ramp** gap bonus.

Balance Up and Over

Perform a manual from the base of the banked walkway, going up, over, and down the other side (in either direction).

Use the quarter pipes near the base of the footbridge to trick out the Special Meter and to gain speed, then tap into a manual and roll up and over the footbridge to the other side. It's a relatively long manual, and the steepness of the footbridge slows down forward momentum significantly at the top. Just keep tapping Up and Down on the controls to maintain balance, then expect to fly down the last portion of the footbridge to complete the goal and to earn the **Up and Over Manual** gap bonus.

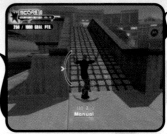

GUEST GOALS

SHRIMP VENDOR'S STATS

Category	Rating
Air	10
Spin	10
Lip	10
Ollie	10
Run	10
Speed	10
Flip	10
Switch	10
Rail	10
Manual	10

THE ROTISSERIE

The Shrimp Vendor is a skating mastermind and features an amazing Special Trick called the Rotisserie. It's a grab-based move that showcases his quick reflexes. Watch as he launches into the air and twirls the board mid-flight as fast as can be. Switching off to the Shrimp Vendor opens a new Special Trick Slot.

Shrimp Slap

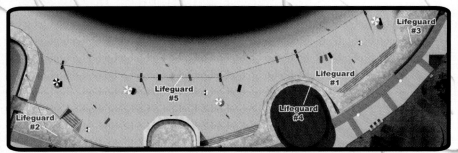

No one is swimming because of the sharks in the water, so the lifeguards are bored. Give them something to do by slapping 5 of them with cold, slimy shrimp.

Skate over to the boardwalk near the lifeguard station and pick up some shrimp from the box near the yellow wall. There are a total of 5 lifeguards needing to get shrimp-slapped so hop the railing onto the beach and start slinging them shrimp!

The first lifeguard is on the beach in front of the lifeguard station.

Another lifeguard is on the concrete walkway near the locker room entrance by the tide pool.

Skate to the other end of the walkway to find the third lifeguard near the other locker room entrance.

As expected, one of the lifeguards is milling around at the lifeguard station. Skate around the front walkway to find him.

The final lifeguard is out on the beach, walking back and forth near the water's edge. Don't get wet!

Rollin' Rollin' Rollin

Get special and perform 2 Rotisseries over the Lofty Roof Gap between the two center buildings.

Head to the end of the parking lot opposite the tide pool and trick off the quarter pipe to gain speed and to light the Special Meter. Spine Transfer up and onto the roof of the nearest large building. Spine Transfer again on the roof to gain more speed and to break through the glass, and then hit the kicker ramp at the edge of the roof to gap across to the other building.

Quickly perform two Rotisseries while in the air over the **Lofty Roof Gap**. Although the Rotisserie isn't an extremely elaborate Special Trick, it isn't quite as fast as, say, the Double Fistin' so tap into them each quickly. Stay as straight as possible while in the air to avoid an untimely spill.

AUSTRALIA

Training

Boston

Barcelona

Berlin

Australia

New Orleans

Skatopia

Pro Skater

Intro

Skater Basics

Trick Lists

Story Mode

Gaps

Classic Mode

Multiskater

Secrets

Seagull Scatter

Seagulls are nothing more than bags of crap with wings... and your shirt, hair, and lap have proven it time and time again. Scatter 10 seagulls with a single combo.

There are dozens of seagulls all over the place, but scaring 10 of them in a single combo by grinding or manualing past them is no small feat. Although this goal can be completed in any number of ways, there is one line that is a bit easier than the rest.

Climb up onto the ledge by the apartments at the end of the beach opposite the tide pool and hop into a grind on the ledge. Grind past the four seagulls on the ledge and hold the grind out onto the electrical wire over the beach. Grind past the lifeguard station, past two more seagulls, then over to the tide pool. Continue grinding off the wire and onto the rocks above the tide pool to scare three more seagulls. From there, manual along the walkway and Wallie into a grind on the boardwalk railing. Trick across to the next railing to scare the final seagull.

Real Men Flip Stairs

Get focused and pull out a clean 360 Double Heelflip down the big stairs.

Trick out the Special Meter on the quarter pipes near the footbridge, then come to a halt halfway between the stairs and the bridge. Press the Focus Button and ollie down the stairs while performing a 360 Double Heelflip (Right + Flip, Flip) for the **Big Stair Set** gap bonus. Begin the ollie completely perpendicular to the stairs and land equally so. The only way to get the Clean Landing bonus is to land perfectly straight so avoid over-rotating.

ABORIGINE'S STATS

Category	Rating
Air	10
Spin	10
Lip	10
Ollie	1
Run	1
Speed	5
Flip	10
Switch	10
Rail	10
Manual	10

GO-GO SUPER KART!

The Aborigine is riding fast and flying high in his supped-up mini go-kart. Hold the Jump Button down to gain tons of speed, then blast off a ramp to perform his patented Toe Hang trick. He's also able to grind and perform flips too!

Handicap Havoc

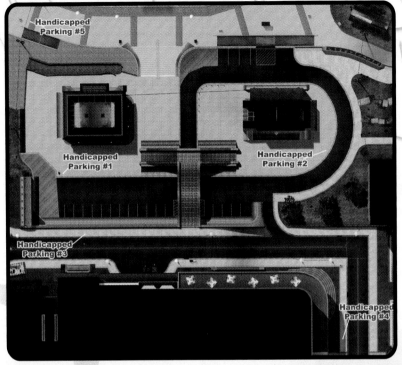

Use the mini go-kart to plow through 5 handicap parking signs that are right in the middle of your skate lines.

The first of the handicap parking signs is in the parking lot by the footbridge, at the end near the tide pool.

Drive under the footbridge, away from the tide pool, to find the next sign where the road curves to the left.

The next handicap parking sign is across the street from the bus stop, near the fire hydrant and crane.

Head down the hill and turn to the right, as if about to drive away from the beach. Another handicap parking sign is on the right side of the road, near the semi-circular steps.

The final sign is on the boardwalk, near the blue wall with all of the graffiti.

Paradise Combo

Now that you've found this beautiful paradise... skate it! Grind all of the outer ledge rocks in a single combo.

Jump over the rubble and drive back through the door for the "Outback Tours" to reenter the paradise area. There are three sections of rock ledges and the Aborigine must grind on all of them in a single combo. Because of the orientation of the ledges feeding into the exit tunnel, it's best to begin the combo just to right of the exit. Hop into a clockwise grind on the lower ledge and then grind and jump around the cave to combo the entire area.

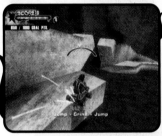

Mini Go-Kart Blast Off

Get some speed in the mini go-kart and air out a 540 spin over the Footbridge Flyover gap.

Steer the mini go-kart over to the parking lot near the footbridge and get some speed off the quarter pipes below the walkway. Hold the Jump Button down for speed and hit any of the four ramps under the footbridge on a steep angle to get the height and distance needed to clear the **Footbridge Flyover** gap. Rotate through the air at least 540-degrees (900-degrees is more than possible) then straighten out the kart for the landing.

AUSTRALIA

Training
Boston
Barcelona
Berlin
Australia
New Orleans
Skatopia
Pro Skater

Intro

Skater Basics

Trick Lists

Story Mode

Gaps

Classic Mode

Multiskater

Secrets

Help Local Skate Rats

This officer has two local skate rats doing curb duty. See if you can find a way to distract him while they make a run for it.

The crane is still parked at the side of the road with Kenny's head dangling from it. Speed past the headless statue and jump into a grind on the right-hand side of the crane. Grind across the red and white striped area to cause the crane to drop Kenny's head. Watch as the head rolls down the road causing the biggest distraction that sad copper has ever seen.

THE SHOWDOWN DOWN UNDER

Thanks to both teams scoring the same number of points, you and Eric Sparrow must compete against one another to decide who stays on the tour. Eric's lame attempt to get back at Nigel Beaverhausen by stealing his clothes netted you the perfect disguise. Don the costume and piss off the locals to get the entire town mad at Nigel. Even better, Eric is sent packing.

There are two more goals that need to be completed with each being worth 500 Goal Points. Although these extra goals do count towards the overall total of Goal Points, this second portion of the Australia chapter is not a separate level.

BEAVER BLAST

A new Special Trick Slot has been added to your repertoire. More important at the moment, however, is the new trick that has been taught to you. The Beaver Blast is a fast flip trick that can be performed out of a single ollie off of flatland. Just make sure there's nothing flammable underneath you!

Piss Off the Construction Workers

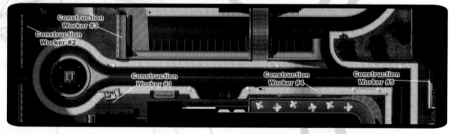

Dress up like Nigel and Beaver Blast 5 construction workers.

Trick out the Special Meter near the fountain, then seek out the 5 construction workers. Ollie over their heads and light their hard hats on fire with a well-timed Beaver Blast.

The first construction worker is on the sidewalk near the crane.

Another construction worker is near the apartment building below the giant emu burger billboard.

Piss Off the Bikini Girls

Grind the wire above the bikini girls to piss them off.

Skate over to the end of the boardwalk opposite the tide pool and climb up onto the ledge near the apartment buildings. Ollie into a grind on the ledge near the seagulls and carefully maintain balance while grinding on the wire strung across the beach. Hold the grind for the full length of the wire to scare the seagulls into crapping on the bikini girls below.

One of the construction workers is pacing back and forth atop the quarter pipe next to Nigel's van. Air off the ramp and Beaver Blast him.

Skate down the hill and ollie up and Beaver Blast the construction worker on the sidewalk near the arcade machine.

The final construction worker is atop the planter at the end of the street to the left of the doors smashed by Kenny's head.

YOUR GOALS

Arcade Machine High Score (25 pts)	
Dance, Dance, Dance (25 pts)	
Riverboat Slapper (25 pts)	
Find the Jester (25 pts)	
Mark Your Territory (25 pts)	
Water Tower Slap (25 pts)	
Raise the Dead (25 pts)	
Save Nawlins (100 pts)	

New Orleans

3000 Goal Points are required to unlock this location.

1000 Goal Points are up for grabs.

Select Chad Muska or Rodney Mullen as a teammate.

Tony Hawk
Guest Skater
From Dance Club
Boombox
Pro Teammate
To Rooftop
Arcade Machine
Secret Skater

PRO GOALS

Nawlins Street Spine (25 pts)	
Wallie the Trolley (25 pts)	
Spine Transfer Combo (25 pts)	
Tag the Big Billboard (50 pts)	
Manhole Manual (50 pts)	
For the Birds (50 pts)	
Gaslamp District (50 pts)	
Big and Focused (50 pts)	

GUEST GOALS

Girls Gone Crazy Parade (50 pts)	
Drop a Hurricane (50 pts)	
Team Challenge (50 pts)	
Balcony Breaker (50 pts)	

SECRET GOALS

Tricycle Vs. Zombie (50 pts)	
Super Trash (50 pts)	
Natas Neversoft (50 pts)	
Sign Spinner (50 pts)	

YOUR GOALS

Arcade Machine High

Find an arcade machine and set a high score.

Unlike in previous cities, the arcade machine in New Orleans is actually tucked out of the way and may be difficult to find. It's on the third floor of the red building on the corner near the dock. Use the quarter pipe on the street to air up into a grind, then ollie out of the grind into the burned-out section of the building. The arcade machine is in the corner.

The high score on this machine is set at 200,000 points. Exit the room in a clockwise grind and drop down onto the rail on the second level. Continue the grind around the building while smashing through the **Nawlins Sign** and the **Green Goddess Sign** gaps. Trick into a Special Grind and balance for at least one or two complete laps around the building. Ollie down into a manual on the street and cap off the combo with a big air combo off one of the many quarter pipes. Revert the landing to add one final trick to the combo.

Begin by linking multiple Sticker Slaps together while descending to the street, then head to the cemetery. Combo numerous Special Grinds while grinding laps around the cemetery. Squeeze in Special Air Tricks when gapping from one section of wall to the other; the Beaver Blast is a very fast trick that is perfect for this.

Sick Mode: 750,000 points in 1:00.

57

Intro

Skater Basics

Trick Lists

Story Mode

Gaps

Classic Mode

Multiskater

Secrets

Dance, Dance, Dance

Locate the boombox and complete the tricks to the beat.

Enter the dance club across the street from the church and roll onto the large multi-colored fan in the floor. Ollie into the air to get blasted onto the roof of the club for the **Dance Floor Skillz** gap. Hop down onto the lower roof and approach the boombox.

This version of the Dance, Dance, Dance goal is just like the one performed in Boston, but it now requires additional tricks such as Impossible, Pop Shove-It, Nosegrab, Indy, Melon, and Tailgrab. Remain stationary, ollie straight into the air and quickly tap into the tricks as they are called out. Listen carefully to the beat and perform the ollie and trick on the beat. Watch the boombox turn red to signify the proper timing.

Riverboat Slapper

Place 3 stickers on the riverboat.

Skate past the street musicians on the dock near the river and ollie over the railing and Sticker Slap the sternwheeler. Repeat this stunt two more times to thoroughly coat the boat in stickers. The riverboat moves further away from the dock with each successive Sticker Slap, so incorporate a No Comply or Boneless when leaping for the third Sticker Slap.

Find the Jester

Locate the King of Mardis Gras. The Jester should be riding around the city somewhere.

The King of Mardis Gras is cruising around the French Quarter atop a parade float resembling a large shark. Keep an eye peeled for the float, then skate over and ollie onto it. The float does occasionally disappear outside of the designated skating area, but you're sure to spot it if you spend some time down by the riverfront. Once the Jester has been found, he heads over to the bar with the courtyard and the ten-foot tall Hurricane glass.

Mark Your Territory

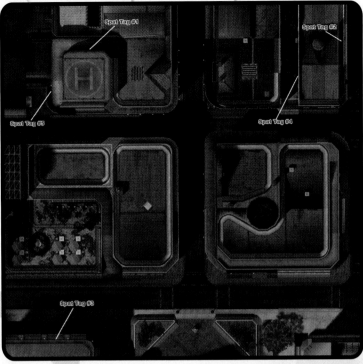

Once again Spat has placed his tags all over New Orleans. Find all 5 of the Spat Tags and place your graffiti tag over them.

Enter the garage elevator near the car and jump into the air to ride the lift to the rooftop. The first Spat tag is on the wall leading up to the helipad.

There is another Spat tag on the backside of the large billboard near the water tower. Take the stairs near the dock to emerge on the roof by the water tower and Graffiti Tag over the Spat.

Air up to the ledge on the building where Tony Hawk stands. Another one of Spat's tags is right there on the wall facing the street.

The fourth Spat tag is on the wall in the alley with the huge garbage dumpster.

The fifth and final Spat tag is in the alley with the spines and "Humidity" banners. Look for it on the wall at the end of the alley nearest the large pink courtyard bar.

Water Tower Slap

Find a way to Sticker Slap the water tower.

Locate the ladder on the side of the yellow building near the road leading from the church to the cemetery. Climb the ladder to the rooftop and hop back onto the board. Skate to the left of the vent, ollie off the ramp at the edge of the roof towards the water tower and press the Jump Button right when about to hit it to Sticker Slap it.

Intro

Skater Basics

Trick Lists

Story Mode

Gaps

Classic Mode

Multiskater

Secrets

Raise the Dead

Raise the living dead by opening all 5 crypts in the cemetery.

Spine Transfer up and over the wall (or smash through the gates) to enter the cemetery. There are five crypts in the cemetery that have human skulls resting atop them. The only way to open a crypt is to grind all of the skulls off of it. The skulls reset themselves 10 seconds after the first one on the particular crypt is knocked off, so start at one end of the row and hold the grind all the way to the other end.

There are three lengthy crypts at ground level. Two of them are near the main entrance gate and the third is to the left (as viewed with your back to the gate). The other crypts are much taller. Use the banked base of the large circular crypt in the center of the cemetery to air up into a grind on the rounded edge to open the fourth crypt. The fifth crypt resembles a tall vert ramp. Ride up the banked wall and grind the pair of skulls off.

> ### CALLING ALL WITCH DOCTORS
>
> Opening all 5 crypts causes the dead to rise, summons the Witch Doctor, and opens a portal to the underworld. All of the pedestrians are transformed into zombies until you "Save Nawlins". The Witch Doctor waits in the cemetery; go see him when it's time to attempt the Special Goals.

Save Nawlins

First, Spine Transfer into the Nawlins underworld. Next, grind the underworld ring. Then, jump off it. Finally, Airwalk over the church statue.

> ### SAVE IT FROM WHAT?
>
> If you're wondering what New Orleans needs to be saved from, then you obviously haven't completed the "Raise the Dead" goal yet. Head to the cemetery and grind the skulls off all five crypts to find out what all the fuss is about.

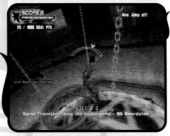

Exit the cemetery and skate straight down the road towards the large underworld portal that opened up in the intersection. Spine Transfer from the edge of the crater to drop **Into the Underworld** and land in a grind on the candle-lit ring in the fiery cauldron below. Hold the grind for a lap or two around the ring and jump off. The skater is catapulted through the night sky towards the church. Charge the quarter pipe beside the statue near the church steps and perform an Airwalk (Down/Right + Grab) while transferring up and over the **Church Statue** from one ramp to the other.

> ### WHEN ZOMBIES ATTACK
>
> There's going to come a time when the crypts need to be re-opened later in this level. Just follow the steps outlined in completing this goal to send the spirits back to the underworld should you tire of seeing drunken zombies stumbling about.

PRO GOALS

Nawlins Street Spine

Spine Transfer over the Nawlins street from one rooftop to the next.

Get up to the roof of the large bar with the courtyard and Spine Transfer off the roof, over the street, and onto the roof of the building with the helipad.

Wallie the Trolley

Perform a Wallie off of the trolley by the river.

Skate up to the side of the trolley and ollie into a Wallride on it for the **Streetcar Ride** gap. Quickly tap the Jump Button to Wallie out of the Wallride to complete this goal. It's best to perform this stunt while the trolley is either moving in the same direction as the skateboard, or while it is stopped. It's difficult to do this trick while the trolley is approaching as it decreases the amount of time available to hit the Wallie.

Spine Transfer Combo

First, Spine Transfer off of the helicopter pad down to the street. Next, Spine Transfer up into the pool on the bar rooftop. Finally, Spine Transfer down into the bar.

Ride the car elevator in the parking garage up to the roof and walk up onto the helipad. The skater at the edge of the roof marks the beginning of the Spine Transfer Combo.

Hit the quarter pipe on the roof and Spine Transfer down to the street below. Quickly hit the Revert Button and Spine Transfer off of the ramp across the street up onto the rooftop bar. Tap the Revert Button a second time and Spine Transfer off the ramp across the roof to land down in the courtyard below. It isn't necessary to manual between the ramps of their close proximity to one another and also because of the incredible speed gained from each successive Spine Transfer. Completing this goal nets the **Helipad Spine1**, **Helipad Spine2**, and **Helipad Spine3** gaps.

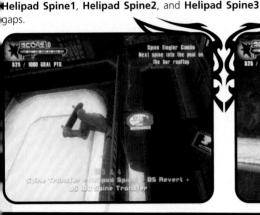

Tag the Big Billboard

Find a way to get up on the ledge and spray a Graffiti Tag on the Mardis Gras billboard.

Spine Transfer up onto the uppermost roof above the courtyard bar, then turn and face the large Mardis Gras billboard. Get plenty of speed and Spine Transfer down into the rooftop directly below the billboard. Hit the ramp across from that landing spot to soar up into the air towards the billboard. Quickly dismount the board while airborne and press the Rotate Right Button to grab the hidden ladder on the side of the building. Climb up to the ledge below the billboard and press the Grind Button to Graffiti Tag it.

Manhole Manual

Perform a manual over 5 small manholes in one combo.

Trick out the Special Meter near the dock, then cross the trolley tracks to the side street and ollie into a manual. Carefully balance the manual while riding across the five small manhole covers. They are positioned in a zigzag pattern starting on the right-hand side of the street. Weave back and forth from right to left to ride over each of them, all the while dodging the revelers. It's best to begin the manual with plenty of speed, as the ride is long and bumpy. Hold the manual to the far end of the street for the **Nawlins Street Manual** gap.

For the Birds

Launch up into the air and give the birds a smack.

Head up onto the roof of the building with the helipad (it's the one with the parking garage) and Spine Transfer down onto the street near the cemetery. Use the speed gained during the drop to launch high into the air off the quarter pipe near the fence across the street and smack the three birds. The birds are lined up in a row so it may take more than one leap to smack all three of them, although rotating through a stretched-out trick like the Stiffy can help extend your reach.

61

Intro

Skater Basics

Trick Lists

Story Mode

Gaps

Classic Mode

Multiskater

Secrets

Gaslamp District

Grind off of 3 gaslamps near the river.

Skate over to the riverfront and ollie into a grind on the purple rails near the planters. Pop off the kinked end of the rail and grind the top of each of the three gaslamps for the **Gas Lamp** gap. The lamps are so small that the grind will only register as a "Kissed the Rail", but that's all it takes. The 3 gaslamp grinds do not need to be performed in a single combo.

Big and Focused

Get focused and land a 100,000 point combo.

Use the ramps in the cemetery to trick out the Special Meter and come to a halt near the vertical crypt. Hit the Focus Button, then ride up the ramp near the outer wall of the cemetery and begin a clockwise grind around the graveyard. The wall naturally curves in an endless loop around the perimeter of the cemetery, creating the perfect place to lay down a monster grind combo. Trick across the occasional break in the wall and land in a different Special Grind each time. It takes less than a full lap around the cemetery to score the necessary 100,000 points.

Sick Mode: Get focused and land a 200,000 point combo.

GUEST GOALS

JESTER'S STATS

Category	Rating
Air	10
Spin	10
Lip	10
Ollie	10
Run	10
Speed	10
Flip	10
Switch	10
Rail	10
Manual	10

THE MANUAL ENTERTAINER

Like many of the other Special Guests, the Jester has insane skating skills. He also has a great Special Manual Trick that is sure to become an instant classic. Watch him hop back and forth from foot to foot while juggling, all the while racking up mega points for a manual. Switching to the Jester unlocks the Manual Entertainer Special Trick, and adds a Special Trick Slot.

Girls Gone Crazy Parade

Ride on the Mardis Gras float and throw beads at 5 crazy girls.

Grab some beads from the girls near the cemetery or the ones near Tony Hawk and head to the riverfront to wait for the parade float. Get off the board, run and jump onto the float and toss a beaded necklace at each of the ladies you pass. Most of the women are standing on the street corners in pairs and there won't be enough time to toss beads at both, so conserve your necklaces and just toss a single strand.

Keep in mind that the Mardis Gras float does leave the skating area so be ready to hop off should it pass the cemetery or where Tony Hawk is standing. Take the moment to pick up some more necklaces and hop back onto the float after it turns around.

Drop a Hurricane

Acid Drop into the world's largest drink.

Skate through the tunnel opposite the alley with the "Humidity" banners into the courtyard bar and pop off the pink and gray curb towards the large glass. Hit the Spine Transfer Button while in the air to Acid Drop right into the enormous Hurricane.

Team Challenge

3 team members must land a Special Trick inside the church courtyard area.

Enter the church courtyard with your skater, the Pro Teammate, and the Jester and perform any Special Trick you desire. Use the quarter pipes near the statue to launch into a quick Special Air or ollie into a Special Manual on the grass. The only requirement is that three different team members must each perform a Special Trick and it must be landed successfully inside the courtyard.

Balcony Breaker

Break 3 balconies around the city in one combo.

The buildings near the center of the city each have flimsy wooden balconies wrapping around them and each of these balconies can be broken by either airing up through them by jumping off a planter, or by Wallriding under and doing a Wallie right up through them. Some of the buildings have several floors of balconies and it's possible to Wallie up through multiple floors.

This goal can prove to be quite challenging due to the requirement that three balconies must be busted in a single combo. It's very easy to run out of room and need to turn around and come back for a second pass. Fortunately, there is a way to work this into a combo that isn't all that difficult.

Begin by the gate to the cemetery and head down the central street. Wallie off the yellow building on the left to break through the first floor balcony, then quickly ollie across to a manual on the building across the street (continue in the same direction). Wallie up through the balcony here, then leap down onto the street near the church and land in a manual. Carefully trick off the quarter pipe near the church, Revert to a manual, and head back down the center street in the other direction while keeping the combo alive. Hit the planter on the right to pop up through the balcony to complete the challenge.

RESET THE BALCONIES

After every few failed attempts at this goal, the balconies may need to reset. Although they reset over time, it's possible to speed up the process by skating around the cemetery for a few seconds, or by heading into the dance club and ollieing while on the fan. By the time you get back down off the roof, the balconies should be back to normal.

WITCH DOCTOR'S STATS

Category	Rating
Air	10
Spin	10
Lip	10
Ollie	10
Run	10
Speed	10
Flip	10
Switch	10
Rail	10
Manual	10

VOODOO TRICYCLE

The Witch Doctor rides a tricked-out tricycle and can pull off an astonishing number of tricks on it. Not only can the Witch Doctor jump and do Wheelies, but he can also grind, and perform Barspins (Flip Button) and Superman Seat Grabs (Grab Button). The real benefit in being the Witch Doctor lies in his voodoo powers that allow him to combat the undead. Only he can rid Nawlins from the Zombie invasion!

Tricycle Vs. Zombie

WAKE THE DEAD

This goal can't be completed without zombies. The only way to get some zombies is to awaken the dead. Return to the cemetery and grind across all of the skulls atop the crypts to open the 5 crypts one more time.

All the Mardis Gras participants have been transformed into zombies and it's up to the Witch Doctor to destroy them. Cruise around town on the tricycle and drive straight into all of the zombies encountered. Drive through 10 of them to complete the goal. The zombies aren't hard to find at all, and there are more than just 10 of them. Cruise around the perimeter of the city and then cut through the central streets to the main intersection.

NEW ORLEANS

Training
Boston
Barcelona
Berlin
Australia
New Orleans
Skatopia
Pro Skater

Intro

Skater Basics

Trick Lists

Story Mode

Gaps

Classic Mode

Multiskater

Secrets

Super Trash

Grab a tricycle and perform a Superman Seatgrab over the big dumpster.

The dumpster is in the alley near the cemetery and riverfront and although it's quite long, the Witch Doctor can leap over it so long as he gets a slight running start. Hold the Jump Button down for speed and air off the kicker-like edge of the dumpster. Press the Grab Button while in the air to perform the Superman Seatgrab to complete the goal and to score the **Dumpster Dive** gap bonus.

Natas Neversoft

Natas Spin the Neversoft eye on the cemetery fence for 10 seconds.

Ride up the quarter pipe in front of the main gate to the cemetery and hop into a Natas Spin (Rotate Right + Grind Button) atop the metal Neversoft logo. Carefully tap to the Left and Right to balance atop the pole for 10 full seconds.

Sign Spinner

Spin 3 signs by grinding right through them.

Cross the road from the cemetery and use the quarter pipe to the left to air into a grind on the railing of the building near the dumpster alley. Grind the rail to the left to spin the **Green Goddess Sign**. Hold the grind around the corner and back towards the intersection in the center of the French Quarter to hit the **Nawlins Sign**.

Jump off the railing after spinning the first two signs and ride up the sloped fire escape to the balcony on the building with the parking garage. Jump into a grind on the railing of to spin **Boo Ya's Sign** directly across from the Nawlins Sign.

The Wheel of Loogies has spoken and you have one chance to help pull your team to victory. Manage to land these insane tricks and the total score for both teams will become equal. This stunt is worth 1000 Goal Points so it's time to either put up or go home. Which is it going to be?

YOU STILL GOOD WITH HELICOPTERS?

Nobody will ever forget that footage of you airing it out over the helicopter in Hawaii last year—even if Eric did try to steal it. Regardless, Tony and the guys are counting on you to pull out some even bigger stunts with a helicopter here in New Orleans. Rodney will be piloting the thing so, umm, best of luck.

The Equalizer

Grab onto the helicopter's skid. Acid Drop into the pool below. Air up and grab the helicopter again. Acid Drop again. Spine over the helicopter.

The first step is to get to the helipad without being thrashed by the security guards on the rooftop. Skate over to the main intersection in the center of the city and go through the doors under the Boo Ya's sign to gain the roof. Come to a stop opposite the large wall to the left of the security guard. Spine Transfer up and over that wall to the helipad to avoid the first guard. Hop off the skateboard while in the air and sprint past the security guard on the helipad. Jump up and grab onto the bottom of the helicopter.

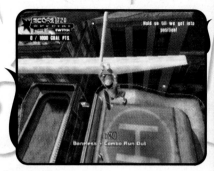

The helicopter flies over to another rooftop. Let go and press the Spine Transfer Button to Acid Drop into the rooftop pool below. Cross the roof and launch out of the other side. Hop off the board while in the air and press the Rotate Right Button to grab back onto the helicopter to complete this stunt.

The helicopter moves one more time. Drop from the helicopter and Acid Drop into the pool on the rooftop below. Cross the pool to the far side and Spine Transfer from one rooftop to the other for the **Nawlins Street Spine** gap. The catch is that the helicopter will be positioned between the two buildings so you had better not slow down!

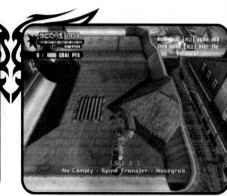

LOCAL FLAVOR

Playin' Some Dixie

No trip to Nawlins is complete without taking in some street music. Head to the waterfront and skate up to the three-piece band near the riverboat and press the Grab Button to get them to play. They'll keep playing that sweet Dixieland music until you tell them to stop.

Coming to a Frat Party Near You!

Arguably the most (in)famous Mardis Gras ritual has to do with the inexplicable craving female partygoers have for plastic beaded necklaces. Their willingness to do just about anything for these trinkets provides spectators with a very *revealing* look into women's fascination with jewelry—even that of the ten-for-a-dollar variety. Grab some beads from the box near the cemetery (or from the lady near Tony Hawk) and use them to entice the ladies on the street into, well, you can figure it out…

65

Intro

Skater Basics

Trick Lists

Story Mode

Gaps

Classic Mode

Multiskater

Secrets

YOUR GOALS

- Arcade Machine High Score (25 pts)
- Locate the Chainsaw (25 pts)
- The Legend of Big Foot (25 pts)
- Zipline Toss Drop (25 pts)
- Launch the Firework (25 pts)
- Tag the Big Billboard (25 pts)
- Mark Your Territory (25 pts)
- Find Ryan Sheckler (25 pts)

PRO GOALS

- Tree Top Spin and Bomb (25 pts)
- Mountain Top Manual (50 pts)
- Lumberjack Combo (25 pts)
- Spine the Mine (50 pts)
- Skatopia Spine Combo (50 pts)
- Downhill Line (50 pts)
- Jump to the Weather Balloon (50 pts)
- Scrape the Hives (50 pts)

GUEST GOALS

- One Long Electric Wire (50 pts)
- Shack Attack (50 pts)
- Over the House (50 pts)
- Zipline Wire Bomb (50 pts)

SECRET GOALS

- Skatopia Transfer (50 pts)
- Grow Some Plants (50 pts)
- A Clear Path (50 pts)
- Manual Up a Slope (100 pts)

SKATOPIA

4500 Goal Points are required to unlock this location.

4000 Goal Points are up for grabs.

Tony Hawk is your teammate.

Guest Skater -
Jesse James

Mineshaft

Vertical Zipline

Secret Skater

Arcade Machine

To Upper Half Pipe

Pro Teammate

To Top of Mountain Bam Margera

Inclined Zipline

YOUR GOALS

Arcade Machine High Score

Find an arcade machine and set a high score.

Climb the face of the mountain to the ledge just below the outhouse at the summit and walk into the mineshaft. The arcade machine is in an alcove on the left. This final arcade machine has a high score of 300,000 points and you have 1:00 to beat it.

Jump down off the mountain and grind the right-hand quarter pipe towards the entrance gate. Trick off the end of the ramp to a grind on the ledge near the Skatopia sign and quickly trick into a Special Grind on the edge of the ramps straight ahead. Loop back around to the right and trick across back to the front of the Skatopia sign. Trick out of this short grind into a manual and steer it straight through the green shack.

Continue the combo by tricking off the quarter pipes atop the mountain. Touch down to end the combo and if more points are needed, launch into a lengthy Special Grind atop the electric wire, or on the edge of the lengthy quarter pipe.

Sick Mode: 1,000,000 points in 1:00.

Head to the top of the mountain and start up a combo on the quarter pipes and pop into a Special Grind on the electric wire. Get Focused and switch up the grind to maintain focus. Trick out of the grind into a Special Manual at the bottom and use the quarter pipes there for more points.

Locate the Chainsaw

Jesse James will build you a gas-powered skateboard to shred these hills with, but he needs an engine first. Go find him a chainsaw.

Jesse James is standing beside the large barn near the pond. Talk to him to learn about his need for a chainsaw, then head out to find it for him.

The chainsaw is actually quite tricky to find, unless you think about where one would use a chainsaw. Head to the top of the mountain and hop off the board near the upper edge of the mineshaft. Jump onto the tree and climb to the top of it to find the missing saw.

The Legend of Bigfoot

Some say he is just a legend. The locals say that they have seen him.

Just as Jesse James finishes building the gas-powered skateboard, Bigfoot leaps out of nowhere and runs off with it. Now it's up to you to find Bigfoot. Return to the ledge on the cliff face where the vertical zipline is and walk in a clockwise direction from it. Bigfoot is hanging out by the tree below the large billboard. Once found, he waits behind the house.

Zipline Toss Drop

Take a ride on the zipline up the mountain face, and then Acid Drop into the unfinished dome of the school bus park.

There are two different ziplines at Skatopia and only one of them can be used to complete this goal. Skate over to the base of the cliff, where it faces the large garage, and climb the ladder to the ledge. Hop into the air and grab onto the zipline by pressing the Rotate Right Button. The zipline rockets straight up the mountain face, sending the skater soaring into the air. Press the Spine Transfer Button to Acid Drop into the pool atop the hill for the **Zipline Drop** gap.

Launch the Firework

Catch your board on fire and then light the firework fuse.

The large firework is atop the roof of the barn and the only way to light it is to air up to the roof via the **Garbage Blast**. Head up the hill above the propane bonfire and skate down towards the fire and ollie off the mound towards the barn. The explosive blast from the fire sends the skater flying onto the roof of the barn. Once there, skate over the firework's fuse to launch it.

No Time to Climb

Those looking to light the board on fire and manually climb up to the roof of the barn are out of luck. The fiery skateboard extinguishes just seconds after riding through the fire. The only way to get to the roof in time to light the fuse is by hitting the **Garbage Blast**.

Tag the Big Billboard

Can you place a masterpiece on the cliff face? Climb up to the ledge, but don't fall off.

The billboard is on the cliff, directly below the unfinished dome. Walk off the edge of the mountain peak to drop into a hanging position and shimmy over to the billboard. Drop straight down to the narrow ledge at the base of the sign and press the Grind Button to Graffiti Tag it.

SKATOPIA

Training
Boston
Barcelona
Berlin
Australia
New Orleans
Skatopia
Pro Skater

Intro

Skater Basics

Trick Lists

Story Mode

Gaps

Classic Mode

Multiskater

Secrets

Mark Your Territory

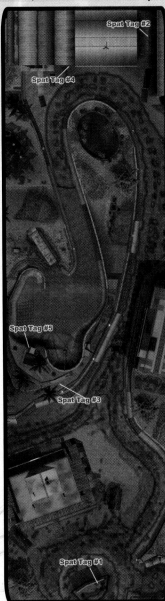

Who does Spat think he is leaving his tag all around the grounds of Skatopia? Find all 6 Spat tags and spray over them with your graffiti tag.

The first Spat tag is located on the back of the large Skatopia billboard near the entrance to the park.

There is a Spat tag on the eave of the barn's rooftop. Climb the ladder near the bowling pins behind the barn to reach it.

Walk along the ledge of the mountain face near the lower entrance to the mineshaft and drop into a hanging position over the edge. The third Spat tag is on the side of the cliff.

Spat made his way to the alley behind the barn, near the bowling lane. Walk around between the L-shaped pool and the barn to find his handiwork and Graffiti Tag over it.

The final Spat tag is on the back of the outhouse at the very top of the mountain. Be careful not to fall down the mineshaft when tagging it.

Find Ryan Sheckler

Ryan is one of the youngest pro skaters, but it doesn't stop him from being one of the best. Meet up with him and he will help you complete some goals.

Ryan Sheckler is hanging out inside the large barn at the back end of Skatopia. Either climb the ladder near Jesse James to enter the loft where he's hiding, or ride up the ramp and enter through the rear.

PRO GOALS

Tree Top Spin and Bomb

Perform a Natas Spin on a treetop, then jump off into an Acid Drop.

Climb to the top of the tree just below the peak of the hill and jump directly into a Natas Spin. Balance the Natas Spin for a few quick revolutions and ollie out of it. Press the Spine Transfer Button to Acid Drop into the quarter pipes at the base of the cliff, behind the house.

Mountain Top Manual

Perform one long manual starting from the school bus park at the top of the hill, and go all the way down to and through the front entrance gate.

Trick out the Special Meter at the top of the hill and roll up to the garden hose stretched across the road. This is the starting line for the Mountain Top Manual. Tap into a manual and carefully balance it the entire length of the road, from the top of the hill down to the gate where Bam is standing. Be extra careful when rounding the corner near the barn, and when trying to negotiate the clutter near the garage. Consider pressing the Focus Button during the latter half of the manual to increase the chances of making it to the finish. Make it out the gate without bailing to score the **Mountaintop Manual** bonus of 15,000 points!

Lumberjack Combo

Grind all 3 logs in one combo.

Ride up the slope under the inclined zipline and Boneless into a grind on the log at the top of the hill. Ollie off the end of the log into a grind on the second log. Balance across this log and ollie onto the third log to complete the combo.

Spine the Mine

Spine Transfer down into the mine shaft.

Skate up to the top of the hill and charge the quarter pipe just to the left of the outhouse. Spine Transfer up and over the outhouse and into the mine shaft for the **Mine Spine** gap.

Skatopia Spine Combo

First, Spine Transfer the cliff edge down into the road below. Next, Spine Transfer into the garage. Finally, Spine Transfer out the other side of the garage.

Skate to the top of the hill and face the quarter pipe on the side above the garage. Spine Transfer off the ramp where the lip of the quarter pipe is painted blue to score the **Cliff Spine** gap. Revert the landing and Spine Transfer into the garage for the **Garage Wall Spine** gap. Revert one more time and angle to the right to air up out of the garage pool. Spine Transfer up and over the edge of the garage to land on the quarter pipe near the grass on the right. Although you actually exited the garage, this still triggers the **Into the Garage** gap bonus.

SKATOPIA

Training
Boston
Barcelona
Berlin
Australia
New Orleans
Skatopia
Pro Skater

Downhill Line

This is a crazy line that goes from the top of Skatopia to the very bottom. It's only for the best skaters. See if you can skate this line in one combo.

Start at the top of the hill, near the incomplete dome, and ollie into a grind on the quarter pipe leading down the hill towards the barn. Ollie out of the grind as soon as you begin grinding over the gray part of the ramp and trick over to a grind on the edge of the pond. Grind partly around the pond, then ollie into a manual and cruise across to a grind on the quarter pipe on the left side of the road. Transfer this grind over to the right-hand side of the pool in the garage (use a manual to keep the combo alive if necessary) then ollie down onto the grass and start manualing towards the trailer.

Wallie off the side of the trailer into a grind on top of it, then air across the gap to the circular quarter pipe up ahead. Grind clockwise around the edge of this ramp and gap across to the ledge near the Skatopia sign. Ride off the end of the grind to complete the combo.

Jump to the Weather Balloon

Find a wooden ramp on the peak of the hill to kick yourself out to the weather balloon.

Drop into the unfinished dome bowl at the top of the mountain and turn around to face it. Ride up the bowl directly under the bug-zapper and Spine Transfer into the tiny wooden ramp on the ledge. Air off the kicker towards the weather balloon and hop off the board and press the Rotate Right Button to grab the rope dangling from the weather balloon.

Scrape the Hives

Scrape the beehives off the walls using Wallrides.

The first of the beehives is on the side of the cliff, around the bend from the vertical zipline. Use the small funbox on the wide part of the ledge to Wallride up and smack it down.

Another beehive is across from the first, on the large cliff marking the boundary of Skatopia. Grind the tall fence near the barn towards the garage and ollie off the end of the fence into a Wallride along the side of the cliff.

One of the beehives is beside the barn, right above the bowling lane. Ollie into a Wallride to knock it down.

Start heading back down the hill and ollie into a grind on the right-hand side of the garage. Wallride up out of this grind to knock the next beehive down.

The final beehive is on the cliff high above the slope with the inclined zipline. Start skating down the slope and hop into a grind on the ledge to the right. Ollie into a Wallride at the cliff to cruise through the final beehive.

GUEST GOALS

RYAN SHECKLER'S STATS

Category	Rating
Air	10
Spin	10
Lip	10
Ollie	1
Run	1
Speed	5
Flip	10
Switch	10
Rail	10
Manual	10

SWIMMING WITH SHARKS

Young Ryan has some tremendous skating abilities, especially when it comes to balance. This is a good thing, given the nature of some of these Guest Goals. Switching to Ryan opens an extra Special Trick Slot, and the hysterical Swimming With Sharks Special Grind trick. As if trying to maintain balance while grinding didn't provide enough pressure, now there's the threat of a shark attack to deal with too. Whatever you do, don't fall.

Shack Attack

Here's a challenge for you. Start a combo and skate through one of the two shacks. Continue the combo back down here and skate through the other shack. No walking in this combo or you'll be disqualified!

Start behind the Skatopia sign by tricking off one of the quarter pipes and Reverting to a manual. Steer the manual through the green shack to be launched to the top of the hill. Land in a manual and transition to a counter-clockwise grind on the outer edge of the quarter pipe. Carry the grind back around the front face of the cliff and leap through the air down towards the red shack in the distance. Land in a manual, trick off the quarter-pipe on the left, and Revert to one final manual. Hold the manual long enough to steer into the red shack to complete the goal. This also earns the **Shack Combo** gap bonus.

SKATOPIA

Training
Boston
Barcelona
Berlin
Australia
New Orleans
Skatopia
Pro Skater

One Long Electric Wire

See if you can grind the electrical wire line from the very top to the very bottom.

ENDURANCE GRINDING PREPARATION

Begin the attempt at the electrical wire grind by tricking out the Special Meter down by the large Skatopia sign. Once the Special Meter is lit (for focusing purposes) enter the green shack to be instantly transported to the top of the hill, in line with the ramp that pops you onto the wire.

Skate to the top of the hill and gain some speed off the quarter pipes there. Get a full Special Meter and do not get into the Switch stance. Air off the small kicker near the start of the electrical wire (to the left of the garden hose) and land in a 50-50 grind. Tap to the Left and Right on the controls to maintain balance past the half pipe and around the corner near the barn. You're on your own through this first section, but help is coming.

Tap the Focus Button after grinding past the barn to slow down the motion and to make it easier to balance. Focus normally runs out after 5 seconds or so if you are to stay in the 50-50 grind. Keep the Special Meter lit, and the skater in Focus, by tapping into other grinds. Double-tap the Flip, Grab, and Grind Buttons to switch up the grind to avoid running out of Focus. Continue maintaining balance during the grind and you're home free in no time!

Intro

Skater Basics

Trick Lists

Story Mode

Gaps

Classic Mode

Multiskater

Secrets

Over the House

Spine Transfer or Acid Drop off of the cliff face to get speed. Then skate off the slanted boards to launch over the house.

Hop off the board at the top of the hill and walk past the outhouse towards the edge of the cliff above the house. Jump off the edge and press the Spine Transfer Button to Acid Drop into the ramps at the base of the cliff. Carry all of this speed into the kicker ramp behind the house to soar up and **Over the House** to complete the gap.

Zipline Wire Bomb

In one combo, grind down the zipline wire and then Acid Drop into the ramps below.

Start near the bonfire and skate up the hill towards the large log under the end of the zipline. Boneless into a grind on the log, then ollie off the end of the log into a grind on the zipline wire. Quickly leap out of the grind and press the Spine Transfer Button to Acid Drop down into the ramps at the base of the slope for the **Drop From the Wire** gap. It's important to leap early, as momentum may cause the skater to overshoot the ramps.

SECRET GOALS

BIGFOOT'S STATS

Category	Rating
Air	5
Spin	10
Lip	10
Ollie	10
Run	1
Speed	10
Flip	10
Switch	10
Rail	10
Manual	10

MOTORIZED SKATEBOARD

Bigfoot may have run off with Jesse James's latest invention, but you get to use it anyway. Bigfoot may not have all the abilities of his nimbler homo-sapien cousins, but his Hairy Foot Grab and Bigfoot Flip air tricks more than make up for it.

Skatopia Transfer

Perform a ramp-to-ramp vert transfer all the way across the entrance to Skatopia.

Skate down the hill past the garage and to the left of the red shack. Air off the quarter pipe on the left and transfer across the entryway to the ramp behind the large Skatopia sign. Land this transfer to complete the goal and to score the **Sign Transfer** gap bonus.

Grow Some Plants

Use Bigfoot's green power to grow the plants.

Some of the locals are trying to get some plants to grow but the seeds aren't taking. Skate around with Bigfoot and perform a Bigfoot Flip over each garden spot to help the plants sprout to life.

The first patch of seeds is at the bottom of the hill, directly in front of the inclined zipline. Look beside the house to find it.

Skate up the slope and past the bonfire to find the second patch of seeds trying to grow. It's to the left of the incomplete full pipe.

The final patch of plants needing attention is on the plateau near the pond. Skate past the pond towards the cliffs and Bigfoot Flip over it.

A Clear Path

Bigfoot cleared a path on this slope. Manual down the slope and catch some big air. Jump off that piece of plywood.

This actually a fairly tricky challenge due to the speed of the motorized skateboard. Roll all the way to the edge of the narrow slope while holding Down on the controls to keep on the brakes. Tap into a manual just as Bigfoot starts the descent and hold the Jump Button to prepare for the leap. Fly off the ramp at the base of the hill to catch the requisite big air and score the **Big Ramp Manual** gap.

Manual Up a Slope

Using the chainsaw powered skateboard, manual up the slope.

Skate over to the base of the large slope and use the small ramp before the incline to pop over the ledge into a Chainsaw Manual on the hill. Balance the manual all the way to the top of the slope to complete this goal.

BOMBS AWAY!

Tony's team may have won the World Destruction Tour, but Bam is not going out like a chump—he's going to blow this place sky high! It's time for you to skate as Bam and complete five goals that all but assure the total annihilation of Skatopia. Consider it the cherry atop a sundae of global mayhem. Each of the goals are worth 200 Goal Points and they are all required for continuing the story of these weary world-travelers.

Spin Bomb

Grind the Spin Bomb 4 times to activate.

Jump up onto the house near the entrance to the Skatopia area and climb the metal beam in the center of the Spin Bomb. Step out onto the metal platform at the top and hop into a grind on the outer edge of it. Carefully balance around the Spin Bomb for 4 complete laps to activate it.

SKATOPIA

Training
Boston
Barcelona
Berlin
Australia
New Orleans
Skatopia
Pro Skater

Intro

Skater Basics

Trick Lists

Story Mode

Gaps

Classic Mode

Multiskater

Secrets

Rockets Battery

4 Natas Spins in a row to activate.

Locate the enormous box of rockets on the side of the cliff near the garage and ride up the ramp towards the blue rocket tips. Ollie into a Natas Spin on one of the rockets, then ollie into a Natas Spin on a second rocket. Natas Spin on four different rockets in a single combo to activate this firework.

Fountain O Glory

Grind down the fuse to activate.

Get speed on the quarter pipes downhill from the firework, then Boneless off the base of the firework up into a grind on the upper edge of it (use a Vert Wallplant for added height if necessary). Grind around the edge towards the green fuse and grind all the way down the fuse to activate it. This goal cannot be completed by grinding up the fuse; you must start at the top.

Box Bombs

Hit 8 boxes in 2 combos.

The boxes are positioned in a pyramid-like configuration in front of the barn and they must be jumped onto by foot or by ollie to activate. The trick is to activate all 8 boxes in just 2 combos. Fortunately, the Caveman makes it easy to activate several boxes quickly!

Trick into a manual and slowly approach the stack of boxes. Ollie into the air and hop off the board for the Combo Run Out maneuver. Quickly hop across the tops of as many boxes as possible before the Caveman timer runs out. Leap up and hop back on the board to keep the combo alive to sneak in another box or two. Once the first combo is over, skate away and observe which boxes still need to be activated. Hop back into a manual to start a combo, then ollie up and Combo Run Out one more time. Hop across the unlit boxes and ollie back into a manual before the timer runs out. Activate all of the upper boxes early in the combos so you have a chance at activating any remaining ground-level boxes with an ollie or two.

Giant Bomb

Climb to the top of the Giant Bomb to activate.

Skate to the top of the hill and hop off the board. Double Jump up onto the Giant Bomb, then quickly jump again to reach the top of it. The weight of Bam on top of the Giant Bomb is all it takes to activate this mega-explosive.

DOG LOVERS UNITE!

Thanks to Bam's heroics, Skatopia is about to blown clean off the map. There's only seconds to go before the giant explosion, but the animals are all milling about with no idea of their impending demise. Leave it to Tony to care for the helpless.

Evacuate the Dogs

When time reaches zero, the bombs are set to go off. Save yourself, by rescuing as many critters as you can.

It's up to you to save Tony Hawk, and the dogs of Skatopia, from the bombs! This is a very difficult goal with a margin for error of a fraction of a second. There are only 5 seconds on the clock and you must get from the top of the hill down the road and out the gate. A 1 second time bonus is added for each dog you get to follow you.

Hold the Jump Button down the entire time for speed and continuing to practice the line. The only way down the hill is to skate by each and every dog as efficiently as possible. It's also important not to allow the cat on the road to slow you down. Look at the accompanying map for the locations of the dogs and just keep practicing that escape route. It's not easy, but it is doable.

NOBODY LEFT BEHIND

Tony might get an award for saving all of those dogs, but he somehow forgot about you! Bam is willing to spot your team an extra 1,000 Goal Points if you save yourself with a giant course-wide combo. This is the last goal in Story Mode—don't give up now!

Escape Line

Combo downhill to the Skatopia sign.

Skate straight ahead towards the quarter pipe and Spine Transfer into the L-shaped half pipe near the barn for the **End Spine** gap. Ride up into a grind on the lip of the ramp. Transfer the grind off the end of the ramp and into a grind on the concrete quarter pipe leading up the hill towards the incomplete dome. Make small hops to maintain momentum, but keep the grind going as far as possible. Ollie off the edge and Acid Drop down towards the garage on the left. Spine Transfer over the **Garage Wall Spine** and then Spine Transfer out the other side. Revert to a manual on the grass and ride up the ramps on the left into a clockwise grind to the exit. Congratulations, you completed Story Mode!

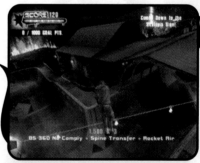

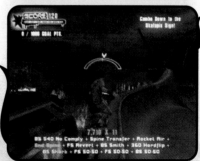

SKATOPIA

Training
Boston
Barcelona
Berlin
Australia
New Orleans
Skatopia
Pro Skater

Intro

Skater Basics

Trick Lists

Story Mode

Gaps

Classic Mode

Multiskater

Secrets

YOUR GOALS	
N/A	
PRO GOALS	
N/A	
GUEST GOALS	
N/A	
SECRET GOALS	
N/A	

PRO SKATER

Complete Story Mode to unlock this bonus location.

Circuit #2
Elevator from Lower Floor

Alien   Circuit #1

To Cargo Area

Monkey
Idol #5   Native #2

Grind These Ropes
To Collapse Statue

Portal to
Ancient Temple   Elevator to
Upper Floor

Monkey Idol #3

Portal to Hell

Monkey Idol #4

Monkey Idol #1

Cargo Area

Monkey Idol #1

Portal to Space

Native #1

ALIEN SPACE STATION

Dance With the Devil

Upon completing the World Destruction Tour, the scene shifts to an alien space station. Grind up to the balcony overlooking the main cargo area and ride the lift to the upper floor. Once there, talk to the alien about activating the red circuitry.

Activate the Red Circuitry

There are two red panels flanking the walkway leading away from the lift on the uppermost floor of the space station. Although the blue rails seem to lead to these panels, they are too high to be of any use.

The only way to activate the panels is to return to the balcony below and skate across to the other side of the room. Grind the railing along the balcony and quickly side-jump into a grind on the red rail. Transfer the grind up to the blue rail, then to the green rail. Hold the grind around the bend and up the incline towards the red panel and Sticker Slap it to activate it. Repeat these steps in the other direction to activate the other panel. Once both panels have been activated, the cargo bay doors open and a portal appears. Jump through the portal to reach an ancient temple deep in the jungle.

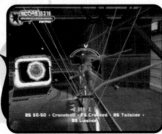

ANCIENT TEMPLE

The native on the left of the main steps warns of what happens to those who deface the monkey idols. Another native on a ledge inside advises you not to grind near the ropes.

Tagging Monkey Idols

There are five monkey idols in and around the temple. The first two monkey idols are on the outside of the temple, one on either side of the stairs. Hop off the board, walk up to the idol, and Graffiti Tag it. There's no better way to anger the gods than with a can of spray paint.

Enter the temple and head to either side to find the third and fourth monkey idol. They are on the ground floor, between the large torches on the wall. The fifth and final monkey idol is on the upper balcony, directly behind the enormous monkey statue.

Tag all five monkey idols to open a portal to hell. Use the ropes to climb out onto the suspended platform in the center of the temple and make a running leap into the fiery portal above the temple entrance.

So Long Support Ropes

There are many ropes inside the temple, but only two that are responsible for supporting the enormous monkey statue. Air up to the balcony to the left of the monkey statue. Hop into a grind through the rope leading from the walkway to the monkey statue. Hold the grind clockwise around the ledge and trick across the gap to continue the grind for the **Hop the Pools** gap and to grind through the second gap.

Once both support ropes have been cut, the monkey statue wobbles and its enormous stone ball crashes down onto the floor. This creates a large crater in the floor, which just so happens to be perfect for skating.

THE PITS OF HELL

Hell has enormous pools, numerous ledges, and plenty of ramps that provides all the boost necessary to get airborne. Looking for something else to do? Head to the upper level and talk to the imp near the skeleton sticking out of the ground.

Satan's Secret Chamber

The imp's boss wants the runes lit up and it's up to you to do it. There's a broken rib bone sticking out of either side of the large ribcage flanking the walkway. Ride up the ramp and leap into a lip trick atop each of the broken ribs.

Now that the ribs are out of the way, and the quarter pipe has collapsed a little, it's time to start lighting the runes. Jump off the crumbled quarter pipe section and Sticker Slap the rune on the pillar behind where the rib bone was. Repeat this for both of the runes and then watch as the door to the back room opens.

Ollie into the fiery mouth of the statue on the wall to gain access to the back room. Once there, enjoy the endless scoring lines made possible by the rotisseries and couches. Also, don't forget to enter the side room so the boss can show his appreciation for all your hard work.

PRO SKATER

Training
Boston
Barcelona
Berlin
Australia
New Orleans
Skatopia
Pro Skater

GAPS

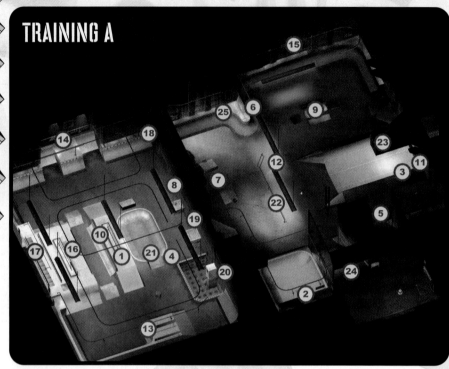

TRAINING (25 GAPS)

TRAINING A

GAP #	GAP NAME	POINTS	MAP
1	RAIL POP	25	A

Ollie into a grind on the rail atop the funbox.

| 2 | BEAM LIP | 50 | A |

Leap into a lip trick on the wooden beam above the pool in the corner of the initial area.

| 3 | HALF PIPE LIP | 50 | A |

Lip trick on the half pipe.

| 4 | POOL 2 POOL | 50 | A |

Grind the lip of the pool in the large area and transfer the grind to the ledge near the water.

| 5 | QP TRANSFER | 50 | A |

Vert between the quarter pipes on either side of the large slopes near the starting point.

| 6 | RAIL 2 LIGHT | 50 | A |

Transfer a grind from a sprinkler pipe onto the overhead lighting.

| 7 | RAMP HOP | 50 | A |

Gap across the two kicker ramps near the puddle and arcade machine.

| 8 | RED BUTTON WALLRIDE | 50 | A |

Wallride across the large red button on the wall near the garage door.

| 9 | CAR HOP | 75 | A |

Use the ramps near the parked taxi cab to leap over the car in either direction.

| 10 | FUNBOX SPINE | 75 | A |

Spine Transfer over the large funbox and into the concrete pool in the center of the large skatepark area.

| 11 | GOING UP | 75 | A |

Grind the rail on the wall near the half pipe towards the starting point and air off the kinked end of it into a grind on the sprinklers.

| 12 | LIGHT HOP | 75 | A |

Transfer a grind between two overhead lights in initial skating area.

| 13 | HIPPIN | 100 | A |

Hip Transfer the quarter pipes against the back wall of the large skatepark area.

| 14 | RECESSED TRANSFER | 100 | A |

Vert transfer between the two quarter pipes in the alcove.

| 15 | SPRINKLER LIP | 100 | A |

Air off the quarter pipe behind the taxi cab into a lip trick on the sprinkler pipe above.

| 16 | UPPER RAIL | 100 | A |

Air off the end of the large funbox near the wall and land in a grind on the central sprinkler pipe near the ceiling.

| 17 | HIGH WIRE | 150 | A |

Air out of the snack room, through the glass, and into a lip trick on the wire high above.

| 18 | OTHERSIDE 1 | 150 | A |

Grind the sprinkler pipe above the blue quarter pipe towards the cracked wall. Ollie through to the newer skatepark area.

| 19 | OTHERSIDE 2 | 150 | A |

Grind the sprinkler pipes past the roll-ins near the starting point and around towards the hole in the upper wall. Transfer the grind through the hole to the sprinkler in the newer area.

| 20 | PASSAGE HOP | 150 | A |

Grind the sprinklers towards the alcove on the wall above the large banner. Ollie out of the grind and into one on the rail in the alcove.

| 21 | BIG OLE LIP | 200 | A |

Air out of the concrete pool in the newer area and lip trick on the sprinkler pipe high above.

| 22 | BIG RAIL | 200 | A |

Grind the full length of the rail to the left of the half pipe in the initial skating area.

| 23 | OVER THE HALF PIPE | 200 | A |

Air off the ramp on the side of the half pipe and soar through the observation room to the other side of the half pipe. Clear it in a single bound!

| 24 | DOWNWARD MANUAL | 300 | A |

Manual down the slope near the starting point.

| 25 | HOLY SHI... | 3,000 | A |

Hop into a grind on the edge of the blue quarter pipe near the half pipe and grind it counter-clockwise all the way through the hole in the wall to the other room.

BOSTON (40 GAPS)

BOSTON A

11	BOSTON COMMON STAIRS	100	B

Ollie down the entire set of stairs leading down into the park near the statue of Washington.

12	BROWNSTONE TRANSFER	100	A

Transfer over the entrance of the apartment building to the right of the construction site.

13	CAR HOP	100	A

Ollie over a car.

14	HOSPITAL TRANSFER	100	

Air up onto the roof of the hospital from the concrete vert ramps at either end of the building.

15	LIBRARY MANUAL	100	B

Tap into a manual while approaching the revolving doors of the library. Balance through the interior of the library and out the other side.

16	LIBRARY MURAL	100	B

Use the concrete vert ramps on the side of the library to air up and over the large mural.

17	MURAL RIDE	100	B

Wallride the mural on the side of the library.

1	LEDGE HOP	25	A

Transfer a grind from one tall ledge to another while skating around the park.

2	RAIL HOP	25	A

Transfer a grind between the two blue rails near the sidewalk in front of the State House.

3	BUS STOP POP	50	A

Grind the shorter of the two blue rails near the State House and air off the kinked end into a grind atop the bus stop.

4	DUMPSTER UP	50	A

Air off the green dumpster in the alley near the library and land in a grind on one of the upper ledges.

5	FENCE LIP	50	C

Lip trick on the blue fence above the concrete barricades around the construction site.

6	HOSPITAL VOLCANO SPINE	50	A

Spine Transfer up and over either of the large brick cone structures in front of the hospital.

7	PLANTER 2 PLANTER	50	A

Grind the edge of the planters near the cannons and ollie into a grind on the other.

8	PLANTER UP	50	A

Air off the planter on the side of the church near the street and land in a grind on the ledge above.

9	SUBWAY SPINE	50	B

Spine Transfer over any of the three subway station entrances.

10	TEA PARTY TRANSFER	50	C

Spine Transfer into the Boston Tea Party ship.

BOSTON B

Intro

Skater Basics

Trick Lists

Story Mode

Gaps

Classic Mode

Multiskater

Secrets

18   RIBOFF LIP   100   B

Use the quarter pipe to the right of the State House stairs (as viewed from the street) to air into a lip trick on the rail.

19   STATEHOUSE STAIRS   100   B

Ollie down either set of steps leading up to the entrance of the State House.

20   SUBWAY MANUAL   100   A

Manual into any of the subway entrances and balance the manual through the subway station and out the other door.

21   TEA BOMB   100   C

Climb the ladder to the top of the crow's nest on the Boston Tea Party ship and Acid Drop down to the main deck.

22   WASHINGTON AIR   100   B

Spine Transfer over the Washington statue in the center of the park.

23   BANK TRANSFER   200   B

Transfer from the concrete ramp at the base of the Riboff Bank through the grate in the wall and into the bank interior.

24   FLIRTING WITH DISASTER   250   D

Enter the subway and Sticker Slap the back wall across the tracks from the platform.

25   ROOF SPINE   250   B

Spine Transfer between the roof of the church and the building with the scaffolding in front of it.

26   STATEHOUSE STAIR SPINE   250   B

Spine Transfer up and over the statues and the stairs in front of the State House front door. Use the ramps on either side of the stairs.

27   TH TRANSFER   250   A

Transfer between the two recessed ramps flanking the Tony Hawk portrait.

28   WIRE TRANSFER   250   A

Grind the wire strung between the roof of the church and the building near the Tony Hawk portrait.

29   BIG DIG BIG AIR   500   A

Hop off the yellow curb under the hospital near the construction site and fly over the massive vent under the suspended portion of the building. This will blow the skater up to the large chutes to the left of the construction site.

30   BOSTON BY WIRE   500   A

Grind the length of the electrical wire starting from the blue rail on the side of the hospital. Grind around the park and back towards the church.

31   CHURCH SIGN SLAP   500   A

Wallride the back of the church and Sticker Slap the church sign near the roof.

32   READING IS FUN   500   A

Grind the blue rail on the side of the church above the massive vent and ollie across the street and grind on the roof of the library.

33   RIBOFF 2 CHURCH   500   A

Grind the yellow rail on the side of the Riboff Bank facing the State House and ollie across the street to a grind on the peak of the church's roof.

34   STREET CROSSING   500   A

Air off the plywood ramp atop the library and cross the street to the construction site. Land on the ramps in the construction site.

35   WALL SLAP   500   B

Grind the edge of the curving brick wall behind the Riboff Bank and ollie off the end. Sticker Slap the sign above the ATM and land back in a grind on the brick wall.

36   YELLOW PIPE CLIMB   500   A

Grind the fence in front of the construction site and ollie out of the grind and grab onto the yellow ladder leading up the side of the building. You must dismount the board while in the air.

37   APARTMENT SPINE   1,000   A

Spine Transfer through the glass ceiling and windows of either apartment at the Brownstone building.

38   HIGH SLAP   1,000   B

Grind the upper yellow rail around the side of the Riboff Bank towards the building near it. Ollie off the end of the rail, Sticker Slap the wall beyond it, and land back in a grind on the rail.

39   I'M A LITTLE TEAPOT   2,000   A

Grind the top of the quarter pipe to the right of the Tony Hawk portrait and leap into a grind on the teapot sign. From there, jump and either grind or Natas Spin on the light pole.

40   BANK DROP   5,000   B

Skate through the Riboff Bank interior and ollie out the far side. Acid Drop onto the back of the subway station in the plaza near the metal sculpture.

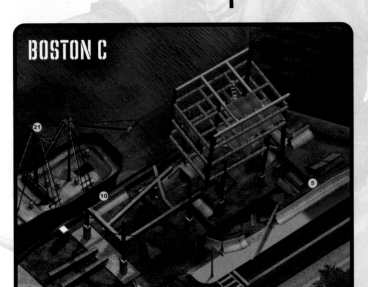

BOSTON C

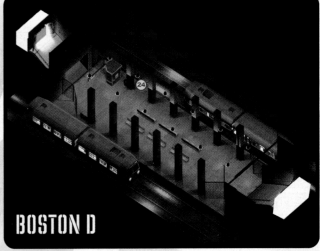

BOSTON D

BARCELONA (33 GAPS)

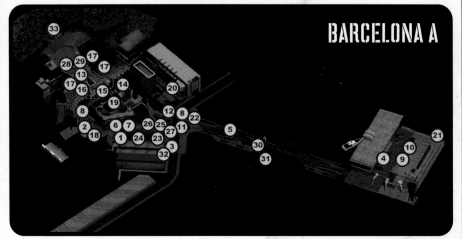

BARCELONA A

| 21 | NIXON PLANT | 100 | A |

Sticker Slap the large, red, Nixon sign near the waterfront.

| 22 | RAMBLA DEL AGUA | 100 | A |

Ollie into a grind on the angled sign near the crate of tomatoes by the bridge. Transfer this brief grind to the large red rail on the bridge.

| 23 | SANTS AWNING | 100 | A |

Air off the plywood ramps near the street and land in a grind on the metal beams above the picnic area in front of Estacion Sants.

| 24 | SANTS BENCH FLIP | 100 | A |

Grind or skate on one of the picnic tables or benches in front of Estacion Sants and flip trick off of it.

| 25 | SANTS BENCHES | 100 | A |

Hold-Grind across all of the benches near Estacion Sants. Hop into a grind on either end, but be sure to grind across all eight benches.

| 26 | SUBWAY MANUAL | 100 | A |

Start skating towards a subway entrance and tap into a manual before the downward slope. Balance the manual down the hill and out the other side of the station.

| 27 | TICK TOC | 100 | A |

Grind the metal awning near Estacion Sants and ollie into a Sticker Slap on the hanging clock.

| 28 | WORLD'S LONGEST BENCH | 100 | A |

Skate to the rear of Parc Guell and grind the lengthy bench with all of the curves in it.

| 29 | DRAGON'S TAIL | 300 | A |

Ollie into a grind on the dragon statue's head and grind across the dragon and gap into a grind from its tail onto the World's Longest Bench.

| 30 | RAMBLA NO TERRANO | 300 | A |

Ollie into a grind on the rails of the bridge and successfully grind from one end of the bridge to the other without setting down on the bridge. Transfer grinds between the various red rails to make the journey without breaking the combo.

| 31 | ARGHHH! | 500 | A |

Grind the netting near the water under the drawbridge. This will free the boat and allow the bridge to close.

| 32 | BUTTERFINGER! | 1,000 | A |

Grind across the top of the Butterfinger machine near the arcade machine.

| 33 | TOWER 2 TOWER | 2,000 | A |

Enter the tram tower near Parc Guell and grind the length of the cable from the tower there to the one near the waterfront.

| 1 | BENCH HOP | 25 | A |

Transfer a grind from one bench to another in front of the Estacion Sants.

| 2 | LEDGE HOP | 25 | A |

Grind the ledge in front of the hospital and ollie across to another ledge.

| 3 | RAIL HOP | 25 | A |

Transfer a grind across two rails near the Estacion Sants.

| 4 | AC BOOST | 50 | A |

Enter the open doors of the cinema near the waterfront to get launched out the vents on the roof. Land in a grind on the rope.

| 5 | BRIDGE RAIL TRANSFER | 50 | A |

Grind any of the red rails on the bridge and ollie into a grind on a different rail.

| 6 | LEDGE 2 RAIL | 50 | A |

Grind the ledge near the lengthy row of benches and ollie into a grind on the rail near the building beside it.

| 7 | RAIL 2 LEDGE | 50 | A |

Transfer a grind between from a railing to a grind on a wall or ledge.

| 8 | TAKING OUT THE TRASH | 50 | A |

Leap into a grind or Natas Spin on any of the trash cans around the city.

| 9 | BESOS | 100 | A |

Tap into a manual near the concrete rollers (the Besos Waves) and manual from one end to the other without interruption.

| 10 | BESOS FLIP | 100 | A |

Skate through the Besos Waves rollers and flip trick up and over the railing at the end.

| 11 | CAR HOP | 100 | A |

Ollie over any car on the road.

| 12 | CATAPULT LAUNCH | 100 | A |

Enter the castle across the street from the bridge and get launched from the catapults on the roof. Can also skate into one of the launching baskets on the catapults.

| 13 | DRAGON'S BREATH | 100 | A |

Jump inside the mouth of the dragon statue.

| 14 | FAN BOOST | 100 | A |

Get launched from the giant fans atop the building near the large billboard.

| 15 | GUELL ENTRANCE | 100 | A |

Transfer a grind between the two walls with the white and brown striped ledges.

| 16 | GUELL PLANTER DRAGON TRANSFER | 100 | A |

Transfer up and over the two walkways near the dragon statue by airing between the quarter pipes near the planters. Get speed for the jump by Spine Transferring down from above.

| 17 | GUELL PLANTER SPINE TRANSFER | 100 | A |

Spine Transfer up and over any of the three planters in the Parc Guell area.

| 18 | HOSPITAL TRANSFER | 100 | A |

Air between any of the quarter pipes in front of the hospital building. Transfer over the steps on either side of the fountain.

| 19 | LA PERDRERA SPIRAL | 100 | A |

Grind the length of the spiral rail in the La Perdrera building from the roof to the floor. The grind must be continuous.

| 20 | MAMO FLIP | 100 | A |

Grind or skate on the ledge in front of the MAMO building and ollie into a flip trick.

Intro

Skater Basics

Trick Lists

Story Mode

Gaps

Classic Mode

Multiskater

Secrets

BERLIN A

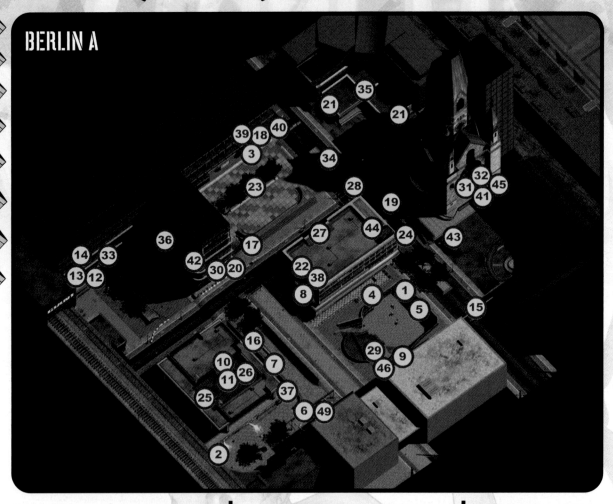

1	AUSFARHT LIP	25	A

Leap into a lip trick on the rail above the AusFarht Center sign.

2	LEDGE HOP	25	A

Grind the ledge around the bend and hop into a grind on the ledge near the Galleria building.

3	LEVEL 1 LIP	25	A

Air into a lip trick on the lower pink ledge of the building near the plaza with the gray and pink tiles.

4	RAIL HOP	25	

Transfer a grind from one rail to the other near the AusFarht Center.

5	AUSFARHT TRANSFER	50	A

Use the ramps on either side of the AusFarht Center entrance to transfer up and over the doorway.

6	AWNING LIP	50	A

Air off the concrete barricade into a lip trick on the gray "Downzked" awning support.

7	BENCH 2 LEDGE	50	A

Grind the bench on the side of the Galleria building and ollie to a grind on the ledge.

8	DROPOFF LIP	50	A

Air into a lip trick on the ledge below the "Afropick" sign.

9	FOUNTAIN MANUAL DOWN	50	A

Manual down the ramped walkway leading to the AusFarht Center entrance.

10	GALLERIA SPINE DOWN	50	A

Spine Transfer off the roof of the Galleria into the pool inside the secret area.

11	GALLERIA SPINE UP	50	A

Spine Transfer from the pool in the secret area onto the roof of the Galleria building.

12	GOLD LIP 1	50	A

Air into a lip trick on the lower ledge of the building near the Oktoberfest area.

13	GOLD LIP 2	50	A

Air into a lip trick on the middle ledge of the building near the Oktoberfest area.

14	GOLD LIP 3	50	A

Air into a lip trick on the upper ledge of the building near the Oktoberfest area.

15	HITTIN' THE PIPE	50	A

Air off the quarter pipe in the street and lip trick on the large blue water pipe above the road near the zoo.

16	LEDGE 2 BENCH	50	A

Grind the ledge near the Galleria and hop into a grind on the bench.

17	LEDGE 2 RAIL	50	A

Grind the steps across the street from the Berlin Platz and ollie to a grind on the fence below the giant billboard.

18	LEVEL 2 LIP	50	A

Air into a lip trick on the middle pink ledge of the building with the pink and gray tiles in the plaza.

19 OVER THE PIPE HOP   50   A

Grind the edge of the trench in front of the church and side-jump over the pipe and grind the other side of the trench.

20 RAIL 2 LEDGE   50   A

Grind the fence under the big billboard and ollie to a grind on the steps to the right of it.

21 SONATA SPINE   50   A

Spine Transfer up to or down from the roof of the ornate gold building to the left of the church.

22 VENT TRANSFER   50   A

Air over the large vent on the roof of the Berlin Platz building via the quarter pipes on either side.

23 WIRE LIP   50   A

Lip trick on the wire above the trees in the center of the plaza with the pink and gray tiles.

24 WIRE POP   50   A

Pop off the planters in the street near the church and grind the wire near the trees.

25 ART DROP   75   A

Transfer off the roof of the Galleria, over a satellite dish, and into the pool inside the secret area.

26 ART LIP   75   A

Leap out of the pool in the Galleria secret area and lip trick on either of the colored pipes.

27 ROOFTOP TRANSFER   75   A

Use the quarter pipes on the roof of the Berlin Platz building to vert transfer over both of the kicker ramps.

28 CAR HOP   100   A

Ollie over any car on the roads of Berlin.

29 FOUNTAIN ESCAPE   100   A

Grind the edge of the fountain near the starting point and ollie to a grind on the railing above the arcade machine.

30 HIGH LIP   100   A

Air off the barricade in the street below the giant billboard and lip trick on the ledge above.

31 INTO CHURCH   100   A

Spine Transfer into the church from either side.

32 OUT OF CHURCH   100   A

Spine Transfer out of the church from either side.

33 SECOND TIER   100   A

Grind the lower ledge of the gold building near the Oktoberfest party and pop off the kinked edge to a grind on the middle ledge.

34 SMACK MY B!*@H UP!   100   A

Pop off the edge of the planter in the street by the church and Sticker Slap the giant posters of the soldiers.

35 SONATA HIP   100   A

Hip Transfer the flat section of the roof in the center of the ornate gold building near the church.

36 THIRD TIER   100   A

Grind the middle ledge of the gold building near the Oktoberfest party and pop off the kinked section to a grind on the upper ledge.

37 WALL DROP   100   A

Grind the Galleria ledge towards the ruined wall near the street. Air off the kinked end of the ledge and Acid Drop onto the other side of the wall.

38 BACKDOOR DROP   150   A

Spine Transfer down from the roof of the building with the vent. Perform the trick to the left of the vent, so as to drop past the "Afropick" sign.

39 LEVEL 3 LIP   150   A

Air into a lip trick on the uppermost pink ledge of the building with the pink and gray tiles in the plaza. Get speed with a series of Spine Transfers starting from the roof of the building across the street.

40 CHECKPOINT TRANSFER   200   A

Air transfer from the ramp in front of the checkpoint (to the left of the ornate gold building) onto the concrete quarter pipe in front of the pink building.

41 LOW CHURCH LIP   200   A

Air into a lip trick on the lower edge on the side of the church.

42 TO THE GALLERIA   200   A

Grind the uppermost ledge of the gold building near the Oktoberfest party in a clockwise direction. Towards the end of the ledge, transfer to grey ledge to the left. Jump off the end of it and land in a grind on the Galleria rooftop.

43 WALL HIP   200   A

Hip Transfer the two wall fragments near the zoo and church.

44 AUSFARHT DROP   300   A

Transfer from the quarter pipe on the roof of the building with the vent down to the ramp below the AusFarht Center sign.

45 CHURCH DROP   400   A

Grind the uppermost ledge of the zoo in a counter-clockwise direction and ollie of the end into an Acid Drop into the church. Reach this ledge via the water pipe in the street.

46 FOUNTAIN MANUAL UP   400   A

Manual up the ramp walkway from the AusFarht Center entrance to the starting point.

47 EXTREME CHURCH LIP   500   B

Acid Drop inside the church and lip trick on any of the ledges.

48 LADDER SKILLZ   500   B

Air off the quarter pipe in the church, hop off the board while in the air, and grab onto the ladder.

49 OWNED!!!   500   A

Grind up the yellow rails of the awning near the "Downzked" sign and knock off the letters to reveal the word "owned". Can also grind across the top of the sign to knock down the letters as well.

GAPS

BERLIN B

INFORM YOURSELF

Intro

Skater Basics

Trick Lists

Story Mode

Gaps

Classic Mode

Multiskater

Secrets

AUSTRALIA (40 GAPS)

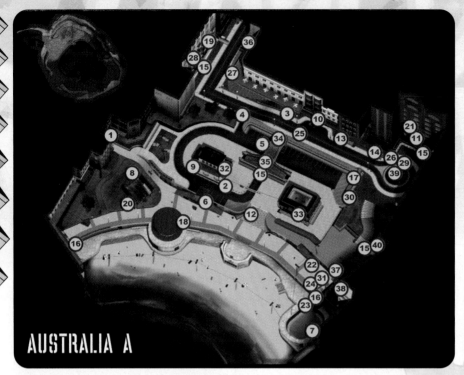

AUSTRALIA A

1	BALCONY LIP	25	A

Air off the quarter pipe at the end of the sidewalk and lip trick on the U-shaped balcony railing.

2	CHAIN GANG	25	A

Transfer a grind between the ledge of the building with the spine ramps on the roof and the chain rail near the corner.

3	HOMEMADE HANDRAIL	25	A

Transfer a grind between the ledge in front of the arcade machine and the fallen lamppost. Must wake the crane operator to knock over the lamppost.

4	LEDGE DROP	25	A

Grind the tall wall alongside the street and ollie off the end into a grind on the small brick ledge.

5	LEDGE HOP	25	A

Transfer a grind between any two adjacent ledges throughout the area.

6	RAIL 2 RAIL	25	A

Transfer a grind between any two railings near the boardwalk area where the graffiti is.

7	ROCK LIP	25	A

Air out of the tide pool and lip trick on the rocks jutting out from the side near the building.

8	9 POINT LANDING	50	A

Grind the edge of the concrete quarter pipe near the grass with the wooden boards on it. Ollie off the end of the ramp over the sidewalk and grass and into a grind on the rail set up near the mini-ramp.

9	ARCHWAY ROOF TAP	50	A

Air off the ramped portion of the planter near the yellow building with the arches and land in a grind on the roof edge above the arches.

10	BALCONY HOP	50	A

Grind the edge of the balcony near the bus stop and side-jump to a grind on the planters.

11	BALCONY LOFTY LIP	50	A

Air off the quarter pipe at the base of the building near the statue and lip trick on the upper balcony.

12	BIG STAIR SET	50	A

Clear the large set of stairs in the middle of the boardwalk with a single ollie.

13	BUS STOP HOP	50	A

Pop off the ramped ends of the bus stop and land in a grind on the awning above the shops.

14	CRANE VAULT	50	A

Air off the ramped edge of the crane into a grind on the red or green awning.

15	G'DAY RAMP 2 RAMP	50	A

Transfer between two quarter pipes. Can be done in multiple areas, but especially easy to hit near the statue of Kenny.

16	HIGH 2 LOW TRANSFER	50	A

Transfer from the upper ramp on the boardwalk to the lower one nearest the beach. Can be done at either end of the course.

17	HOT WIRE LIP	50	A

Air up from the quarter pipe near the statue to a lip trick on the wire above the parking lot.

18	LIFE GUARD ROOF TAP	50	A

Grind the handrail near the boardwalk and air off the kinked end of it into a grind on the lifeguard station roof.

19	LOW BAY WINDOW LIP	50	A

Air off the pink and white checkerboard ramp to a lip trick on the lowest bay window.

20	10 POINT LANDING	75	A

Grind the fence-like railing near the mini-ramp in the direction of the beach. Ollie off the end and gap over the boardwalk and down into a grind on the rail that wraps around the base of the lifeguard station.

21	BALCONY CLIMB	75	A

Grind one of the railings on the fire escape that has a kinked end on it. Ollie off the end, Sticker Slap the wall nearby and land in a grind on the railing *above* the one you were originally on.

22	CAN SKIP	75	A

Skate towards any of the spinning garbage can and ollie into a grind on it (Kiss the Rail) and quickly skip across it into a grind on a nearby rail or ledge.

23	COPING JUMP	75	A

Grind the coping on the lower quarter pipe at the end of the boardwalk near the tide pool and ollie into a grind on the lip of the pool.

24	LOW 2 HIGH TRANSFER	75	A

Transfer from the upper ramp on the boardwalk to the lower one nearest the beach. Can be done at either end of the course.

25	CAR HOP	100	A

Ollie over any of the cars on the road. Can also ollie over the parked cars in the parking lot.

26	FOUNTAIN TOUCHDOWN	100	A

Air off the base of the crane and land in a grind on the edge of the fountain.

27	FROM BRASS OVER 10	100	A

Grind the brass railing away from the road barricade and ollie off the end. Clear the entire curved set of stairs and land in the street.

28	HIGH BAY WINDOW LIP	100	A

Air off the checkered quarter pipe across from the curved set of stairs and lip trick on the upper bay windows.

29	PEACE OUT!	100	A

Air off the fountain and land in a Natas Spin on the fingers of the Kenny statue.

30	TC'S GRASS GAP	100	A

Ollie from the brick area near the Kenny statue and clear the grass slope. Land in the parking lot below.

31 BIG COPING JUMP   150   A

Grind the coping on the upper quarter pipe at the end of the boardwalk near the tide pool and ollie into a grind on the lip of the pool.

32 LOFTY ROOF GAP   150   A

Skate the roof of the building with the spine ramps on it and air off the kicker at the end. The fan boost will propel you through the air to the other building. Acid Drop into the rooftop bowl for the gap.

33 TC'S AWNING   150   A

Pop off the ledge in front of the building near the logs and grind the awning.

34 FOOTBRIDGE FLYOVER   200   A

Use the concrete quarter pipes on either side of the footbridge to air up and over the actual bridge.

35 UP AND OVER MANUAL!   200   A

Get some speed and manual up the walkway to the top of the footbridge. Maintain balance and continue the manual down the other side.

36 BIG STREET CROSS   250   A

Skate around the balcony past the restaurant tables and air from the quarter pipe in the corner down onto the one on the other side of the street.

37 BIGGUN'S RAMP 2 RAMP   250   A

Transfer from the highest quarter pipe to the lowest one near the tide pool. Grind the logs in front of the building for speed and hit the quarter pipe on a hard angle to the right.

38 CHECK YOUR PANTS!   250   A

Climb the ladder on the side of the apartment building near the emu burger billboard and run to the far end of the ledge. Jump up and Acid Drop from the uppermost ledge to the tide pool below.

39 PEACE OFF!   250   A

Ollie into and out of a Natas Spin on Kenny's fingers to complete the "Kenny's Real Feelings" goal.

40 NO @$%#@$%# WAY!!!   5,000   A

Grind the ledge above the emu burger billboard (near the wall of glass) towards the beach and ollie off where it bends. Land in a grind on the handrail on the ground that leads down to the tide pool.

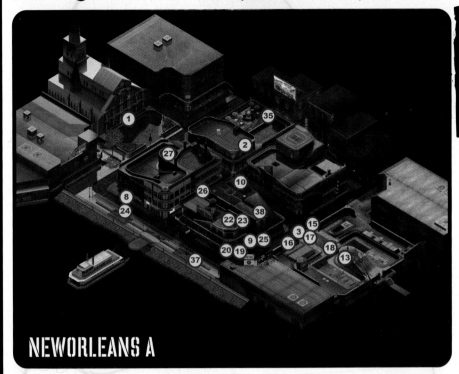

NEW ORLEANS A

1 CHURCH STATUE   25   A

Vert transfer over the statue in front of the church.

2 INTO THE UNDERWORLD   25   B

Raise the dead by opening the 5 crypts in the cemetery, then Spine Transfer into the cavern that opens in the center of town.

3 NAWLINS STREET SPINE   25   A

Spine Transfer from the roof of the building with the helipad to the one in front of the church.

4 GRAVE GATE TRANSFER   50   A

Vert transfer from one of the side quarter pipes in front of the cemetery to the ramp in between the gates.

5 HELIPAD SPINE1   50   B

Spine Transfer from the helipad down onto the side street below.

6 HELIPAD SPINE2   50   B

Spine Transfer from the street below the helipad up onto the rooftop pool under the large billboard.

7 HELIPAD SPINE3   50   B

Spine Transfer from the rooftop pool below the billboard to the courtyard bar.

8 POLE POP   50   A

Grind on (Kiss the Rail) a pole in front of McDonald's and pop into a grind (Kiss the Rail) on another pole without touching the ground.

9 ALLEY TRANSFER   100   A

Vert transfer between the ramps flanking the entrance to the garbage alley where the purple banner is.

10 BIG EASY ROOF GAP   100   A

Jump between the rooftops of the two buildings on either side of the street near the cemetery.

11 BOO YA'S SIGN   100   B

Grind through the "Boo Ya's Bottomless Topless" sign on the balcony in the center of town.

12 CAR HOP   100   B

Ollie over a car or the parade float.

13 CRYPT KEEPER   100   A

Spine Transfer up and over the large circular crypt in the cemetery.

14 DUMPSTER DIVE   100   B

Clear the entire dumpster in the alley with a single leap. Use the ramped edges of the dumpster to take flight.

15 GRAVE GATES TRANSFER   100   A

Vert transfer across the front gates of the cemetery. Spine Transfer down from a rooftop and use the quarter pipe to the right or left to gap all the way past both gates to the other ramp.

16 GRAVE WALL SPINE   100   A

Spine Transfer over the front wall of the cemetery into the street.

Intro

Skater Basics

Trick Lists

Story Mode

Gaps

Classic Mode

Multiskater

Secrets

NEWORLEANS B

17   GRAVE WALL TRANSFER   100   A

Vert transfer from ramp to ramp over either of the cemetery gates, but perform the trick while in the cemetery, not in the street.

18   GRAVEYARD TRANSFER   100   A

Vert transfer between the brick quarter pipes that flank the grassy slope in the center of the cemetery.

19   GREEN GODDESS DOOR TRANSFER   100   A

Vert transfer over the door to the Green Goddess establishment on the corner near the water, across from the cemetery.

20   GREEN GODDESS SIGN   100   A

Grind the awning of the Green Goddess building across from the cemetery and smash the neon sign on the corner.

21   NAWLINS SIGN   100   B

Grind the awning of the yellow building in the center of town and smash through the large neon Nawlins sign.

22   ONTO THE ROOF RAMP   100   A

Vert transfer from the quarter pipe on the roof of the Green Goddess building to the one on the platform above the doors.

23   OVER THE ROOF RAMP   100   A

Vert transfer up and over the ramp atop the doors on the roof of the Green Goddess building.

24   STREETCAR RIDE   100   A

Wallride the streetcar near the waterfront.

25   VEGAS SHOW DOOR TRANSFER   100   A

Transfer up and over the doorway to the shop to the right of the dumpster alley, as viewed from the cemetery.

26   OVER THE ALLEY TRANSFER   200   A

Transfer over the dumpster alley from one rooftop to the other using the quarter pipes.

27   DANCE FLOOR SKILLZ   250   A

Enter the nightclub and skate onto the dance floor (directly across from church). Ollie into the air while on the dance floor to get boosted through the ceiling to the rooftop.

28   HUMIDITY DROP   250   C

Air off either kicker ramp in the alley with the "Humidity" banners and Acid Drop onto the far side of the spine ramp.

29   HUMIDITY LIP   250   C

Air up from either spine ramp and lip trick on one of the "Humidity" banners.

30   WIRE LIP   250   B

Leap into a lip trick on the wire above the concrete ramps at the end of the river near the cemetery.

31   AIR BOAT SIGN SLAP   500   B

Pop off a grind on the lengthy crypt in the cemetery and Sticker Slap the large air boat billboard.

32   HIP BONE   500   B

Skate through the alley to the left of the cemetery and Hip Transfer off the quarter pipe onto the ramp inside the cemetery.

33   HUGE ALLEY DROP!   500   B

Air off the quarter pipe on the roof of the Green Goddess building and transfer down to the quarter pipe at the edge of the dumpster alley.

34   NAWLINS STREET MANUAL   500   B

Manual the length of the street that cuts through the center of the town, either starting or finishing near the riverboat.

35   OBRIEN'S BALCONY MANUAL   500   A

Manual down the entire length of the walkway at the courtyard bar.

36   SUPER DUPER LIP   500   B

Spine Transfer down from the rooftop across the street and air from the street into a lip trick on the edge of the ramp atop the helipad.

37   GAS LAMP   1,000   A

Grind one of the purple rails near the streetcar tracks and pop off the end into a grind on a gas lamp.

38   SMOKE BOMB   1,000   A

Jump from the wood propped up on the smoky chimney and Acid Drop into the cemetery across the street.

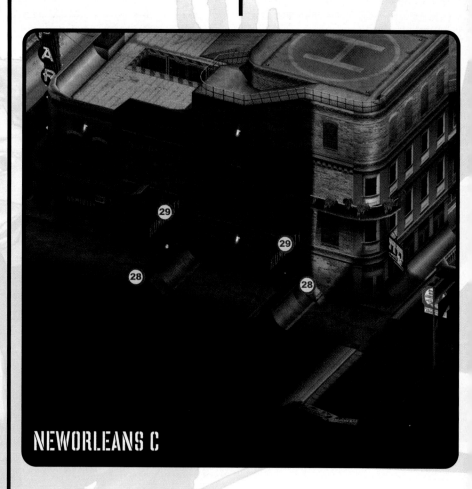

NEWORLEANS C

SKATOPIA (43 GAPS)

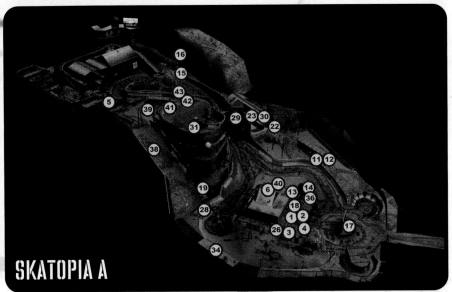

SKATOPIA A

1 DOWNSTAIRS   1   A

Run down the stairs on the front porch of the house.

2 UPSTAIRS   1   A

Run up the stairs on the front porch of the house.

3 GREEN SHACK   5   A

Grind the roof of the small green shack.

4 HOUSE STEP   5   A

Grind across any of the steps leading up to the front porch of the house.

5 GARBAGE BLAST   10   A

Air off the explosive garbage fire by ollieing while skating over it.

6 A-FRAME GRIND   50   A

Grind the peak of the house's roof.

7 BARN POOL HIP   50   B

Hip Transfer the corner of the L-shaped pool behind the barn.

8 BARN RAMP MANUAL   50   B

Manual down the walkway ramp on the side of the barn.

9 END SPINE   50   B

Spine Transfer out of the corner of the L-shaped pool to the concrete quarter pipes at the rear of the property.

10 GARAGE POOL MANUAL   50   B

Manual the length of the garage. Tap into the wheelie and balance it past the pool and out the other side.

11 MOBILE HOME DROP   50   A

Hit the wooden ramp on the side of the mobile home and Acid Drop down into the concrete ramp on the other side.

12 MOBILE HOME WALL BOMB   50   A

Grind the concrete quarter pipe downhill toward the mobile home and WalliePlant off the side of the mobile home for air. Acid Drop into the semi-circular bowl in the distance.

13 OVER THE PORCH DROP   50   A

Leap from the ramps on either side of the house on an angle. Soar over the corner of the house and Acid Drop into the ramps near the front steps.

14 SHACK 2 SIGN   50   A

Grind the roof of the red shack and ollie into a grind on the ledge around the base of the Skatopia sign.

15 SIDE BOMB   50   A

Air off the ramp near the mountainside uphill from the garage and Acid Drop on an angle into the concrete quarter pipe near the road.

16 SIDEWALL BOMB   50   A

Grind the fence towards the mountain on the side of the barn and Wallride the rock face. WalliePlant off the cliff and Acid Drop into the concrete quarter pipe by the dirt road.

17 SIGN SPINE   50   A

Spine Transfer over the Skatopia sign in either direction.

18 STAIR TRANSFER   50   A

Vert transfer over the stairs in front of the house.

19 BIG SLOPE HIP TRANSFER   100   A

Skate down the big slope under the inclined zipline and Hip Transfer from the ramp under the mineshaft entrance to the one at the base of the cliff.

20 BOWLING MANUAL   100   B

Manual the length of the bowling alley behind the barn.

21 CAR HOP   100   B

Ollie over the car when it drives by.

22 HELLSKULL GAP   100   A

Grind the lower interior ledge of the garage and ollie to a grind on the mobile home.

23 HUGE SHACK GAP   100   A

Grind the rail on the roof of the garage and ollie off the end into a grind on the roof of the red shack.

24 OVER THE ROAD GARAGE BOMB   100   B

Air off the funbox on the ledge above the "Free Land" sign and Acid Drop into the pool inside the garage.

25 POND X 5   100   B

Grind five laps around the pond.

26 PORCH MANUAL   100   A

Manual the ground under the front porch of the house. Don't bang your head on the steps!

27 CLIFF SPINE   200   B

Spine Transfer from the bowl atop the mountain down onto the road beside the garage.

28 DROP FROM THE WIRE   200   A

Grind the inclined zipline cable down the big slope and ollie into an Acid Drop on the small ramps at the base of the slope.

29 GARAGE WALL SPINE   200   A

Spine Transfer from the dirt road up and over the garage wall. Land in the pool inside the garage.

30 INTO THE GARAGE   200   A

Spine Transfer into or out of the garage on the side facing the edge of the map.

31 MINE SPINE   200   A

Spine Transfer over the outhouse at the top of the mountain and into the mineshaft. There is a ramp at the base of the shaft that makes this possible.

32 OVER THE HOUSE   200   B

Hit the ramp behind the house with enough speed to launch up and over the entire house. Acid Drop down from the cliff to get enough speed.

33 SIGN TRANSFER   200   B

Vert transfer from the quarter pipes on either side of the Skatopia sign to the banked ledge behind the sign.

34 WEIRD TRANSFER   200   A

Hit the base of the ramps to the left of the house on an angle and Hip Transfer onto the quarter pipe near the cement mixer by the fence.

Intro

Skater Basics

Trick Lists

Story Mode

Gaps

Classic Mode

Multiskater

Secrets

35 ZIPLINE DROP 200 B

Ride the vertical zipline into the air and Acid Drop into the mountaintop bowl.

36 SHACK COMBO 500 A

Skate through either the red or green shack and stay in a combo all the way back down the mountain and manual into the other shack to combo the both of them. See the corresponding goal in the Story Mode chapter for specific instructions on accomplishing this feat.

37 WATER PIPE GRIND 500 B

Grind the entire length of the water pipe on the side of the mountain. It's on the ledge directly above the "Free Land" sign and ends near the big slope.

38 MANUAL 1.BIG SLOPE 2.CEMENT MIXER 3.FRONT GATE 1,000 A

Tap into a manual on the big slope and carefully balance it down the hill. Stay to the right and roll past the cement mixer, around the path near the fence, and down to the front gate.

39 OUT THE BUS, GRIND 2 TREES, GRIND HOUSE 1,000 A

Enter the bus atop the mountain to get teleported out the other end. Land in a grind on the angled trees on the big slope. Grind two of the trees, then ollie to a grind on the edge of the house.

40 SIDEWAYS HOUSE LAUNCH 1,000 A

Air up and over the house in the sideways direction. Acid Drop off the mobile home to get enough speed.

41 TOP GRIND 1,000 A

Grind the entire length of the concrete quarter pipe that starts at the top of the mountain and ends near the Skatopia sign. Use Focus!

42 MOUNTAINTOP MANUAL 15,000 A

Tap into a manual at the top of the mountain near the garden hose stretched across the road and balance it all the way down the road and out the front gate. Again, use Focus!

43 HUGE ELECTRIC WIRE 20,000 A

Pop off the kicker ramp near the garden hose atop the mountain and land in a grind on the electric wire. Grind the length of the wire all the way to the bottom of the course near the Skatopia sign.

SKATOPIA B

PRO SKATER (31 GAPS)

PROSKATER A

1 LEDGE HOP 25 A

Grind the ledge in the bottom of the space station and transfer the grind to another ledge.

2 RAIL HOP 25 A

Transfer a grind from the yellow and green quarter pipe to the green rail above it.

3 WIRE HOP 25 A

Transfer a grind between any two of the red, green, and blue wires in the space station.

4 SPINE THE LANDING PAD 40 A

Spine Transfer over the main landing pad. Can be done while the spacecraft is still there.

5 CRANELESS 50 A

Grind the red or blue wire towards where the giant crane is and ollie across the break in the wires to continue the grind.

6 HOLO BOY 50 A

Ollie from one side of the control room to the other while passing through the hologram.

7 LEDGE 2 RAIL 50 A

Transfer a grind from the ledge around the walkway to the handrail overlooking the landing pad.

PROSKATER B

23 TRIPLE RAIL SKIP — 200 — A

Grind the handrail on the side of the walkway near the crane and transfer the grind across both gaps in the rail.

24 SPACE LEAP — 250 — A

Transfer a grind across the large gap where the main bay door is. Get a lot of speed and ollie out of the grind to carry the distance.

25 HOP THE POOLS — 400 — B

Transfer a grind between the ledges of the two pools on the balconies behind the large monkey statue.

26 CLEAR THE MONKEY — 600 — B

Grind the ledge of either lower pool and ollie off the end and soar all the way past the monkey statue and land in a grind on the other pool.

27 CABLE MAN — 750 — A

Air off the small quarter pipe in front of the main hangar door of the space station and lip trick on the cable above.

28 CUTTING EDGE — 750 — B

Leap into a lip trick on the monkey statue's sword.

29 MONKEY TRANSFER — 750 — B

Vert transfer from the quarter pipe on either of the balconies above the monkey statue down to the ramp at the base of the statue.

30 SPINE DROP — 2,000 — A

Spine Transfer up through the glass of the observation deck (where the hologram is) and Acid Drop down to the ramp at the base of the landing pad.

31 SNAKE ACID LIP — 3,500 — B

Acid Drop down into the snake pit (after toppling the monkey statue) and air up into a lip trick on the highest ledge of the column on the opposite side.

8 TEMPLE PLATFORMS — 50 — B

Air from one kicker ramp to the other.

9 PORTAL HOP — 50 — B

Grind the ledge towards the large portal outside the temple and ollie past the portal to continue the grind on the other side.

10 RAIL 2 LEDGE — 50 — A

Grind the handrail on the walkway above the landing pad and ollie into a grind on the ledge near the wall.

11 RAMP TRANSFER — 100 — B

Spine Transfer over the main entrance ramp outside the temple.

12 TEMPLE WALL TRANSFER — 50 — B

Spine Transfer down from the upper patio outside the temple to the ground below.

13 CABLE PLANT — 75 — A

Grind the red or blue rail near the elevator. Grind towards the portal where the rail begins to bend.

14 CLEAR THE ENTRANCE — 75 — B

Grind the ledge inside the temple, near the entrance and ollie past the opening and land in a grind on the other side.

15 CLEAR THE FIGHTER — 75 — A

Vert transfer up and over the entrance to one of the side hangars.

16 STAR TRANSFER — 75 — A

Ride the lift to the upper level and cross to the lookout room. Transfer between the quarter pipes on the walkway and the ones on the floor.

17 HOP THE HELL BEAMS — 80 — C

Grind the beams high above the ground in the hell area and transfer from one to the other.

18 HIGH LIP — 100 — A

Skate into one of the side hangars and lip trick on the upper ledge above the quarter pipe.

19 RUBBLE JUMP — 150 — B

Grind off the rock rubble to the left of the large monkey idol and air up to the platform above.

20 SPINAL COLUMNS — 150 — B

Spine Transfer through the holes in the center of the giant columns.

21 GO TO HELL — 175 — C

Spine Transfer down into the hell pit in the center of the area.

22 DOUBLE MONKEY — 200 — B

Transfer a grind across all three quarter pipe lips in front of the large monkey statue. Grind, jump, grind, and jump again into a final grind.

PROSKATER C

Intro

Skater Basics

Trick Lists

Story Mode

Gaps

Classic Mode

Multiskater

Secrets

THE TRIANGLE (22 GAPS)

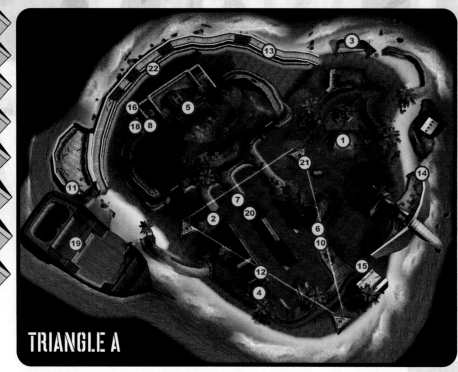

TRIANGLE A

1	KICK 2 BLADE	25	A

Leap from the large kicker into a grind on the blade of the helicopters with the missiles.

2	LEDGE 2 LOG!	25	A

Grind the rock ledge and ollie to a grind on the log under the half pipe platform.

3	LIFEBOAT GAP	25	A

Transfer a grind from any nearby ledge to a grind on the edge of the sunken lifeboat.

4	LOG 2 LEDGE	25	A

Grind the log under the half pipe platform and ollie into a grind on a nearby rock ledge.

5	WEE CHANNEL GAP	25	A

Air over the roll-in channel on the government fort in the side of the mountain.

6	BLADE 2 LEDGE	50	A

Grind the blade of the smaller helicopter and transfer the grind to a nearby rock ledge.

7	CROSSING YOUR ROCK FINGERS!	50	A

Transfer a grind between the coping of the half pipes and the rock ledges that are shaped like the letter "W".

8	HIGH TO LOW	50	A

Transfer from the upper quarter pipe to the lower on the side of the government building, near the walkway.

9	INTO THE CORE!	50	B

Grind the floor vent inside the secret area and pop off the kinked end into a grind on the power line above.

10	LEDGE 2 BLADE	50	A

Grind the rock ledge and ollie into a grind on the smaller helicopter's blade.

11	MAN OVERBOARD!	50	A

Spine Transfer out of the corner structure into the stern of the pirate ship.

12	MINI HIP!	50	A

Hip Transfer from the half pipe ramp up to the mini-ramp on the platform above. Can also be performed in the other direction.

13	WALL CROSSING	50	A

Grind one side of the wall and hop into a grind on the other ledge.

14	WING 2 ROCK HOP!	50	A

Grind the wing of the crashed plane and ollie into a grind on the rocks near the nose cone from the jet.

15	WINGIN' IT!	50	A

Grind the back edge of the W-shaped rocks nearest the beach and hop into a grind on the wing of the plane.

16	CANYON JUMP	75	A

Grind the edge of the quarter pipe at the base of the government center (the one on the side) and hop across to a grind on the ledge at the base of the wall.

17	AROUND THE CORE!	100	B

Enter the interior secret area and grind the length of the power line near the ceiling through one tube and out the other.

18	LOW TO HIGH	100	A

Transfer from the lower quarter pipe on the side of the government building up to the quarter pipe on the walkway.

19	PIRATE SHIP LIP	100	A

Air up into a lip trick on the beam of the pirate ship.

20	WIDE CHIN GAP	100	A

Vert transfer from the half pipe with the riser to the W-shaped rock ledges near the mountain.

21	POWER TAP!	150	A

Air off the triangular base of the antenna and land in a grind on the power line.

22	MOTHER SHIP LIP	250	A

Spine Transfer down off the government building and air up from the base of the lengthy wall and lip trick on the UFO.

TRIANGLE B

SCHOOL (47 GAPS)

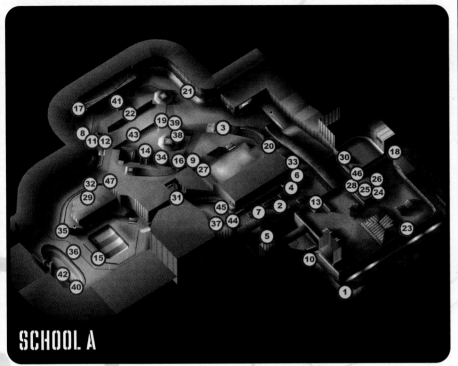

SCHOOL A

1	GARBAGE OLLIE	50	A

Grind the dumpsters in the corner behind the gym and ollie over the lone dumpster when exiting the grind.

2	GIMME GAP	50	A

Grind down the side of the awning at the starting point and transfer the grind to one of the planters.

3	KICKER GAP	100	A

Ollie the gap in the two kicker ramps at the base of the lengthy staircase.

4	PLANTER GAP	100	A

Transfer a grind between two of the planters on the ground below the starting point.

5	STRANGE TRANSFER	123	A

Vert transfer quarter pipe under the sky bridge and land in a grind on the nearest planter.

6	BRICK 2 METAL	150	A

Grind the ledge near all of the planters and ollie to a grind on the handicap ramp's rail.

7	PLANTER 2 BENCH	200	A

Transfer a grind from one of the planters to a picnic table.

8	SMALL TRANSFER	200	A

Vert transfer between the two curving quarter pipes to the left of the shed with the rail on top of it.

9	DITCH SLAP	250	A

Air off the kicker near the canal and land on the other side.

10	DUMPSTER RAIL GAP	250	A

Grind up the rail propped against the dumpsters and ollie off the end to clear the dumpsters. Then land in a grind on the other side of the dumpsters.

11	FUNBOX TO RAIL TRANSFER	250	A

Air off the large funbox near the playground wall and land in a grind on the edge of the curving quarter pipe.

12	FUNBOX TO TABLE TRANSFER	250	A

Air off the funbox near the playground wall and land in a grind on the picnic table.

13	MINI GAP	250	A

Head up to the roof of the gym and grind the edge of the wall. Transfer the grind over the break in the wall where the rail is and continue grinding.

14	AIR BRIDGE	300	A

Use the footbridge over the canal as a ramp and air off the inclined portion to the ground on the other side.

15	RAIL 2 RAIL	300	A

Transfer a grind across the two railings on the ground between the two pools.

16	MANUAL THE BRIDGE	350	A

Manual up and over either of the footbridges near the canal.

17	QP 2 METAL	400	A

Air off the quarter pipe near the playground wall and land in a grind on the rail atop the roof.

18	RIDE THE CORNER	400	A

Make a left at the gymnasium entrance and skate into the alley. Wallride along the outer wall of the corner in the alley up ahead.

19	TRIANGLE 2 TRIANGLE	400	A

Transfer a grind from one triangular rail near the playground wall to the other with an ollie.

20	HANDICAP RAIL	500	A

Grind the length of the railing near the handicap ramp in front of the gym.

21	PARK GAP	500	A

Air between the two quarter pipes against the wall near the kicker ramps and playground wall.

22	PLAYGROUND RAIL	500	A

Grind the length of the rail atop the playground wall.

23	ROOF BOMB	500	A

Skate up to the roof of the gymnasium and Spine Transfer from the roof down to the ramps directly behind the gym.

24	AIR CONDITIONER HIP	750	A

Hip Transfer the large square air conditioner unit on the roof of the gym.

25	M TO THE AIR	750	A

Manual across the top of the large air conditioning unit on the roof of the gym.

26	OVER THE AIR CONDITIONER	750	A

Use the ramp beside the air conditioner to launch up and over the large air conditioner on the roof of the gym.

27	RAIL TO RAIL TRANSFER	750	A

Grind the ledge towards the canal, ollie across the canal, and continue grinding on the other ledge.

28	ROOF 2 AWNING	750	A

Boneless off the top of the air conditioning unit on the gym roof to the large awning heading down the stairs.

29	FLAT ROOF DROP	800	A

Acid Drop off the lower roof near the shallow swimming pool. Make sure to run and jump out to reach the ramp.

30	LIP THE KICKER EDGE	800	A

Leap up from the quarter pipe near the gymnasium entrance and lip trick on the kicker ramp perched atop the roof above.

31	HALL PASS	1,000	A

Skate down the hill under the starting point and grind the rail from the grass up to the ledge. Air off the end of the grind, through the opening, and land in a grind on the ledge on the other side.

32	HUGE RAIL	1,000	A

Grind the lip of the yellow and black quarter pipe from near the canal to where it ends by the high dive.

Intro
Skater Basics
Trick Lists
Story Mode
Gaps
Classic Mode
Multiskater
Secrets

33   MANUAL THE HANDICAP SLOPE   1,000   A

Manual down the handicap ramp under the awning near the stairs.

34   OVER A FOOTBRIDGE   1,000   A

Drop into the canal and hit the ramp divider and air up and over the footbridge without touching it.

35   QP 2 POOL EDGE   1,000   A

Grind the lengthy yellow and black quarter pipe under the low roof building and ollie off the end of it into a grind on the diving pool.

36   SWIM TEAM GAP   1,000   A

Boneless from one swimming pool to the other.

37   HUGE LEDGE 2 HIGH RAIL   1,100   A

Start grinding down the hill under the starting point and ollie into a grind on the rail that leads from the grass up to the roof across the path.

38   T 2 DITCH   1,250   A

Pop off the curving triangular rail and fly over the pyramid funbox and into the canal.

39   T LAUNCH 2 T   1,250   A

Pop off the curved triangular rail and land in a grind on the other triangular rail.

40   WALLRIDE OVER BUTTERFINGER!   1,250   A

Wallride up and over the Butterfinger vending machine in the corner near the high dive.

41   BIG KICK 2 METAL!   1,420   A

Air off the large funbox near the playground wall and land in a grind on either of the rails atop the metal roof.

42   LIP DIVER   1,500   A

Air up out of the dive pool and lip trick on one of the lower diving boards.

43   2 BRICK!   1,750   A

Pop off the long, straight triangular rail and land in a grind atop the playground wall.

44   MANUAL THE BIG SLOPE   2,000   A

Tap into a manual on the ground under the starting point and balance it all the way down the slope towards the swimming pools.

45   LONG ASS RAIL   2,500   A

Grind the entire ledge leading from the top of the slope down to the kicker ramp near the lap swimming pool.

46   SICK HIP TRANSFER   5,000   A

Hip Transfer from the edge of gymnasium roof, to the right of the air conditioning unit, down onto the quarter pipe at the base of the wall near the gym entrance.

47   DROP THE GIANT BOMB!   6,000   A

Grind the rail across to the roof near the slope and climb up onto the uppermost rooftop. Run towards the corner over the yellow and black quarter pipe and Acid Drop down onto it.

PHILADELPHIA (54 GAPS)

PHILADELPHIA A

1   EASY POST HOP   10   A

Ollie over one of the posts near the building with the observation deck.

2   POST HOP   50   A

Ollie over one of the posts connected with chains.

3   STATUE HOP   50   A

Gap from one of the concrete curved curbs to the other.

4   TRACK SMACK   50   A

Grind the lengthy yellow rail on the ground near the skatepark and ollie onto the other.

5   BOOB TO BOX   69   A

Head to the back left corner of the concrete skatepark and transfer from the large hump to the funbox.

6   BENCH GAP   100   A

Grind the ledge near the benches and ollie over a bench to continue the grind.

7   CAR HOP   100   A

Ollie over any of the cars on the road.

8   FUNBOX WHEELIE   100   A

Manual up and over the large funbox near the starting point.

9   HOBO GRIND   100   A

Hop into a grind on the yellow rail on the left of the skatepark and grind the entire length of it.

10   PHILLYSIDE BIG BOWL LIP   100   A

Lip trick on the tall bowl near the lengthy spine that sticks out into the park.

11   PHILLYSIDE HOP   100   A

Air off the kicker in front of the skate park near the street and leap over the wall to enter it.

12   PHILLYSIDE HP LIP   100   A

Lip trick on the coping on the half pipe.

13   PHILLYSIDE MID BOWL LIP   100   A

Lip trick on the top of the middle bowl on the right-hand side of the park.

14 PHILLYSIDE NEW BOWL LIP   100   A

Lip trick on the back of the concrete skatepark.

15 PILLAR HOP   100   A

Grind the edge of the bowl in the back corner of the skatepark and ollie over the block near the pillar to continue the grind.

16 PLANTER TRANSFER   100   A

Grind the outer edge of the planter towards the stairs and ollie across the sidewalk to a grind on the other ledge.

17 RAILING TO PLANTER   100   A

Grind the railing of the balcony and ollie down to a grind on the planter.

18 STAIR SET   100   A

Ollie down the set of stairs across from the building with the balcony.

19 THPS SIGN GAP   100   A

Air off the kicker and clear the THPS sign near the fountain.

20 UP THE SMALL STEP SET   100   A

Ollie up the set of steps across from the building with observation deck on the corner.

21 WORLDS MOST OBVIOUS GAP   100   A

Transfer the two kicker ramps to the right of the starting point.

22 JUST VISITING   150   A

Grind the ledge of the planter across from the benches and ollie off the end into a grind on the planter to the right near the small steps.

23 PLANTER DOUBLE PILLAR GAP   150   A

Grind the planter alongside the street and ollie over the two posts and continue the grind on the other planter.

24 SHORT STAIR   150   A

Grind the length of the upper fountain step. This is the one closest to the THPS sign.

25 FUNBOX TRANSFER   250   A

Grind the rail box on the side of the funbox at the skatepark and ollie into a grind on the yellow rail.

26 LONG STAIR   250   A

Grind the length of the longest fountain step. This is the lower one near the THPS sign.

27 MEDIUM STAIR   250   A

Grind the length of the middle fountain step.

28 PHILLY HP TRANSFER   250   A

Spine Transfer between the half pipe and the bowl in the concrete skatepark.

29 TELEPHONE CO. GAP   250   A

Ollie over the railing on the balcony and land in a grind on the telephone wire. This is at the building on the corner.

30 AWNING GRIND   500   A

Pop off the semi-circular statue into a grind on the blue awning.

31 CHILLIN ON THE BALCONY   500   A

Air off the angled curb and fly onto the balcony of the building near the staircase.

32 CONCRETE TRANSFER   500   A

Vert transfer between the two bowls on either side of the spine ramp in the skatepark.

33 DEATH FROM ABOVE   500   A

Grind the lengthy electric wire from the building with the balcony out over the fountain. Drop off the wire and land in a grind on the center of the fountain.

34 FLATLAND TECHIN'   500   A

Tap into a manual near the small set of steps and balance it all the way to the large set of stairs in the opposite corner of the plaza.

35 FLY BY WIRE   500   A

Grind the entire length of the wire that is strung up above the fountain.

36 GRIND UP DEM STAIRS   500   A

Grind up the shortest handrail on the large set of stairs in the corner of the plaza. Then ollie up to the top of the stairs.

37 LITTLE CORNER GRIND   500   A

There is a rail on the walls in the corner of the city opposite the skatepark. Grind the length of this rail.

38 MANUAL STIMULATION   500   A

Manual over the rollers in the skatepark.

39 PILLAR FIGHT   500   A

Air off the edge of the pillar in the back left corner of the skatepark.

40 THPS FOUNTAIN GAP   500   A

Ollie down the fountain steps and land in a grind on the edge of the fountain.

41 TRAIN HARD   500   A

Grind the back edge of the skatepark nearest the train tracks and fence.

42 FOUNTAIN PING   750   A

Air off the kicker ramp near the edge of the fountain and land in a grind on the central ring of the fountain.

43 WORLDS SECOND MOST OBVIOUS GAP   750   A

Boneless off the kicker ramp near the starting point and fly over the landing ramp to the handrail on the stairs. Land in a grind for the gap.

44 COOL QP TRANSFER   800   A

Transfer between the two quarter pipes against the back fence of the skatepark.

45 GRIND OF FAITH   1,000   A

Grind the pipes leading out towards the center of the fountain, ollie through the water spray, and land in a grind on the other pipes.

46 MANUAL MID STAIR LEDGE   1,000   A

Manual the length of the middle fountain step.

47 AIR THE FUNBOX   1,100   A

Hit the funbox near the starting point and air off the ramp portion and clear the rest of it.

48 FLATLAND TECHIN' TO THE STREET!   1,100   A

Manual the entire length of the plaza from the small stair all the way past the planters and benches to the other end.

49 LEDGE 2 HANDRAIL   1,100   A

Grind the planter across from the benches and air into a grind on the railing on the observation deck.

50 BEHIND THE PILLAR   2,000   A

Vert Transfer behind the pillar that is positioned in front of the two bowls on the right-hand side of the skatepark.

51 STICKER SLAP THE THPS SIGN   2,000   A

Pop off the kicker in front of the THPS sign and Sticker Slap the sign.

52 MANUAL BIG STAIR LEDGE   2,500   A

Manual the length of the lower fountain step. This is the longest one of the three.

53 ROCKIN' THE STAIRS   2,500   A

Tap into a manual beside the fountain and make a series of ollies and manuals in a clockwise direction to combo your way up the steps around the perimeter of the fountain.

54 MANUAL SMALL STAIR LEDGE   5,000   A

Carefully manual the small fountain step. It's the upper step and you must manual between the edge of the step and the chain and posts.

INFORM YOURSELF

DOWNHILL JAM (18 GAPS)

Intro

Skater Basics

Trick Lists

Story Mode

Gaps

Classic Mode

Multiskater

Secrets

DOWNHILL JAM A

1	25FT	25	A

Air out of the underground launch ramp at the base of the slope and soar through the air for 25 ft.

2	MANUAL THROUGH THE HP!	100	A

Manual the length of the concrete half pipe.

3	OVER THE GIANT GRATE!	100	A

Use the humps near the lower portion of the course to soar up and over the large grate in the floor.

4	50FT	150	A

Air out of the underground launch ramp at the base of the slope and soar through the air for 50 ft.

5	LIP BAR	250	A

Air into a lip trick on the bar that extends across the break in the wall.

6	RAIL 2 RAIL	250	A

Transfer a grind between the two triangular rails near the start of the course.

7	75FT	450	A

Air out of the underground launch ramp at the base of the slope and soar through the air for 75 ft.

8	NEVERSOFT ELEC. CO. GAP	500	A

Air off the quarter pipe at the base of the rocks into a grind on the upper observation deck near the bottom of the course.

9	PIPE 2 TRIANGLE	500	A

Grind the raised pipe on the right-hand side just down the slope from the starting point. Ollie off the end and land in a grind on the triangular rail.

10	HIGH UP TRANSFER	800	A

Transfer the large gap in the path that loops around past the "Globe" sign.

11	HIT LEDGE LEFT	800	A

Grind the right-hand rail past the large arch in the rocks and ollie off the end to a grind on the ledge on the left.

12	HIT LEDGE RIGHT	800	A

Grind the left-hand rail past the large arch in the rocks and ollie off the end to a grind on the ledge on the right.

13	100FT	1,000	A

Air out of the underground launch ramp at the base of the slope and soar through the air for 100 ft.

14	HUGE WATER HAZARD GAP	1,000	A

Ollie from the ground near the two lengthy pipes and, instead of grinding across the water hazard, air all the way to rocks on the other side of the cavern.

15	SMACK THE POLE	1,112	A

Air off the third kicker ramp that you come to and grind the short rail sticking out of the side of the rock formation.

16	QP 2 PIPE	4,000	A

Air off the quarter pipe to the right of the water hazard and land in a grind on the pipes extending over hazard.

17	BOX 2 BOX	6,969	A

Gap from one funbox to the other on the ledge above the finish line.

18	KICKER 2 PIPE 2 PIPE 2 PIPE!!	10,000	A

Start on the first rock formation and pop off the kicker to a grind on the rail sticking out of the rocks. Carry the grind off this rail and onto the pipes up ahead. Lastly, ollie off this grind onto the pipe that runs across from left to right.

LOS ANGELES (74 GAPS)

LOSANGELES A

| 1 | DOORWAY HOP | 50 | A |

Grind the brick ledge behind the tower building and transfer the grind across the gaps where the doors are.

| 2 | BURRITO CARNITAS | 100 | A |

Grind the blue ledge of the car wash.

| 3 | BURRITO GRANDE | 100 | A |

Vert transfer up and over the entrance to the car wash.

| 4 | BUSTIN CHERRIES! | 100 | A |

Grind the upper edge of the pink theatre building and ollie into a grind on the rail sticking out from the purple tower.

| 5 | CAR HOP | 100 | A |

Ollie over any car on the street.

| 6 | COLD CHILLIN' | 100 | A |

Vert transfer between the two large quarter pipes facing the car wash.

| 7 | DOWN THE STAIRS | 100 | A |

Ollie down one of the sections of stairs in front of the library.

| 8 | EAST SIDE! | 100 | A |

Ollie clear across the street from the tower building back towards the library.

| 9 | EASTERN TREMOR! | 100 | A |

Grind the long rail down the slope behind the library.

| 10 | GOIN' BALLISTIC | 100 | B |

Air off the rooftop half pipe into the air.

| 11 | GRIND ILLIN' | 100 | B |

Transfer a grind across the edge of the two large quarter pipes facing the car wash.

| 12 | HOTEL LIP SMACKIN' | 100 | B |

Leap into a lip trick on the ledge of the Morehead Hotel.

| 13 | HUNG OVER | 100 | B |

Use the ramps on either side of the door to transfer up and over the Morehead Hotel sign.

| 14 | INDIANA STYLE! | 100 | A |

Manual through the yellow shack from the side by the street towards the purple shack.

| 15 | KIOSK! | 100 | A |

Spine Transfer the kiosk near the car wash.

| 16 | LIP WASH | 100 | A |

Air up the front of the car wash and lip trick on top of the white sign.

| 17 | NORTHERN WASHER LIP | 100 | A |

Air off the quarter pipe near the circular fountain and lip trick on the window washer scaffold to the right.

| 18 | NORTHERN TREMOR! | 100 | A |

Grind the rail on the side of the library stairs facing the starting point.

| 19 | NOSE BLEED TIME | 100 | B |

Air out of the rooftop half pipe on the tower and get very high in the air.

| 20 | OVER THE YELLOW STONE SHACK | 100 | B |

Grind the edge of the yellow shack towards the bank and air off the angled portion of the wall. Clear the rest of the yellow shack to get the gap.

| 21 | PERSHING RAMP | 100 | B |

Grind the ledge alongside the yellow shack and gap across the ramp down to the street and land in a grind on the steps on the corner.

| 22 | PURE AIR! | 100 | B |

Hit the "They're Grate" gap to open the grates on the library. Drop into the library and gap across from one ledge to the other.

| 23 | PURPLE SKIPPIN' | 100 | B |

Air over the purple half pipe lengthwise.

| 24 | PURPLE TRANSFER | 100 | B |

Vert transfer between the narrow purple quarter pipe and the half pipe.

| 25 | RAIL SKIP! | 100 | A |

Grind the white ledge down the slope from the starting point and ollie across the street into a grind on the left-hand rail inside the library tunnel.

| 26 | SOUTHERN WASHER LIP | 100 | B |

Air off the quarter pipe near the fountain and lip trick on the window washer scaffolding on the left side.

| 27 | SOUTHERN TREMOR! | 100 | A |

Grind the rail on the side of the library steps near the many newspaper vending machines.

| 28 | SQUEAKY CLEAN! | 100 | A |

Transfer a grind between the two rails inside the car wash.

| 29 | THEY'RE GRATE! | 100 | B |

Grind the lengthy, curving brick ledge behind the tower building. This will open the grates on the floor nearby and on the library roof.

| 30 | TOWER LOCKIN' | 100 | B |

Transfer from the rooftop half pipe on the tower to the quarter pipe on the ground behind it.

| 31 | TOWER POPPIN' | 100 | B |

Transfer from the rooftop half pipe on the tower to the quarter pipe on the ground near the fountain.

| 32 | TOWER RAIL SWAP! | 100 | B |

Grind the rail near the staircase behind the tower and ollie into a grind on the handrail on the walkway above.

| 33 | TOWER SOUTH | 100 | B |

Grind the railing on the walkway on the side of the tower building and gap across where the break in the railing is for the stairs.

| 34 | TRIPLE X HOP! | 100 | B |

Grind the ledge in front of the theatre and ollie across to a grind on the edge of the bank.

| 35 | WEST SIDE! | 100 | B |

Ollie across the street without touching it from the library to the tower building.

| 36 | WESTERN TREMOR! | 100 | A |

Grind the rail inside the library.

| 37 | WIRE RIDIN 1! | 100 | A |

Air into a grind on the wire where it connects to the Morehead Hotel. Start grinding towards the tower building.

Intro

Skater Basics

Trick Lists

Story Mode

Gaps

Classic Mode

Multiskater

Secrets

38   YELLOW CUTTER!   100   A

Ollie through the hole in the yellow stone shack.

39   YELLOW FALL!   100   B

Drop through the hole in the roof of the yellow stone shack.

40   BUNKER   200   A

Ollie down the slope at the starting point without touching the grass.

41   DON'T FALL!!!   200   B

Grind the edge of bank's roof and ollie over to the roof of the theatre.

42   HOT, HOT, HOT!   200   B

Grind the quarter pipe towards the fire truck and ollie into a grind on the side of the truck.

43   OVER THE FOUNTAIN!   200   A

Ollie over the circular fountain.

44   OVERPASS LEAP   200   A

Trigger the earthquake and air from the plywood ramp on the overpass to the bank's roof.

45   PASSIN' GAS   200   A

Transfer a grind from the edge of the car wash roof to the large sign near the sidewalk.

46   RIDIN' THE XXX!   200   B

Grind the edge of the marquee on the theatre.

47   SHOOTS N' LADDERS!   200   B

Grind the ladder on the fire truck.

48   TO THE LADDER   200   B

Air off the kicker on the sidewalk and land in a grind on the fire truck ladder.

49   TOWER RAILS GAP   200   B

Grind the railing on the walkway behind the tower building and gap across where the large set of stairs is. Continue grinding on the other side.

50   VENTING FRUSTRATION   200   B

Vert transfer out of the quarter pipe behind the tower building and transfer up to the grate by the brick building.

51   WASHIN' WINDOWS   200   A

Air out of the quarter pipe to the right of the fountain and grind the window washing scaffold above.

52   WIRE RIDIN' 2!!   200   A

Continue grinding the wire from the Morehead Hotel towards the tower building past the first Wire Ridin' gap.

53   ALL THE WAY   300   A

Ollie down both sets of stairs in front of the library.

54   ELECTRIFIED!   300   A

Pop off the curved ledge beside the fountain and land in a grind on the electrical wire overhead.

55   NICE MOVE!   300   B

Grind up fire truck ladder and transfer to a grind on the ledge in front of the Morehead Hotel. Then side-jump off the end to grind the roof near the billboard.

56   WIRE DROP   300   A

Grind the wire from the Morehead Hotel to the tower building and drop off the end into a grind on the edge of the fountain.

57   WIRE RIDIN' 3!!!   300   A

Grind the entire length of the wire from the Morehead Hotel to the tower building.

58   FOUNTAIN HOP   400   A

Transfer a grind from the semi-circular ledge beside the fountain to a grind on the fountain.

59   ROLL HUMP JUMP   420   B

Skate behind the library and ollie down the slope near the office building.

60   FROM PURPLE TO STREET!   500   A

Air out of the purple half pipe and land in a grind on the street curb.

61   MANUAL CUT LEDGE   500   A

Manual the length of the brick ledge alongside the yellow stone shack.

62   MANUAL DOWN THE BUNKER!   500   A

Manual from the starting point down the grass slope to the street.

63   NACHOS 'N QUESO Y'ALL   500   A

Spine Transfer from the roof of the carwash, over the white sign, and down onto the quarter pipe near the entrance.

64   PRODUCTION DROP   500   A

Walk through the entrance of the liquor store near the car wash to be teleported to the roof of the theatre.

65   RIDICULOUS SPINE   800   B

Spine Transfer from the large vert ramp behind the car wash to the one on the side of the tower building.

66   MANUAL UP THE BUNKER!   1,000   A

Get speed off the side of the library and manual up the grassy slope to the starting point.

67   ORANGE WALLIE 2 STREET   1,500   A

Enter the orange half pipe and Wallie off the side wall of it into the street near the library.

68   MANUAL DECK OVER PILLARS   2,150   A

Manual from the yellow stone shack to the purple half pipe and ollie over the pillars and into the street near the corner.

69   POST TO STAIR!   2,500   A

Natas Spin on one of the pillars on the corner near the purple shack and ollie off into a manual. Manual across the street and grind the stairs.

70   MOREHEAD LEDGE   3,000   B

Manual the entire length of the ledge on the front of the Morehead Hotel.

71   POST TO WIRE!   5,000   B

Grind (Kiss the Rail) on a one of the pillars on the corner near the purple shack and ollie off into a grind on the wire above the street.

72   HUGE LAUNCH!!!   10,000   B

Transfer from the quarter pipe near the fountain to the one on the ground on the other side of the rooftop half pipe.

73   OH YEAHH! YOU ARE GOOD!   10,000   B

Grind the purple wall near the street (behind the palm trees) and ollie off and Sticker Slap the XXX marquee.

74   FIRETRUCK STOMP!!   10,069   B

Hit the zip ramp near the purple shack and air across the street and down the road to the fire truck. Land in a grind on the fire truck to complete the gap.

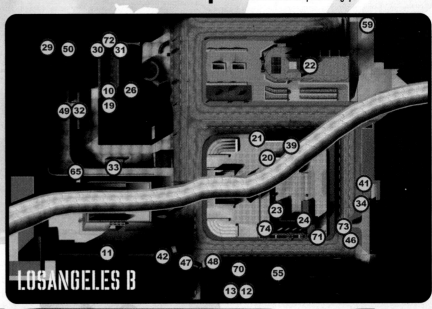

LOSANGELES B

CANADA (63 GAPS)

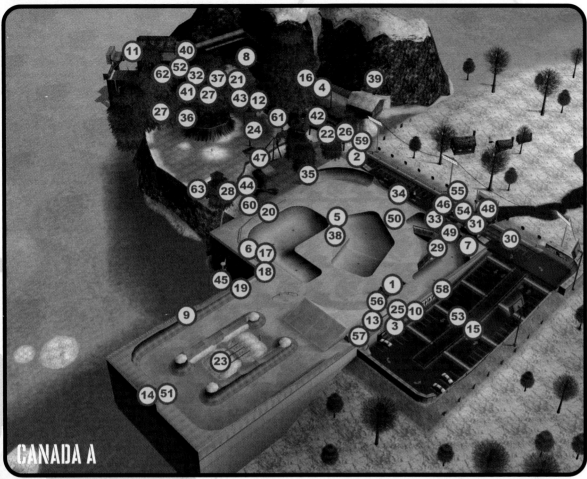

CANADA A

---

1 FUNBOX HOP   10   A

Gap over the funbox composed of two kicker ramps.

2 OVER THE BLADE   25   A

Transfer up and over the starting point using the ramps on either side.

3 ...JUST WENT BANKRUPT   50   A

Grind the Hurley International billboard on the way back up the hill in the parking lot and drop into a grind on the handrail on the ground.

4 ALL THAT GLITTERS   50   A

Grind the rope on the left side of the walkway leading away from the cabin and ollie into a grind on the right-hand rope.

5 BOWL TO BOWL   50   A

Grind the edge of the bowl nearest the totem pole and side-jump to a grind on the middle bowl.

6 BOWL TO RAIL   50   A

Grind the edge of the bowl closest to the totem pole and transfer the grind to the metal rail in the corner.

---

7 CUT THE CORNER   50   A

Grind the fence to the right of the starting point and ollie into a grind on the triangular platform in the corner above the pool.

8 DEAD MAN'S SLIDE   50   A

Transfer a grind across the two logs that are positioned against the side of the mountain, near the walkways.

9 FENCE TRANSFER   50   A

Grind the lengthy quarter pipe in the skatepark and transfer the grind to the chain link fence.

10 IPO FUNDING   50   A

Grind the handrail towards the banners and ollie into a grind on top of one of them.

11 LOAD AND GO   50   A

Air out of the hydraulic ramp into the covered half pipe up above.

12 LOOK, MA! NO TALENT   50   A

Grind the rope around the edge of the walkway that encircles the large tree and gap across the break in the rope.

---

13 MANUAL TRANSMISSION   50   A

Manual the length of the ledge in the skatepark directly above the banners by the parking lot.

14 OVER THE HUMP   50   A

Grind the chain link fence up and over the hump where it rises behind the roll-ins.

15 PARKING LOG MINI GAP   50   A

Grind the handrail in the center of the parking lot and gap across the small break in the center to continue the grind.

16 PROSPECTOR PATH   50   A

Grind the rope on the walkway leading away from the cabin and ollie into a grind on the log to the right.

17 RAIL BANK SHOT   50   A

Grind the metal rail in the corner near the totem pole and transfer the grind to the red rail.

18 RAIL CHEATER   50   A

Grind the red rail near the totem pole and transfer the grind to the lengthy metal one nearby.

Intro

Skater Basics

Trick Lists

Story Mode

Gaps

Classic Mode

Multiskater

Secrets

| 19 | RAIL STOMP | 50 | A |

Grind the coping on the lengthy quarter pipe and ollie out of the grind and into one on the red rail near the totem pole.

| 20 | RAIL TO BOWL | 50 | A |

Grind the metal rail in the corner near the totem pole and ollie to a grind on the edge of the pool.

| 21 | STILL BOOTLEGGIN' | 50 | A |

Keep to the left where the elevated walkway forks and ollie across the gap to the walkway on the other side of the ditch.

| 22 | TREE AIR GAP | 50 | A |

Ollie from the wooden platform behind the starting point to the walkway that goes through the tree.

| 23 | WE DON'T NEED NO STEEENKING RAILS | 50 | A |

Gap from one snowdrift to the other in the center of the skatepark.

| 24 | AROUND THE HORN | 100 | A |

Grind the rope that loops around the large tree.

| 25 | BANNER AD DOT COM | 100 | A |

Transfer a grind from one banner to the other.

| 26 | CLIMB THE TREE | 100 | A |

Air off the ramp at the starting point and land on the small wooden platform in the tree behind it.

| 27 | CORRAL GAP TRANSFER | 100 | A |

Use the snowdrifts as quarter pipes and vert transfer over the cleared sections of the corral around the large tree.

| 28 | CORRAL TO TREE GRIND | 100 | A |

Grind the edge of the corral towards the skatepark and ollie across the stream into a grind on the fallen tree.

| 29 | CROOKED EXTENSION | 100 | A |

Skate up out of the L-shaped pool near the parking lot and lip trick on the back of the funbox.

| 30 | CURB HOPPIN | 100 | A |

Gap between grinds on the curb in the upper parking lot and the triangular parking block.

| 31 | DOZER BLADE GAP | 100 | A |

Grind the curb towards the large bulldozer and ollie across the break in the curb and land in a grind on the other side.

| 32 | ENIM DETNUAH EHT | 100 | A |

Grind the curving rail away from the walkway with the generator and gap into a grind on the corral.

| 33 | FENCE EXTENSION | 100 | A |

Ride up out of the pool nearest to the parking lot and lip trick on the chain link fence.

| 34 | FENCE HOPPIN | 100 | A |

Transfer grinds across the chain link fence to the right of the starting point and the funbox or rail on the upper parking lot.

| 35 | FLYING FENCEMAN | 100 | A |

Grind the edge of the large quarter pipe in the corner of the skatepark nearest the starting point. Transfer the grind to the fence leading towards the totem pole.

| 36 | GRIND THE PINE | 100 | A |

Grind the giant tree trunk in the center of the corral and ollie into a grind on the outstretched limb of the tree.

| 37 | HITCH KNOT GAP | 100 | A |

Grind the rope on the walkway above the corral to where the walkway forks. Stay to the left and transfer the grind across the break to the other side.

| 38 | LIGHT IT UP! | 100 | A |

Spine Transfer between the pool in the center of the skatepark and the one near the totem pole.

| 39 | MINE CART LAUNCH | 100 | A |

Grind the rail on the mine car tracks nearest the mountain and ollie off the end into a grind on the power line near the cabin.

| 40 | PICKAXE SLUICE | 100 | A |

Ollie out of the covered half pipe to the ramp leading up to the mine car tracks.

| 41 | THE HAUNTED MINE | 100 | A |

Grind the edge of the corral in a clockwise direction and ollie into a grind on the rail that curves around towards the generator.

| 42 | THE OLD WING DAM | 100 | A |

Grind across the logs on the dilapidated bridge behind the cabin.

| 43 | THE PANHANDLER | 100 | A |

Air out of the corral and pause in a lip trick on the rope for the walkway above.

| 44 | TREE TO CORRAL GRIND | 100 | A |

Grind the fallen tree and ollie over the streambed and into a grind on the corral.

| 45 | AHHH! MY HEAD! | 200 | A |

Ollie off the fence and grind the totem pole.

| 46 | CAR GAP | 200 | A |

Use the kickers in the parking lot to air over the parked cars.

| 47 | THERE'S GOLD IN THEM THAR HILLS | 200 | A |

Hit the kicker ramps to transfer over the streambed.

| 48 | AIR OVER THE BLADE GRIND | 250 | A |

Grind the wooden fence towards the bulldozer blade and ollie up and over it to continue the grind on the fence.

| 49 | ANTENNA STOMP | 250 | A |

Grind the antennae sticking out from the back of the funbox near the corner pool. Try to Spine Transfer up out of the fun box.

| 50 | AURORA BURLY-ALIS | 250 | A |

Spine Transfer between the pool in the center of the skatepark and the large one near the corner of the parking lot.

| 51 | BREEZY CHANNEL GAP | 250 | A |

Vert transfer over the roll-ins in the back of the skatepark.

| 52 | CHAINSAW BUZZIN' | 250 | A |

Grind the second of the logs alongside the mountain and ollie into a grind on the rail near the generator.

| 53 | CROSSOVER THE EASY WAY | 250 | A |

Grind the handrail in the center of the parking lot while skating downhill and ollie across to the rail on the other side.

| 54 | CURB BOMB | 250 | A |

Pop off the kicker ramp near the parked cars and land in a grind on the curb.

| 55 | FENCE BOMB | 250 | A |

Pop off the kicker ramp near the parked cars and land in a grind on the wooden fence.

| 56 | FUNBOX TO RAIL STOMP | 250 | A |

Ollie off the funbox with the two facing kicker ramps and land in a grind on the large corner quarter pipe.

| 57 | GO LONG AND GRIND | 250 | A |

Grind the fence to the right of the starting point until it turns then jump into a grind on the ledge above the banners.

| 58 | PARK TO LOT LAUNCH | 250 | A |

Grind the fence above the banners and ollie down to a grind on the railing in the lower area of the parking lot.

| 59 | SAP SLAPPER | 250 | A |

Air off the ramp at the starting point and into a grind on the wooden walkway in the trees behind it.

| 60 | BUCK WILD | 500 | A |

Spine Transfer out of the creek bed near the waterfall into the pool in the corner of the skatepark.

| 61 | WHOA. THAT WAS COOL. | 500 | A |

Boneless out of the corral and land in a grind on the log bridge over the icy water.

| 62 | SAVED BY THE GENERATOR | 1,000 | A |

Grind the second log on the side of the mountain and ollie directly into a grind atop the generator (not the railing, but the actual generator).

| 63 | THE LOG QP! | 5,000 | A |

Grind the entire length of the corral from one end to the other.

AIRPORT (35 GAPS)

AIRPORT A

| 1 | CLAIM HOP! | 50 | A |

Transfer a grind between the escalator coming down from the heliport and the rail in front of it.

| 2 | HELIPORT BAGGAGE | 50 | A |

Grind one side of the baggage conveyor belt and hop into a grind on the other side.

| 3 | RAIL HOP | 50 | A |

Transfer a grind from the grey ledge to a red rail.

| 4 | WALKWAY HOP | 50 | A |

Grind one side of the moving walkway and ollie to a grind on the other side.

| 5 | DRAINING THE VEIN | 100 | A |

Grind across the rails and the urinals in the restroom.

| 6 | DROPPIN' SCIENCE! | 100 | A |

Combo a series of grinds across the overhead lights that start above the first escalator and angle to the right, then continue all the way to the security checkpoint.

| 7 | ESCALATIN' THE SITUATION | 100 | A |

Vert transfer over the escalators coming down from the heliport.

| 8 | GATE HOP! | 100 | A |

Grind the red rails near the gates and ollie across the gap to the next red rail.

| 9 | ILLUMINATIN' | 100 | A |

Ollie off the first bank of pay phones and grind the lights overhead.

| 10 | LAST HIGH LIGHT! | 100 | A |

Air off the rail between the last set of escalators and land in a grind on the final set of overhead lights.

| 11 | LIGHT HOP! | 100 | A |

Gap between grinds on two different lights in the basement area.

| 12 | LIGHT POP! | 100 | A |

Transfer a grind from the ledge around the basement wall to one of the lights.

| 13 | LIGHTEN UP! | 100 | |

Air off the second bank of payphones and land in a grind on the overhead lights.

| 14 | LOCAL CALL | 100 | |

Grind up and over the first bank of payphones.

| 15 | MULIN' | 100 | A |

Air over the security checkpoint in the area by the baggage carousel.

| 16 | MUSICAL CHAIRS | 100 | A |

Grind one set of couches near the gates and ollie into a manual. Cross the floor and ollie into a grind on another set of chairs all in the same combo.

| 17 | O THE S | 100 | A |

Air over the security scanners before heading down the final set of escalators to the gates.

| 18 | OFF THE COUCH | 100 | A |

Manual from one end of the terminal to the other. Get speed off the quarter pipe at the end, above the spiral ramp and manual past all of the couches.

| 19 | S LOOK OUT!! | 100 | A |

Grind the entire rail leading into the ladies restroom, then transfer to the ledge above the sinks.

| 20 | SPIRAL STAIRS NORTH | 100 | A |

Grind the railing on the northern spiral ramp.

| 21 | SPIRAL STAIRS SOUTH | 100 | A |

Grind the railing on the southern spiral ramp.

| 22 | SPOTTED BAGS | 100 | A |

Lip trick on the ledge between the escalators near the baggage carousel.

| 23 | TAKIN' THE HIGH ROAD | 100 | A |

Air off the kinked end of the first set of escalators and land in a grind on the overhead light.

| 24 | THROUGH THE PAD! | 100 | A |

Grind the conveyor belt through the helipad and transfer the grind to the escalator handrail.

| 25 | WALKWAY RIDE1! | 100 | A |

Grind the length of the first moving walkway.

| 26 | WALKWAY RIDE2! | 100 | A |

Grind the length of the second moving walkway.

| 27 | X-RAY | 100 | A |

Ollie over the right-hand counter near the starting point and manual the conveyor belt into the x-ray machine.

| 28 | FLYING HIGH IN THE SKY | 200 | A |

Air off the narrow computer terminals and lip trick on the large sign overhead.

| 29 | THE HARD WAY UP! | 200 | A |

Wallie into a series of grinds across the lockers and eventually up onto the lights.

| 30 | ECONOMY CLASS LIP | 250 | A |

Air out of the basement into a lip trick on the lowest red rail.

| 31 | GATE TRANSFER! | 300 | A |

Ollie from the edge of the couch, over one of the gate entrances, to a grind on the rail on the other side.

| 32 | BUSINESS CLASS LIP! | 500 | A |

Air out of the basement and lip trick on the upper red rail.

| 33 | START TO FINISH!!! | 600 | A |

Start a combo by sticker slapping the entrance of the airport. Grind through the men's bathroom and keep the combo intact all the way to the bottom of the final escalator.

| 34 | HELICOPTER HOP! | 2,000 | A |

Grind through the x-ray machine and pop off the kicker and clear the helicopter in a single leap.

| 35 | MANUAL THE SLOPE! | 5,000 | A |

Tap into a manual and balance on two wheels down the upper slope near the first set of escalators.

BARCELONA

0 Goals required to unlock this location.

5 Stat Points available.

Hit Bull
With a Tomato

Grind Rope to
Free Boat & Close Bridge

COURSE GOALS

High Score - 30,000 Points
Pro Score - 60,000 Points
Sick Score - 100,000 Points
High Combo - 10,000 Points
Collect S-K-A-T-E
Collect C-O-M-B-O
Collect 5 Tapas
Get the Secret Tape
Manual the Subway
Grind the World's Longest Bench

SCORING GOALS

There are plenty of places to score big at Barcelona, with the Parc Guell area being a prime location. Link together multiple aerial tricks while Spine Transferring over the Guell Planters for huge combos

Conversely, those who prefer lengthy grind combos are sure to have a field day grinding across the bridge to the waterfront area. Grind the netting in the water to free the boat and get the bridge closed and then grind the various red rails from one side to the other for plenty of points.

Sick Mode: The High Score (100,000), Pro Score (200,000), Sick Score (300,000) and High Combo (75,000) requirements are each tougher than on Normal mode, but the Parc Guell area and the lengthy grind across the bridge are still the best spots to hit. Link together multiple Guell Planter Spine Transfer gaps while airing it out back and forth amongst the trees for additional points and to up the multiplier. Similarly, link a couple Bridge Rail Transfer gaps together while grinding across the bridge and cap off the run by taking a dip in the pool by the waterfront.

COLLECT S-K-A-T-E

S Ollie onto one of the bus stops in front of the Estacion Sants.

K Continue in a clockwise direction from the "S" towards the Parc Guell. The "K" is above the quarter pipes on the left, near the building with the scaffolding.

A Boneless into a grind on the white and brown striped wall. Grind to the edge of the wall and ollie across the entrance to the Parc Guell to pluck the "A" out of the air and to continue the grind towards the bull.

T Continue past the bull to the museum. Grind the leftmost ledge on the walkway and ollie off of it into the street to snag the "T".

E Get some speed and cross the street towards the angled sign near the start of the bridge. Grind the angled sign and ollie into a grind on the upper red rail to grab the final letter and to score the **Rambla del Agua** gap.

COLLECT C-O-M-B-O

Hop into a grind on the ledge to the left of the starting point to get the "C". Ollie across to the railing near the La Perdrera building for the **Ledge 2 Rail** gap and to get the "O" and the "M". Grind around the corner, then ollie down into a manual.

Manual towards the "B" up ahead and Wallie off the wall into a grind on top of it to continue the combo through the fourth letter. Ollie out of the grind back into another manual and continue straight ahead towards the quarter pipe at in the corner to get the final "O".

Intro

Skater Basics

Trick Lists

Story Mode

Gaps

Classic Mode

Multiskater

Secrets

COLLECT 5 TAPAS

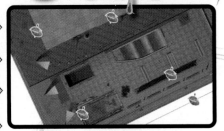

The first Tapas is on the yellow railing near the bridge, on the waterfront side.

Spine Transfer into the skating pool area by the waterfront to pluck the Tapas out of the air above the edge.

Pop off the pink brick planter into a grind on the awning of the cinema to get the third Tapas.

Wallie into a grind atop the lengthy wall in the center of the waterfront plaza area.

Drop down onto the walkway near the water and grind the railing in a clockwise direction. Round the corner and ollie out onto the cable strung along the water surface to pick up the final Tapas.

MANUAL THE SUBWAY

Tap into a manual while skating towards one of the subway entrances and balance the manual down the ramp into the subway station. Continue tapping Up and Down on the controls to maintain balance as the skater reappears exiting another subway entrance. Manual up and out of the other station to get the **Subway Manual** gap and to complete the goal.

GRIND THE WORLD'S LONGEST BENCH

Skate to the rear of the Parc Guell area, towards the tower for the sky tram. There is a patio area just below the tram tower that has an incredibly long, wavy stone bench. Skate to one end of it and ollie into a grind on it. Balance the grind all the way to the other end without falling to complete the goal and to score the **World's Longest Bench** gap bonus.

GET THE SECRET TAPE

The Secret Tape is atop the central red rail high above the bridge. Although it's possible to grind the outer rails towards the center and make the transfer to the center one to get the Secret Tape, there is a much easier way.

Head to the waterfront area and enter the tram tower to pop up on top of the tower. Face the bridge, then run and ollie into a grind on the right-hand cable. Balance the grind towards the bridge and once over the red rail with the Secret Tape, ollie straight up and allow the skater to fall below the cable. Press and hold the Grind Button once below the cable to grind the red rail towards the Secret Tape.

AUSTRALIA

Complete 6 Goals at Barcelona to unlock this location.

5 Stat Points available.

COURSE GOALS

High Score - 65,000 Points
Pro Score - 130,000 Points
Sick Score - 200,000 Points
High Combo - 30,000 Points
Collect S-K-A-T-E
Collect C-O-M-B-O
Smash 5 Flower Pots
Get the Secret Tape
Find and Hit 5 G'Day Ramp Transfers
Bust All 5 Yellow Street Lamps

Doorway to Paradise

Natas Spin on Fire Hydrant to Make Crane Operator Break Wall

SCORING GOALS

Australia has several good places to throw down some big combos. Those who excel in lengthy grinds should certainly enjoy the rails flanking the boardwalk and the high wire that stretches from one end of the beach to the other. There's also the ledge near the street and the circular base of the statue and fountain. Meanwhile, those who like to score in the half pipe have numerous ramps to choose from. The mini-ramp is conducive for stringing big combos together, as are the large quarter pipes in the parking lot near the footbridge.

When it comes time to lay down a big combo, consider Spine Transferring up into the building near the mini-ramp and hitting the **Lofty Roof Gap** over to the other building. Trick into a grind on the edge of the rooftop pool and Acid Drop down to the sidewalk. Keep the combo alive by manualing into a lengthy grind on the boardwalk railings.

Sick Mode: The High Score (150,000), Pro Score (300,000), Sick Score (450,000) and High Combo (100,000) requirements remain obtainable with just a few tweaks to the above tips. For starters, incorporate Special Grinds and Special Manuals into each scoring combo. If possible, Special Grind a few laps around the edge of the lifeguard station or the statue's base, then quickly tap into other grinds to quickly boost the multiplier. Also consider hitting the rooftop ramps and the Lofty Roof Gap but work on keeping the scoring line alive by Hip Transferring among the many concrete quarter pipes in the plaza below.

COLLECT S-K-A-T-E

S Follow the directions for obtaining the "T". While still on the roof, hit the **Lofty Roof Gap** dead center to grab the "S" while landing on the building with the rooftop pool.

K The "K" hovers above the right-hand quarter pipe near the barricade that marks the end of the skating area on the street.

A Climb the fire escape near the koala statue to the second level and Caveman into a clockwise grind on the railing to get the letter.

T Spine Transfer up and over the Butterfinger billboard to reach the roof of the building's roof. Spine Transfer over the middle spine ramp on the roof to pluck the "T" out of the air.

E The "E" is on the wire that stretches across the beach. Either grind from the apartment buildings over to it, or climb one of the lamp posts and hop into a grind on the wire right near it.

COLLECT C-O-M-B-O

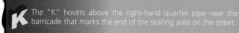

Ollie into a grind on the handrail in the parking lot, near the lifeguard station. Grind to the right, grab the "C", then ollie across the gap to continue on towards the "O" and "M". Jump down into a manual and ride up the narrow quarter pipe at the end of the sidewalk. Transition to a grind on the edge of the wall and balance along the apartment building towards the "B". Side-jump over to the other ledge to another grind and grab the "O" in the distance.

SMASH 5 FLOWER POTS

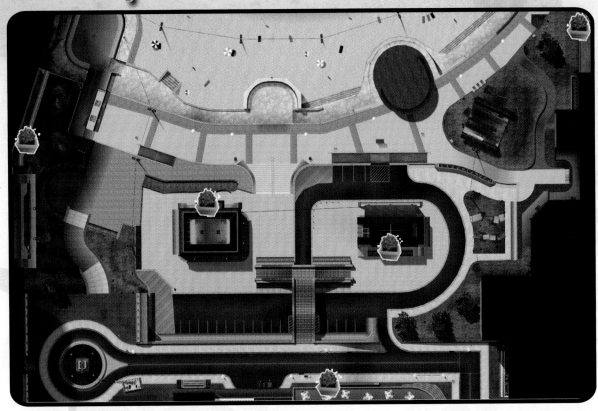

The first flower pot is on the back of the building with the spine ramps on the roof. Grind the ledge alongside the parking lot towards the mini-ramp.

Loop around to the front of the building with the rooftop pool and grind the steps leading up to its entrance.

The final flower pot is on a balcony under the enormous emu burger billboard. Grind the balcony of the yellow building and ollie into a grind on the final balcony, nearest the tide pool.

Another flower pot is on the ledge of the apartment buildings at the end of the beach opposite the tide pool.

The fourth flower pot is on the short ledge near the arcade machine and bus stop.

GET THE SECRET TAPE

Climb the fire escape near the koala statue all the way to the uppermost level and ollie into a clockwise grind on the railing. Transfer the grind across the gap in the balconies to snag the Secret Tape.

FIND AND HIT 5 G'DAY RAMP TRANSFERS

Go through the tunnel under the footbridge and turn around. Air between the two ramps flanking the black banner on the footbridge to score the first **G'Day Ramp 2 Ramp** gap.

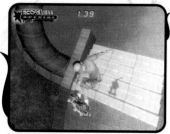

Transfer over the steps from the narrow concrete quarter pipe to the circular bowl-like area near the logs.

Skate up towards the apartment buildings near the koala statue and air transfer between the ramps near the entrance to the one with the fire escape.

The fourth transfer is also near the koala statue. Air it out between the two ramps alongside the small tree near the circle in the street.

The final **G'Day Ramp 2 Ramp** gap is at the base of the hill, facing the street. Transfer between the two checkerboard quarter pipes flanking the red doors to the apartment building.

BUST ALL 5 YELLOW STREET LAMPS

Climb the taller of the two white street posts near the mini-ramp (the one near the Butterfinger billboard). Shimmy out onto the wire in the direction of the street and jump up into a grind towards the green building. Hold the grind past the Stat Point on the ledge of the building onto the cable connecting the yellow street lamps. Tap Left and Right on the controls to maintain balance while grinding through all five lamps. You may need to ollie once or twice to maintain speed in the uphill portion of the grind.

SKATOPIA

Complete 6 Goals at Barcelona to unlock this location.

5 Stat Points available.

COURSE GOALS

- **High Score - 65,000 Points**
- **Pro Score - 130,000 Points**
- **Sick Score - 200,000 Points**
- **High Combo - 30,000 Points**
- **Collect S-K-A-T-E**
- **Collect C-O-M-B-O**
- **Get 5 Bags of Dog Food**
- **Get the Secret Tape**
- **Front Flip the Skatopia Sign**
- **Hit the 5 Skunk Grinds**

SCORING GOALS

The enormously long concrete quarter pipes and half pipes make it possible to compile valuable grind combos. Grind on the L-shaped pool behind the barn and transfer the grind down into a manual on the dirt road. From there, it's easy to trick into a lengthy downhill Special Grind that can culminate with an aerial combo behind the house.

As for nailing the combo, it's possible to score a quick 200,000 points by linking multiple Spine Transfers together. Start in the bowl atop the cliff and Spine Transfer down to the ground beside the garage. Revert to keep the combo intact and Spine Transfer in, then out of the garage. These three Spine Transfers also net the **Cliff Spine**, **Garage Wall Spine**, and **Into the Garage** gap bonuses.

Sick Mode: The High Score (150,000), Pro Score (300,000), Sick Score (450,000) and High Combo (100,000) requirements are well within the reach of the scoring lines mentioned above. Another line to consider trying begins in the L-shaped pool. Link several aerial tricks together, then leap out of the pool into a grind on the electrical wire. Switch to Focus and carefully grind the length of the wire down to the Skatopia sign while switching between different grinds to increase the multiplier.

107

COLLECT S-K-A-T-E

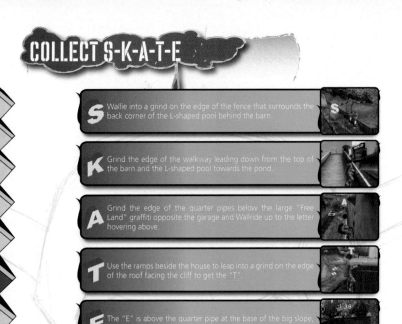

S Wallie into a grind on the edge of the fence that surrounds the back corner of the L-shaped pool behind the barn.

K Grind the edge of the walkway leading down from the top of the barn and the L-shaped pool towards the pond.

A Grind the edge of the quarter pipes below the large "Free Land" graffiti opposite the garage and Wallride up to the letter hovering above.

T Use the ramps beside the house to leap into a grind on the edge of the roof facing the cliff to get the "T".

E The "E" is above the quarter pipe at the base of the big slope, just beside the bottom of the inclined zip line.

COLLECT C-O-M-B-O

Start skating up the hill away from the entrance while keeping to the right-hand side of the park. Turn around and slide into a grind on the concrete quarter pipe near the mobile home to get the "C". Grind downhill in a clockwise direction towards the entrance to pick up the "O". Transfer the grind to the ledge behind the Skatopia sign to obtain the "M".

Here is the tricky part. Hold to the right on the controls while ollieing out of the grind towards the "B" in order to land in a grind on the ledge curving off to the right. Keep the combo alive by grinding the edge of the quarter pipe heading uphill to the right to snag the final "O".

GET 5 BAGS OF DOG FOOD

The first bag of dog food is on the front porch of the house. Use the right-hand ramp to air up and grab it off the deck.

Jump down from the billboard on the side of the cliff to get the next bag of dog food. It's on the same ledge as the entrance to the mineshaft.

Skate into the alley between the half pipe and the barn to find the next bag of dog food.

Exit the pool inside the garage on the uphill side and ride across the bag of dog food sitting on the grass.

The final bag of dog food is atop the hill, near the outhouse.

Intro

Skater Basics

Trick Lists

Story Mode

Gaps

Classic Mode

Multiskater

Secrets

GET THE SECRET TAPE

The Secret Tape is hovering high above the ground against the cliff marking the edge of the big slope. It's possible to grind the edge of the quarter pipe against the cliff and Wallie off the cliff to snag it, but there is an easier way.

Use the vertical zipline to launch high into the air. Acid Drop into the bowl atop the mountain for the **Zipline Drop** gap. Spine Transfer out the other side of the bowl down onto the side of the big slope. Doing so provides more than enough speed to launch from the ramp at the base of the cliff and grab the Secret Tape.

FRONT FLIP THE SKATOPIA SIGN

Grind the logs alongside the road leading into Skatopia to get some speed. Spine Transfer over the Skatopia sign and quickly hold the Grab Button and tap Up, Up on the controls to Front Flip while airborne.

HIT THE 5 SKUNK GRINDS

Head up the hill to the right of the house towards the garage and turn around. Boneless into a grind atop the red shack for the first Skunk Grind.

Air off the embankment behind the Skatopia Sign into a right-hand grind atop the sign. Hold the grind across the wire to the shed with the blue tarp. Hold the grind around the roof of the shed for the next Skunk Grind.

Leap into a grind on the edge of the barn's roof nearest the walkway leading down to the ground. The easiest way over to that edge is to grind the light wire to it.

Grind the edge directly below the large billboard on the cliff face. Climb up the rope ladder from the ledge with the mineshaft entrance to reach it.

The final Skunk Grind is the log at the top of the big slope, under the terminus for the inclined zipline.

COURSE GOALS

High Score - 100,000 Points
Pro Score - 200,000 Points
Sick Score - 300,000 Points
High Combo - 60,000 Points
Collect S-K-A-T-E
Collect C-O-M-B-O
Get the Secret Tape
Madonna the Soldiers
Acid Drop from the 4 Beer Steins
Put the Space Monkey Back Together Again

BERLIN

Complete 6 Goals at Australia or Skatopia to unlock this location.

5 Stat Points available.

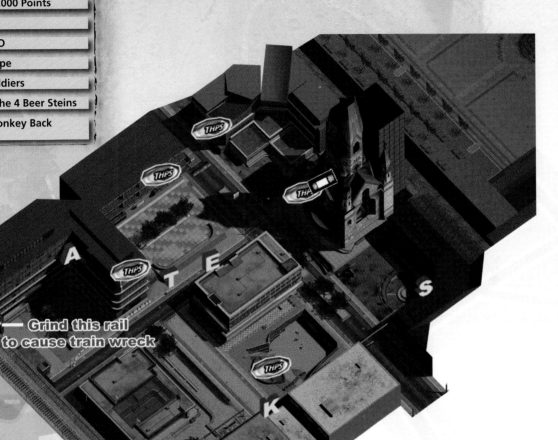

Grind this rail to cause train wreck

BS Wallride • Wallie • Hang Ten Nosegrind • Impossible • Fakie Ollie • Spine Transfer • Nosegrab • 360 Shove-it • BS Revert • Manual • Spine Transfer • One Foot Tailgrab

BS Revert • Manual • Spine Transfer • One Foot Tailgrab • BS Revert • FS Tailslide • Moonwalk Five-0

Nosegrab • BS 50-50 • Kerflip • Moonwalk Five-0 • Double Impossible • Nose Manual • Moonwalk Five-0

SCORING GOALS

Trick out the Special Meter near the fancy gold building and ollie into a Special Grind on the lengthy rail in the center of the street leading down the hill towards the Oktoberfest party. Manual out of the grind and Spine Transfer onto the roof of Gretchen's Bar. Revert to a manual and Spine Transfer back down and trick into another Special Grind on the lower ledge of the office building.

There are plenty of other places to score large quantities of points. For starters, link numerous Spine Transfer gaps together by starting at the zoo and Spine Transferring into and out of the church. Keep the combo alive by Spine Transferring onto the roof of the gold building. Continue the counter-clockwise combo with a Hip Transfer and additional Spine Transfers to get back down to street level.

Sick Mode: The High Score (200,000), Pro Score (400,000), Sick Score (600,000) and High Combo (150,000) requirements can be met all at once with a single back-and-forth combo on the main street in front of the church. Start the combo with a Special Trick off the ramps at either end of the street and Revert to a manual upon landing. Use manuals and grinds to combo the length of the street to the ramp at the far end and go big again with another Special Trick. Use Focus to keep the combo alive as long as possible. This line will net millions of points in a single combo to those with the skill to pull it off.

COLLECT S-K-A-T-E

S Use the ramps at the end of the street near the soldier poster to air into a grind on the water pipe. Grind to the left and ollie into a grind on the upper edge of the zoo and aquarium to get the "S".

K The "K" is floating high above the ramped barricade up the steps from the AusFarht Center. Leap off the ramps to snag it.

A Hold the grind after obtaining the "T" and continue to the left around the ledge of the yellow building. The "A" is in the corner near the box of paint cans.

T Enter the AusFarht Center to teleport to the roof of the nearby building. Skate across the roof diagonally and Boneless over the edge into a grind on the cable stretching out towards the billboard across the street.

E Return to the AusFarht Center to regain the nearby rooftop. Air off the kicker ramp to pluck the "E" out of the air.

COLLECT C-O-M-B-O

Grind the rail along the sidewalk above the entrance to the AusFarht Center and transfer it to the ledge under the awning near the shops. Ollie out of the grind into a manual and pop back into a grind on the steps straight ahead. Transfer the grind across the gap in the stairs to collect the "M". Grind around the bend in the steps and manual across the street towards the gold building. Spine Transfer up to the rooftop to snag the "B" and Revert to a manual to get the final letter above the ramp straight ahead.

No Comply + Nosegrab + BS Tailslide + Impossible

No Comply + Nosegrab + BS Tailslide + Impossible + FS Nosegrind + Manual + BS Noseslide

No Comply + Nosegrab + BS Tailslide + Impossible + FS Nosegrind + Manual + BS Noseslide + Moonwalk Five-0 + Manual + Spine Transfer + Nosegrab

GET THE SECRET TAPE

Spine Transfer into the church and air up to the ladder hanging down from above. Climb the ladder to the ledge and carefully walk around to the other room. Head to the right and step out over the wooden planks towards the outer ledge and continue around the outer ledges in a counter-clockwise direction. Run up the edge of the steeple to the Secret Tape.

MADONNA THE SOLDIERS

Locate the large double-sided poster of the soldiers in the main road in front of the church. Use the ramps at either end of the road and the edges of the medians to gain speed. Once going as fast as possible (Skitchin' is another viable way to get up to speed) hit the front of the median nearest the posters and launch up and over the soldiers' image. Perform a Madonna (Up/Right + Grab Button) while in the air to complete the goal.

ACID DROP FROM THE 4 BEER STEINS

Enter the AusFarht Center to gain the nearby rooftop. Ride up and off the left-hand kicker ramp and press the Spine Transfer Button to Acid Drop down onto the awning.

Climb the ladder near the building with the pink ledges to the top and scamper across the ledge to the right. Jump up and Acid Drop off the upper ledge near the beer stein.

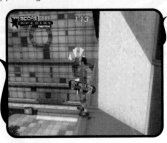

Climb the ladder in the corner of the yellow building opposite the Oktoberfest party. Step off to the right and Acid Drop back down into the plaza from the beer stein.

Spine Transfer into the church and air up to the ladder hanging down from the above. Climb the ladder and step around to the other room. Head to the right and walk across the planks of wood to the outer ledge overlooking the gold building. Acid Drop from this ledge to complete the goal.

Ollie into a grind on the yellow handrail leading down from the starting point to the entrance to the AusFarht Center.

Skate through the entrance to the AusFarht Center to be teleported to the rooftop of the nearby building. Transfer between the two ramps flanking the fan to pluck the next part of the Space Monkey out of the air while hitting the **Vent Transfer** gap.

Use the vent on the roof to boost the skater across to the roof with the satellite dishes. The next Space Monkey part is floating above the ramp straight ahead.

The Space Monkey's head is floating above the roof of the fancy gold building near the church. Spine Transfer onto the lower rooftop, then air off the ramp on the roof to grab the part from the upper edge.

The final Space Monkey part is hovering just above the "Inliners Rule" sign near the Oktoberfest bar.

AIRPORT

Complete 6 Goals at Berlin to unlock this location.

5 Stat Points available.

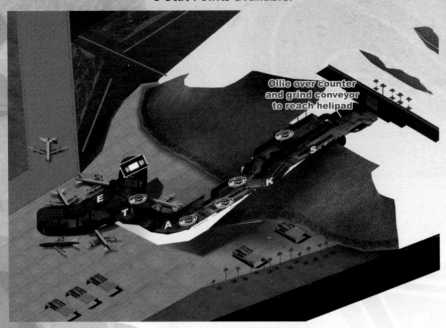

Ollie over counter and grind conveyor to reach helipad

COURSE GOALS

High Score - 125,000 Points
Pro Score - 250,000 Points
Sick Score - 400,000 Points
High Combo - 80,000 Points
Collect S-K-A-T-E
Collect C-O-M-B-O
Crush the Suspicious Suitcases
Nose Manual the Escalator Slope
Nosegrab Over the Copter!
Get the Secret Tape

SCORING GOALS

Those who have played *Tony Hawk's Pro Skater 3* are already aware of the Airport's ability to accommodate high scoring grind-based combo lines. There are three areas in particular that seven-figure combos can be strung together. For starters, there is the international baggage carousel area. Grind the handrails around the periphery of the area back and forth by using the sloped escalator rails to reverse their direction for another pass.

Another potent scoring area is near the north and south terminals where all of the international flags are. Use the red rails to grind laps around the terminals while mixing in Special Manuals and Special Grinds to build valuable combos.

The basement baggage area is arguably one of the best places to lay down lengthy grind combos of all the games in the series. Grind lap after lap across the concrete ledge, the baggage crates, the red rail, and even the light fixtures. With the addition of Focus, there's no end in sight to the grinds possible down in the basement.

Sick Mode: The High Score (250,000), Pro Score (500,000), Sick Score (750,000) and High Combo (200,000) requirements can all be met by hitting up the areas mentioned above. Those skating on Sick Mode simply need to use Focus and keep the combos going a little longer than those playing on Normal Mode. Remember to double-tap the Flip, Grind, and Grab Buttons to switch up the grinds to build the multiplier!

COLLECT S-K-A-T-E

S Ollie off the first bank of payphones into a grind on the lights for the **Illuminatin'** gap and transfer the grind to the second set of lights for the "S".

K Grind the edge of the walkway between the first set of escalators to get the "K" at the bottom.

A Hop off the board and climb the middle palm tree past the security checkpoint. The "A" is atop the tree.

T Leap from above the last set of escalators into a grind on the lights for the **Last High Light** gap and ollie off the end to score the "T".

E Air off either of the vert ramps nearest the center of the terminal and land in a grind on the upper red rail. Grind the rail towards the center of the terminal and ollie across the gap for the "E".

COLLECT C-O-M-B-O

Grind the handrail of the moving sidewalk to snag the "C" and drop into a manual. Pop off the kinked end of the ledge near the escalators and land in a grind on the upper light for the **Takin' the High Road** gap. Transfer the grind to the angled light to the right. Ollie before the end of this light to continue the grind on the lights running parallel with the concourse for the **Droppin' Science!** gap and to continue collecting the letters. Side-jump over to the lights on the right and continue transferring grinds across all of the lights to collect all of the letters. Jump off the final light to snag the last letter.

116

CRUSH THE SUSPICIOUS SUITCASES

Skate into the ladies restroom on the middle section of the airport and smash the suitcases near the stalls.

The fourth suitcase is the easiest to miss as it's on the x-ray machine near the security checkpoint. Hit the **O the S** gap to avoid setting off the alarms, then turn around and crush the suitcase on the conveyor.

The final suitcase is atop the crates basement. Ollie onto the crate and grind across its edge to destroy the luggage.

Ollie the right-hand counter at the starting point and follow the conveyor belt to the first set of suitcases near the helipad.

Grind down the railing from the helipad to the international terminal. The next suitcase is sitting atop the baggage carousel.

Intro

Skater Basics

Trick Lists

Story Mode

Gaps

Classic Mode

Multiskater

Secrets

NOSE MANUAL THE ESCALATOR SLOPE

Skate towards the first of the two sets of escalators and tap into a Nose Manual (Down, Up). Balance the Nose Manual from before the downhill begins all the way to the bottom of the slope, where the ground flattens back out. Score the **Manual the Slope!** gap while performing a Nose Manual to complete the goal.

NOSEGRAB OVER THE COPTER!

Leap over the right-hand counter near the starting point and grind the baggage conveyor to the helipad. Exit the grind and Boneless off the kicker ramp at the end and Nosegrab (Up + Grab Button) while soaring over the helicopter. Land the jump for the **Helicopter Hop** gap.

GET THE SECRET TAPE

Skate down past the escalators to the two terminals and head to the right. Air off the last vert ramp on the left to leap into a right-hand grind on the uppermost red rail. Hold the grind in a clockwise direction around the end of the terminal to get the Secret Tape.

SCHOOL 1

Complete 6 Goals at Berlin to unlock this location.

5 Stat Points available.

Approach door to enter gymnasium.

Climb ladder to reach high dive.

COURSE GOALS

High Score - 125,000 Points
Pro Score - 250,000 Points
Sick Score - 400,000 Points
High Combo - 80,000 Points
Collect S-K-A-T-E
Collect C-O-M-B-O
Set Off 5 Fire Alarms
Smash the 5 School Books
Double Kickflip the Kicker Gap
Get the Secret Tape

SCORING GOALS

School 1 is an original *Tony Hawk's Pro Skater* level and, being such, it doesn't quite have as many areas that are conducive for elaborate scoring lines. However, there are two areas in particular where skaters with good balance and fast fingers can squeeze out some high scoring combos.

Head to the area with the tall wall and funboxes, across the canal from the picnic tables. Use the funboxes to trick into a Special Grind atop the wall. Trick into a manual on the way down and use the quarter pipes to add some aerial flair to the line. Revert the landing and manual back up and over the funboxes to repeat the line in the other direction. Keep this up as long as you can for big points!

After finishing with the wall and funboxes, consider climbing the ladder to the top of the high dive and Acid Dropping into the pool below. Revert the landing and use the speed to link up multiple Special Tricks with the help of some well-timed Reverts and manuals. When speed becomes an issue, slip into a grind on the edge of the pool and double-tap into a host of other grinds to increase the multiplier.

Sick Mode: The High Score (250,000), Pro Score (500,000), Sick Score (750,000) and High Combo (200,000) requirements are quite high, but all of them can be completed with one single combo. Trick into a Special Grind on the edge of the high dive pool and, after a few seconds, initiate Focus. Hold the grind for at least two laps around the pool, then start switching into numerous other grinds to boost the multiplier. You'll eventually reach the maximum Focus time and grind balance will be entirely depleted so quickly trick out of the grind into a Special Manual and either hit up one of the nearby quarter pipes or flip trick out of the manual to end the combo.

COLLECT S-K-A-T-E

S Grind the handrail near the wheelchair ramp alongside the lengthy staircase and ollie through the "S" over to a grind on the brick wall.

K Grind the ledge of the bridge over the canal and ollie out of the grind and up into the air to grab the "K".

A Wallie into a grind atop the lone wall in the picnic area, between the two funboxes.

T The "T" is atop the roof of the small building above the lengthy quarter pipe. Travel counter-clockwise around the course from the picnic area to the swimming area to find it.

E Grind the rail near the shallow swimming pool and ollie off the end of it to grab the "E" out of the air.

COLLECT C-O-M-B-O

Skate towards the picnic plaza and ollie into a grind on the ledge near the picnic tables. Grind through "C" and hit the **Rail To Rail Transfer** gap by ollieing across the break in the rail to continue collecting the letters. Jump to the right immediately after snagging the "M" in order to continue the grind towards the "B". Ollie out of the grind on the lower ledge into one on the coping of the quarter pipe to the left to finish the combo.

Those having trouble with this line may wish to try to collect the letters in reverse order. It might be a little unorthodox, but it follows a slightly less difficult, "downhill" approach to the collection process.

SET OFF 5 FIRE ALARMS

SCHOOL

Barcelona
Australia
Skatopia
Berlin
Airport
School
Downhill Jam
New Orleans
Training
Boston
Canada
Philadelphia
Los Angeles
The Triangle

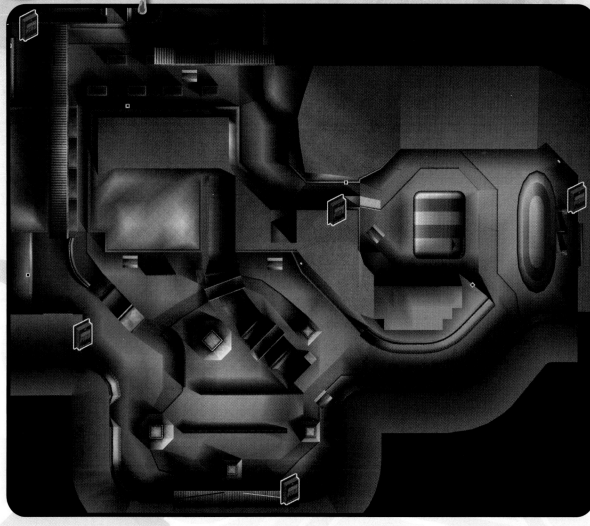

The first fire alarm is on the wall to the left of the gymnasium entrance. Wallride across it to set it off.

Another fire alarm is located on the wall near the bottom of the sloped walkway leading down from the starting point towards the pools.

The third fire alarm is on the wall to the left of the giant movie screen near the high dive.

Skate to the area with the tall wall and the funboxes and Wallride across the fire alarm on the shed behind the wall.

The final fire alarm is on a wall near the picnic area. It's right next to the pair of kicker ramps.

SMASH THE 5 SCHOOL BOOKS

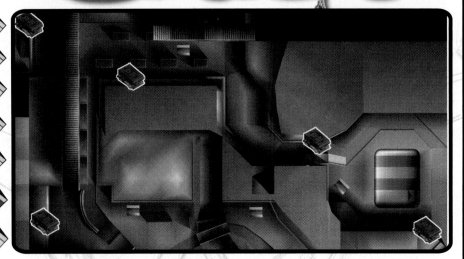

Drop off the awning at the start of the run and grind the ledge to the left of the planters.

Head down to the bottom of the lengthy staircase and grind the ramp on the right to take out the third set of books.

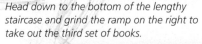

Air off the quarter pipe on the side of the building near the gymnasium entrance and smash the books sitting on the corner of the roof near the skater.

Ollie into a grind on the short wall of the building near the lap-swimming pool. It's to the left of the graffiti artist.

Skate past the pools in a counter-clockwise direction. The last set of books is on the ledge near the large graffiti.

DOUBLE KICKFLIP THE KICKER GAP

Skate down the lengthy staircase leading from the gymnasium to the picnic area to find two kicker ramps. Ollie off one of the ramps and perform a Double Kickflip (Left + Flip, Flip). Land on the other kicker ramp for the **Kicker Gap** bonus and to complete the goal.

GET THE SECRET TAPE

Skate around the side of the gymnasium and ride up either of the two walkways that lead to the rooftop. Use the funbox to air onto the raised portion of the roof and grind the wooden plank for the **Roof to Awning** gap. Skate down the awning (not the one you begin on) to get plenty of speed and Boneless off the end to pluck the Secret Tape out of the air.

DOWNHILL JAM

Complete 6 Goals at Airport or School 1 to unlock this location.

5 Stat Points available.

COURSE GOALS

High Score - 165,000 Points

Pro Score - 325,000 Points

Sick Score - 500,000 Points

High Combo - 100,000 Points

Collect S-K-A-T-E

Collect C-O-M-B-O

Smash 5 Crates

Japan Over the Giant Grate

Manual Through the Puddles

Get the Secret Tape

SCORING GOALS

The best scoring line just so happens to be the one traced out by the COMBO letters. Trick into a grind on the left-hand pipe nearest the starting line and drop down into a grind on the triangular ledge for the **Pipe to Triangle** gap. Hop over to the right to Special Grind the lengthy pipe over the water hazard and trick into a Special Manual. Hit the kicker on the right to leap into a grind on the pipes before tricking down into the concrete half pipe. Work the half pipe back and forth with plenty of quick tricks and rotation. Revert to a manual upon landing each trick and, depending on speed, try to mix in a Special Air Trick or two.

In addition to the line described above, spend as much time as needed in the concrete half pipe to get any remaining points. Use Special Tricks while the skater possesses enough speed, then rely on quick flip tricks and grabs to boost the multiplier. Slip into a Special Grind on the left-hand edge of the half pipe to boost the base score before ending any other scoring lines.

Sick Mode: The High Score (325,000), Pro Score (650,000), Sick Score (1,000,000) and High Combo (250,000) requirements are a bit tougher to accomplish, but can be earned by building as large a multiplier as possible while following the line detailed above. Incorporate as many flip tricks, rolls, and spins as possible when airing in and out of grinds. Also, roll through the finish line in a combo so as to continue it back at the starting point atop the hill—that's the best way to build an enormous combo!

COLLECT S-K-A-T-E

S From the starting point, head down the hill and air off the ramp on the right to land in a grind on the pipes. The "S" is at the end of these first pipes.

K Get some speed by tricking off the ramps at the base of the cliffs near the top of the course, then Boneless off the left hand ramp into a grind on the pipes sticking out of the rocks above the end of the water hazard.

A Ride up the path to the far left and hop into a grind on the lengthy pipe that leads to the top of the dam on the right.

T Exit the concrete half pipe and use the kicker on the right to Boneless into a grind atop the large red and black billboard. Ollie off the end of the sign to snag the "T".

E The "E" is hovering above the ground near the finish line. Stick to the right-hand side when passing by the giant grate and grind the railings near the spectator area. Ollie off the second rail to get the final letter before dropping to the finishing line.

COLLECT C-O-M-B-O

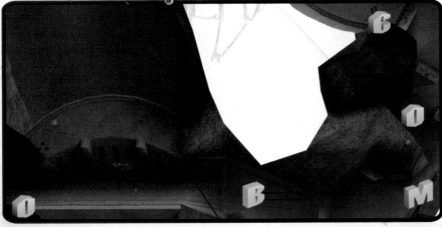

Ollie into a grind on the lengthy pipe that drops down over the water hazard near the top of the course. Ollie off the end of the pipe to snag the "O" out of the air and manual towards the wall straight ahead. Air off the ramp to get the "M" and Revert to a manual upon landing. Balance the manual towards the kicker on the right and air into a grind on the next set of pipes. Pluck the "B" out of the air and land in another manual. Ride up the left-hand side of the concrete half pipe and slip into a grind on the edge. Hold the grind to the very end of the concrete and ollie off to snag the final letter.

SMASH 5 CRATES

The first crate is on the ledge above the pipes near the starting point. Air off the ramp and Wallride up into a grind on the ledge to smash the crate.

The third crate is on top of the dam. Ride up out of the concrete half pipe to the walkway on the upper right side and smash the crate.

The final crate is on the upper ledge above the finish line. Stay to the right when going past the giant grate and smash the crate before ollieing down to the finish line.

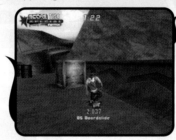

Continue down the hill and Boneless off the left-most kicker ramp to land on the rock formation above the water hazard. The second crate is atop these rocks.

Follow the directions for getting the Secret Tape. On the way there, smash the crate on the ledge following the difficult jump near the "globe" sign.

JAPAN OVER THE GIANT GRATE

Skate down to the bottom portion of the course and locate the two bumps in the center of the area. There is a large grate between these (right before the path dips downhill to the finish line). Jump from the first of the bumps and press Up/Left + Grab Button in the air to perform the Japan maneuver. Depending on how your trick assortment is set up, this may be the Crossbone or some other trick. Regardless the trick mapped to that command, the command required to complete the goal will not change. Land the trick for the **Over the Giant Grate!** gap.

Intro

Skater Basics

Trick Lists

Story Mode

Gaps

Classic Mode

Multiskater

Secrets

MANUAL THROUGH THE PUDDLES

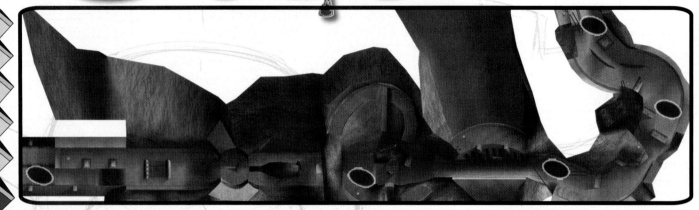

The first puddle is just downhill from the starting point. Tap into a manual and roll through the puddle without falling.

Continue down the hill and stay to the far left. The next puddle is directly in front of the leftmost kicker ramp.

The third puddle is just uphill from the large concrete half pipe. It's right near the two large overhead pipes.

Exit the bottom of the concrete half pipe and stay to the left. Go through the dip in the ground and tap into a manual to ride through the puddle at the crest of the hill.

The final puddle is just feet from the finish line. Stay to the left after the giant grate and ride down the hill and through the dip. Manual through the puddle after the dip to complete the goal.

GET THE SECRET TAPE

Exit the concrete half pipe by skating up the slope to the top of the dam on the right. Grind across the pipe to the ledge in the distance, near the "globe" billboard. Once there, Boneless across the gap to the next ledge (you may need to Wall Jump once or twice to complete the jump) and skate up onto the land bridge near the "almost" billboard. Continue skating along this path in a loop. Leap across the break in the walkway, then ollie off the end to grab the Secret Tape atop the rock spire. Consider hopping off the board when about to land on the rock to avoid missing the Secret Tape, as was commonplace back in the day.

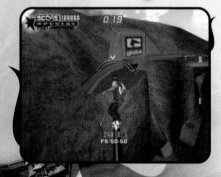

New Orleans

Complete 6 Goals at Downhill Jam to unlock this location.

5 Stat Points available.

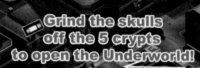

Grind the skulls off the 5 crypts to open the Underworld!

COURSE GOALS

High Score - 200,000 Points
Pro Score - 400,000 Points
Sick Score - 600,000 Points
High Combo - 150,000 Points
Collect S-K-A-T-E
Collect C-O-M-B-O
Japan the Big Crypt
Collect 5 Voodoo Dolls
Smash 5 Crystal Balls
Get the Secret Tape

SCORING GOALS

New Orleans has plenty of places to launch enormous aerial and street-based combos. In addition to the many quarter pipes and makeshift half-pipes on the roofs and in the alleys, there are also the ramps at the base of each of the buildings and near the church. Best of all, it's possible to chain together a series of Spine Transfers from one rooftop down to the street, then back up onto another building.

Like many courses, however, the best scoring can be had by linking together numerous grinds. From the starting point, trick down the road towards the cemetery and manual towards the big crypt in the center. Launch into a big Special Air Trick and Revert to a manual. Carefully slide up the wall to the right of the gate and start a lengthy clockwise grind on top of it. Use lengthy Special Grinds on the long sections of wall to boost the base score. Increase the multiplier by flipping, grabbing, and spinning when ollieing between sections of the wall. The entrance gate and the arch near the dock will pop the skater high enough into the air to safely perform a quick Special Trick. Keep grinding for as long as possible.

Sick Mode: The High Score (400,000), Pro Score (800,000), Sick Score (1,250,000) and High Combo (300,000) requirements can all be achieved by performing the same lengthy cemetery grind described previously. Furthermore, consider starting a second grind combo on the streetcar tracks. Use the rails and benches nearby, then cap it off by Spine Transferring into the churchyard and adding some aerial tricks to the line.

Intro

Skater Basics

Trick Lists

Story Mode

Gaps

Classic Mode

Multiskater

Secrets

COLLECT S-K-A-T-E

S The "S" sits atop the large crypt in the center of the cemetery. Spine Transfer over the crypt to get it.

K Leap onto the roof of the building with the helipad. The "K" is near the edge of the roof, just above the lower ramp.

A The "A" is floating high above the edge of the ramp on the roof nearest the courtyard bar. It's on the side across from the church.

T Grind the balcony of the building on the corner near the church and waterfront to get the next letter.

E Air off the concrete ramps on the corner near the cemetery and waterfront to get the "E" hovering above them.

COLLECT C-O-M-B-O

Ride up the ramp at the base of the building to the left of the church and grind the ledge to the "C" to start the combo. Pop off the kinked end of the sign and aim towards the tree on the right before tapping the Spine Transfer Button to Acid Drop into the churchyard. Revert and manual towards the church entrance and hit the **Church Statue** gap while plucking the "O" out of the air.

Revert back to a manual and carefully wheelie across the street towards the "M". Wallride off the planter where the "M" is and bust through the balcony and Wallie into a grind on the uppermost railing. Grind through the "B" and around the curve in the rail and ollie down into a manual on the road below. Manual straight ahead towards the ramped barricade beyond the alley and leap up and snag the final "O" to complete the goal.

Move into position by entering the dance club across the street from the starting point and ollieing while on the dance floor to get boosted to the building's rooftop. From there, Spine Transfer over the edge down into the street opposite the building near the church. Although this isn't a necessary step, the speed gained from the rooftop Spine Transfer makes it easier to complete the objective.

JAPAN THE BIG CRYPT

Enter the cemetery and trick off the banked walls in the center area to get speed. Charge the large crypt in the center of the cemetery and Spine Transfer over it. Perform a Japan (Up/Left + Grab Button) while airing over the crypt to complete the goal and to snag the **Crypt Keeper** gap.

COLLECT 5 VOODOO DOLLS

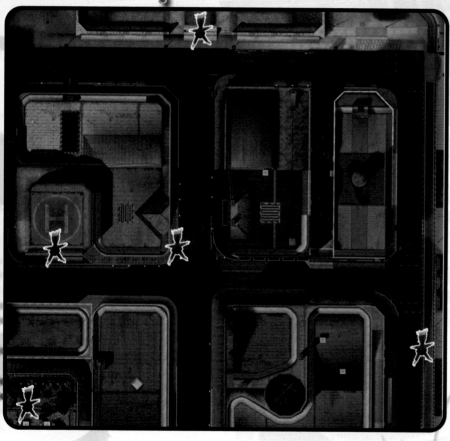

Air into a grind on the electrical wires running above the streetcar. Ollie from the wire closest to the water onto the other to get the next voodoo doll.

Enter the parking garage lift and ollie into the air to be catapulted to the rooftop. The next voodoo doll is just above the quarter pipe on the helipad atop this building.

Grind the uppermost balcony of the building with the parking garage and helipad on it. The voodoo doll is on the corner above the main intersection in the center of town.

Spine Transfer over the main gate of the cemetery to grab the next voodoo doll.

Enter the courtyard bar and shimmy out onto the light wire strung above the enormous Hurricane drink. Climb up onto the wire to get the final voodoo doll.

Intro

Skater Basics

Trick Lists

Story Mode

Gaps

Classic Mode

Multiskater

Secrets

SMASH 5 CRYSTAL BALLS

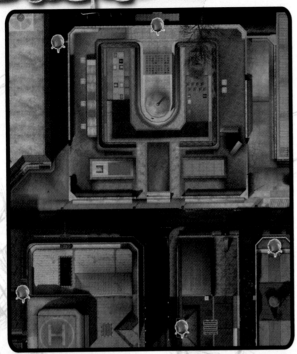

The first crystal ball is high above the ground in the alley with the "Humidity" banners. Spine Transfer off the ramp below it to reach it.

Enter the alley to the left of the cemetery and air off the quarter pipe near the water to get the next crystal ball.

Grind the outermost wall of the cemetery around towards the dock and gap across the arch to snag the next crystal ball.

Exit the cemetery through the main gate and start down the road. Climb the ladder on the left side of the road to the top of the building with the smokestack and water tower. The next crystal ball is at the top of this ladder.

Leap across towards the water tower and spot the crystal ball above the ramp on top of the doorway. Use the quarter pipe on the side to transfer to the ramp above the doors to complete the goal. This also scores you the **Onto the Roof Ramp** gap.

GET THE SECRET TAPE

Climb the ladder on the side of the building opposite the cemetery and get lined up with the narrow board leading to the smokestack. Skate up the board and ollie out into the smoke to grab the Secret Tape. While you're airborne, hit the Spine Transfer Button to Acid Drop into the cemetery for the **Smoke Bomb** gap.

TRAINING

Complete 6 Goals at Downhill Jam to unlock this location.

5 Stat Points available.

SCORING GOALS

Considering that the Training course is an actual skatepark, it should be come as no surprise that there are plenty of areas to score points. This park contains ramps, rails, and pools of all shapes and configurations and can accommodate any skating style. Those looking to string together lengthy aerial routines can score plenty of points in the half pipe and pool. Those looking to grind their trucks bare have miles of sprinkler pipe and coping available.

Those looking to clear off all the goals in a single combo can do so by following this combo. Start by gaining speed off the quarter pipe at the starting point, then tapping into a manual. Balance the wheelie down the slope for the **Downward Manual** gap and air it out over the pipe. Hit the **Car Hop** gap and manual into a clockwise grind on the quarter pipe at the back of the room. Follow the rails around for the **Going Up** and **OtherSide 2** gaps. Land in a Special Grind on the sprinkler pipe in the other room, and click into Focus once balance becomes an issue. Keep the grind going as long as possible, then drop down into a Special Manual and start busting big air tricks on the quarter pipes on the floor. Cap off the run with a dip in the concrete pool or a lengthy grind around its edge.

COURSE GOALS

COURSE GOALS
High Score - 200,000 Points
Pro Score - 400,000 Points
Sick Score - 600,000 Points
High Combo - 150,000 Points
Collect S-K-A-T-E
Collect C-O-M-B-O
Get the Secret Tape
Break All the Sprinklers
Benihana Over the Half Pipe
Grab All the Skateboards

Sick Mode: The High Score (400,000), Pro Score (800,000), Sick Score (1,250,000) and High Combo (300,000) goals can be completed by following the run outlined previously.

131

Intro

Skater Basics

Trick Lists

Story Mode

Gaps

Classic Mode

Multiskater

Secrets

COLLECT S-K-A-T-E

S Turn around at the starting point and air off the center of the quarter pipe to pluck the "S" out of the air.

K The "K" is on the sprinkler pipe between the two ramps leading down from the starting point. Either air up and grab it or pop into a clockwise grind on the pipes by ollieing off the kinked end of the rail near the wall by the half pipe for the **Going Up** gap.

A Leap from the crates to the ladder above the water pool and climb up to the ledge. Shimmy past the large sign to the alcove to the right to find the "A".

T The "T" is hovering above the two quarter pipes in the recessed area in the larger section of the park. Transfer from one ramp to the other to get it and the **Recessed Transfer** gap.

E Follow the directions for finding the Secret Tape and maintain the grind on the sprinkler pipe in the larger skatepark room. The "E" is on the sprinkler pipe above the break room.

COLLECT C-O-M-B-O

Hit the **Ramp Hop** gap near the puddle on the floor to grab the "C" and land in a manual. Grind to the left through the hole in the wall atop the quarter pipe to continue the combo. Pop off the kinked edge to land in a grind on the middle height rail for the "M". Continue grinding around the bend and quickly Wallie up to the uppermost rail in time to grab the "B". Ollie to the light fixtures for the **Rail 2 Light** gap and transfer to the second light for the final letter and the **Light Hop** gap.

GET THE SECRET TAPE

Grind the rails along the wall near the half pipe and air off the kinked end into a grind on the sprinkler pipes above the two slopes near the starting point for the **Going Up** gap. Keep the clockwise grind going by transferring across the breaks in the pipe. Maintain balance while grinding around the corner above the arcade machine and ollie through the hole in the wall to snag the Secret Tape while transferring to the sprinklers in the other room. Land in a grind on the next pipe for the **OtherSide 2** gap and a chance at completing the sprinklers goal, as well as the scoring goals.

BENIHANA OVER THE HALF PIPE

Launch **Over the Half Pipe** and tap into a Benihana (Down/Left + Grab Button) while airborne. Don't attempt this one without sufficient speed, and don't waste a successful leap by holding the trick too long.

BREAK ALL THE SPRINKLERS

There are a total of 19 sprinklers spread across the many pipes near the ceiling and it's up to you to grind across each and every one of them. Fortunately, water sprays out of each broken sprinkler, indicating which ones you've already smashed.

Start the destruction in the first room of the skatepark by leaping airing off the quarter pipe behind the taxicab and landing in a grind to the right. Grind across the sprinkler, over to the light, and on towards the hole in the wall. Break the second sprinkler, then drop back down before leaving the room.

Enter the pool and air into a grind on the sprinkler pipes high above. There are three sprinklers above this pool.

Grind the quarter pipe behind the taxicab in a clockwise direction and air off the kinked rail for the **Going Up** gap. Transfer the grind across the pipes above the slopes and around the bend near the arcade machine. Break the three sprinklers here and gap across to the other room to continue the grind for the **OtherSide 2** gap.

There are ten sprinklers in the larger room and the pipes are all close enough to ollie from one to the next. Hold the grind after hitting the **OtherSide 2** gap and grind in a clockwise loop. Gap across to the next section of pipe and continue the grind back to the ring of pipe over the recessed quarter pipes.

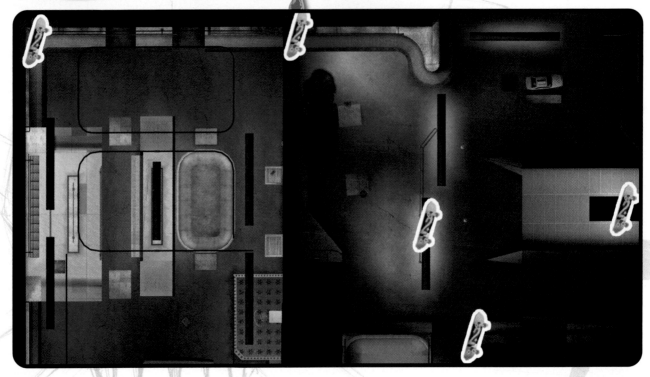

From the starting point, head down the ramp on the left and Wallride along the wall to grab the first skateboard.

Air off the back wall of the original skating area and start a grind to the right on the sprinklers. Transfer the grind onto the lights, then onto the next sprinkler pipe. Continue the grind through the upper whole in the wall leading into the larger skatepark area for the **OtherSide 1** gap and the next skateboard.

Hold the grind from the previous skateboard to the corner near the large yellow tube. Grind counter-clockwise around the uppermost sprinkler pipe to snag the next board or just climb the ladder on the side of the tube.

Launch off the ramps on the outside of the half pipe to soar through the glass of the observation room above. Grab the skateboard while snagging the **Over the Half Pipe** gap.

The final skateboard is between the two light fixtures in the first room. Leap off the quarter pipe behind the taxicab into a grind to the left on the sprinkler. Transfer the grind across the light fixtures to get the board.

BOSTON

Complete 6 Goals at New Orleans or Training to unlock this location.

5 Stat Points available.

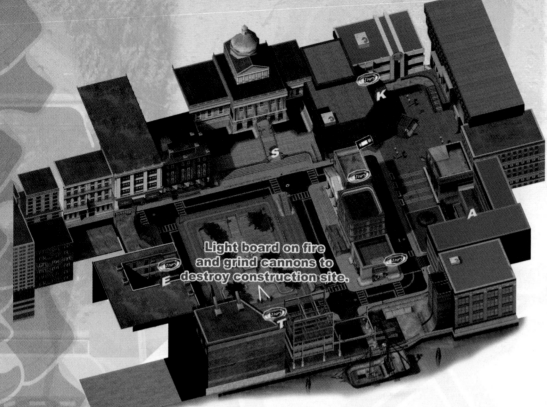

Light board on fire and grind cannons to destroy construction site.

COURSE GOALS

High Score - 235,000 Points	
Pro Score - 350,000 Points	
Sick Score - 700,000 Points	
High Combo - 175,000 Points	
Collect S-K-A-T-E	
Collect C-O-M-B-O	
Smash 5 Tea Barrels	
Get the Secret Tape	
Backflip Down the Common Stairs	
Grind the 5 Pigeon Rails	

SCORING GOALS

Boston is a street skater's paradise. The common area in the center of town has numerous ledges and wires for grinding and the multitude of quarter pipes make it possible to add some quick air tricks to any run. Those looking for a true vert style of skating should head to the Boston Tea Party ship and use it as a floating half pipe. Another option is to use the cannons to collapse the construction site and use the half pipes on the upper floors.

One good line starts right at the starting point for the level. Grind the yellow rail outside of the Jeers bar and **Rail Hop** into a grind on the blue rails near the State House. Pop off the kink in the end of the second blue rail and land in a grind on the rail on the side of the Riboff Bank (above the bus stop). Special Grind around the side of the bank and trick into a Sticker Slap on the wall beyond the end of the rail. Return to another Special Grind for the **High Slap** gap and continue the combo in the opposite direction. Reverse the series of grinds back towards the Jeers bar and use the concrete barricades near the starting point to throw down a big aerial maneuver before heading back off in the other direction once again. Keep the combo going with Focus and Special Manuals to really up the points!

Sick Mode: The High Score (500,000), Pro Score (1,000,000), Sick Score (1,500,000) and High Combo (375,000) requirements have risen again. The combo line described previously can net well over one million points to those who practice it, but there are other options as well. Head to the construction site and use the pipe and stacks of wood in the center to grind back and forth. Use the ramps at either end of the site to reverse direction and Revert to a manual to keep the combo going. Mix in as many quick tricks when ollieing in and out of grinds to boost the multiplier.

COLLECT S-K-A-T-E

S Ollie into a grind on the metal fence surrounding the State House. Grind up and over the arch above the sidewalk to score the "S".

K Wallie into a grind on the brick wall curving around towards the ATM on the side of the Riboff Bank. The "K" is on the wall, near the edge.

A Transfer from the banked walls near the hospital entrance up onto the roof above the entrance. The "A" is on the corner of the roof nearest the construction site.

T Skate over to the construction site and Hip Transfer on the blue bundle of materials in the corner near the large yellow ladder.

E Skate into the apartment house to the right of the construction site and transfer over the front steps to get the "E" and the **Brownstone Transfer** gap.

COLLECT C-O-M-B-O

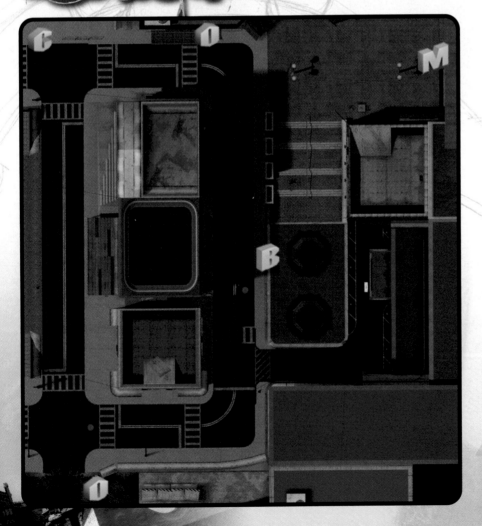

Hop into a grind on the railing in front of the State House to start the combo. Transfer the grind to the next rail and air off the kinked end of it to grind the top of the bus stop for the **Bus Stop Pop** gap. Snag the "O" and drop into a manual on the plaza floor. Manual towards the brick vert ramp with the portrait of Tony Hawk on it. Transfer through the "M" to the other wall and Revert into a manual. Ollie onto the ledge near the street and hold-grind down the hill towards the hospital. Grind the curb near the street in front of the hospital for the "B". Finish off the combo by manualing into a grind on the large blue fence curving away from the hospital towards the ship.

SMASH 5 TEA BARRELS

The first tea barrel is on the sidewalk near the green benches across the street from the mini-ramp on the scaffolding.

Another tea barrel is on the main deck of the Boston Tea Party ship.

The third tea barrel is on the patio up the stairs near the children's museum on the corner near the arcade machine.

One of the tea barrels is on the mini-ramp atop the blue scaffolding.

The final tea barrel is atop the subway entrance near the Riboff Bank.

GET THE SECRET TAPE

The Secret Tape is atop a cable running from the top of the church over to the building in the plaza near the Tony Hawk portrait. The most direct way to get it is to Spine Transfer onto the library, then Spine Transfer from building to building until on the church. Once there, simply grind the cable.

There is a second way to get the Secret Tape. Head up the curving staircase in the plaza behind the Riboff Bank and sneak through the hole in the chain link fence behind the metal barrier. This leads directly to a ledge high up on the nearby building. Although it requires an uphill grind, it's possible to grind up the cable to the Secret Tape from here. Use plenty of ollies to get enough momentum to grind up the wire to the Secret Tape and the **Wire Transfer** gap.

BACKFLIP DOWN THE COMMON STAIRS

Get lined up with the **Boston Common Stairs** and wait for the cars to pass. Hold the Jump Button for speed and ollie down the set of stairs. While airborne, hold the Grab Button and press Down, Down on the controls to Backflip.

GRIND THE 5 PIGEON RAILS

Grind the lengthy blue rail on the sidewalk in front of the State House building.

There are a bunch of pigeons on the wire strung above the two cannons. Either grind the wire down from the roof of the library or pop off the curb into a grind on it.

Wallie into a grind on the brightly colored mural above the stairs to the children's museum. It's also possible to leap into a grind from the lower railing.

Head up the curving brick stairs near the Tony Hawk portrait and hop into a grind on the metal barricade near the chain link fence.

The final pigeon rail is behind the large construction site, near the port-a-potty. Grind the fence separating the ship from the construction yard.

Intro

Skater Basics

Trick Lists

Story Mode

Gaps

Classic Mode

Multiskater

Secrets

CANADA

Complete 6 Goals at Boston to unlock this location.

5 Stat Points available.

Grind past lever to raise ramp.

COURSE GOALS

High Score - 275,000 Points

Pro Score - 475,000 Points

Sick Score - 850,000 Points

High Combo - 200,000 Points

Collect S-K-A-T-E

Smash 5 Snowmen

Collect C-O-M-B-O

Completely Scrape the 5 Icy Rails

FS Boardslide the Entire Log QP

Get the Secret Tape

SCORING GOALS

The skatepark has enormous scoring potential given its many quarter pipes, spines, and bowls. A great way to go about scoring big points in the park is to start off with a couple of Special Tricks on the quarter pipes in the corner of the park, then tricking into a Special Grind on the edge of one of the bowls. Use Focus to maintain balance and grind lap after lap to up the base score. Trick into a Special Manual when the grind balance is used up to up the score even more!

A great line begins right at the starting point. Trick into a grind on the rail to the right and gap back and forth between it, the fence to the right, and the funbox up ahead for the **Fence Hoppin'** bonus. Manual off to the right and trick into a Special Grind on the handrail in the center of the parking lot. Transfer the grind across the gap for the **Parking Lot Mini Gap**. Grind to the end and launch into a Special Air Trick off the quarter pipe before Reverting back to a Special Grind on the handrail again. Work the parking lot back and forth, up and down the hill for a seven-figure combo!

Sick Mode: The High Score (600,000), Pro Score (120,000), Sick Score (1,750,000) and High Combo (450,000) requirements can be met with a few lengthy combos like the two described previously. String as many aerial tricks together in the skatepark before hopping into a Special Grind on the coping of one of the pools and use Focus to keep the combo going. Consider tapping into a few flatland tricks at the end of the run to up the multiplier.

COLLECT S-K-A-T-E

S Grind up the cable stretching from the corner quarter pipe to the top of the large banner in the parking lot. Ollie off the top of the banner to snag the "S" above the parked cars.

K Air off the ramp at the starting point to grab the "K" while soaring towards the trees behind it.

A The "A" is high above the ground where the log quarter pipe abuts up against the tree with the circular walkway around it. Launch off the quarter pipe corral to snag it out of the air.

T Grind the rail near the engine to raise the ramp up into the air at the end of the walkway. Transfer to the ramp and, from there, into the covered shed where the "T" is.

E Air out of the covered shed near the "T" into the chute and ollie out of the chute into a grind on the mine car track nearest the mountain. Hold the grind all the way towards the starting point to find the "E". Land in a grind on the power line for the **Mine Cart Launch** gap.

CANADA

Barcelona
Australia
Skatopia
Berlin
Airport
School
Downhill Jam
New Orleans
Training
Boston
Canada
Philadelphia
Los Angeles
The Triangle

SMASH 5 SNOWMEN

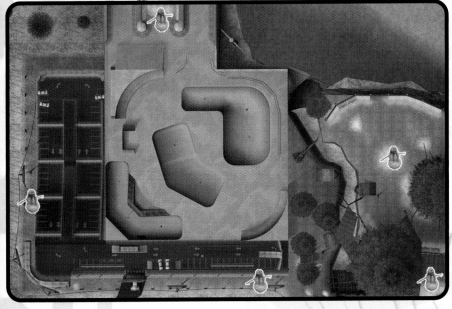

The first snowman is to the immediate left of the starting point. Skate around the wooden fence and thrash it.

Head down the hill in the parking lot and ollie over the wooden fence on the left. The snowman is on the dirt near the corner in the parking lot.

Enter the skatepark area and ride over to where the two snowdrifts are between the spine ramps. One of the snowmen is there.

There is a snowman standing out in the open inside the large tree corral area.

Cross the dilapidated log bridge over the icy stream behind the starting point and smash the snowman on the ground under the walkway.

Intro

Skater Basics

Trick Lists

Story Mode

Gaps

Classic Mode

Multiskater

Secrets

COLLECT C-O-M-B-O

Use the snow bank near the starting point to air onto the cabin. Ollie off the roof to get the "C" and land in a grind on the right-hand edge of the walkway. Transition to a grind on the log to the right for the "O". Ollie over to the log with the "M" near it. Grind off the edge of this log into a manual on the walkway. The "B" is on the rail to the left and the "O" is straight ahead, above the quarter pipe.

COMPLETELY SCRAPE THE 5 ICY RAILS

Grind the upper rail of the pyramid shaped funbox in the corner of the skatepark near the street and parking lot.

The first icy rail is just to the right of the starting point. Ride down the starting ramp and hop into a grind on the fence to the right.

Grind the left-hand rail in the center of the parking lot. Hop across the small break in the rail and grind the lower section on the left.

The final icy rail is in the center of the skatepark. It's one of the three rails sticking out of the two snowdrifts between the spine ramps.

There is a red rail within the skatepark covered in ice. It's located near the corner with the large totem pole.

FS BOARDSLIDE THE ENTIRE LOG QP

Enter the large cleared area, ringed by the log corral and quarter pipes. Slide into the Switch stance and ride up the base of the quarter pipe at the far right end (near the collapsed log bridge) and hold Left + Grind Button to start a FS Boardslide. Carefully balance the FS Boardslide all the way around the perimeter of the log quarter pipe.

Initiate Focus if balancing becomes difficult, otherwise just hold the Jump Button to prepare for the dismount and tap to the Left and Right on the controls for balance. Ollie out of the grind once the **The Log QP!** gap triggers. Consider transferring the grind to the tree sticking out of the ground near the skatepark for the **Corral to Tree Grind** gap.

GET THE SECRET TAPE

The Secret Tape is floating on an iceberg out in the water and only those willing to take a flying leap off a fence will get it. Head to the back of the skatepark, to the left of the large roll-ins. Get some speed and grind the chain link fence behind the ramps from left to right to nab the **Over the Hump** gap. Grind all the way to the corner of the fence and ollie straight off the fence and down onto the iceberg in the distance. The Secret Tape is atop the small pinnacle.

Intro

Skater Basics

Trick Lists

Story Mode

Gaps

Classic Mode

Multiskater

Secrets

PHILADELPHIA

Complete 6 Goals at Boston to unlock this location.

5 Stat Points available.

Grind across top of pole to bring down fence to skatepark.

Thanks to the hold-grind ability introduced in *Tony Hawk's Pro Skater 4*, it's now possible to quickly grind across the many stone benches in the plaza. Tap in different directions while holding the Grind Button to change the type of grind without jumping to build up the multiplier. Ollie into a Sticker Slap on the side of the building and Special Trick back into a Special Grind on the benches to make a return trip. Rack up the **Bench Gap** bonuses while building the multiplier too!

COURSE GOALS

High Score - 275,000 Points

Pro Score - 475,000 Points

Sick Score - 850,000 Points

High Combo - 200,000 Points

Collect S-K-A-T-E

Collect C-O-M-B-O

Smack All the Bags

Smash the 5 Hoagies

Triple Heelflip Over the THPS Sign

Get the Secret Tape

SCORING GOALS

The Philadelphia course was a favorite for many in *Tony Hawk's Pro Skater 2* and retains great grind-based scoring opportunities. One of the best scoring lines at Philadelphia has always involved the lengthy electrical wire that wraps halfway around the course. Trick off the quarter pipe to the right of the building with the observation deck and manual up the walkway into a Special Grind on the wire. Use Focus to make balancing easier and hold the grind around the corner all the way to the far end of the wire. Trick out of the grind into a Special Manual and extend the combo as far as possible with fast flip tricks, grinds, and flatland tricks.

Sick Mode: The High Score (600,000), Pro Score (120,000), Sick Score (1,750,000) and High Combo (450,000) goals require a bit more than a lengthy grind on the power lines. Head over to the half pipe under the bridges and start linking several Special Air Tricks together before slipping into a grind on the coping. Transfer the grind to the yellow rails on the ground and either keep the combo going in the skatepark or Special Manual across the road and up into a grind on the numerous ledges near the fountain.

COLLECT S-K-A-T-E

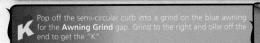

S Grind the ledge to the left of the fountain, as viewed from the starting point, and ollie hard to the right before the end to get the "S". It's also possible to get it following the "A".

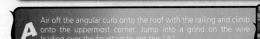

K Pop off the semi-circular curb into a grind on the blue awning for the **Awning Grind** gap. Grind to the right and ollie off the end to get the "K".

A Air off the angular curb onto the roof with the railing and climb onto the uppermost corner. Jump into a grind on the wire leading over the fountain to get the "A".

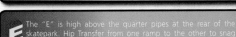

T Ride up onto the observation platform on the corner and grind the electrical wire all the way to the far end of the street to get the "T". Use Focus if necessary and grind across the top of the first utility pole to gain access to the skatepark.

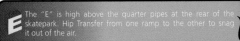

E The "E" is high above the quarter pipes at the rear of the skatepark. Hip Transfer from one ramp to the other to snag it out of the air.

COLLECT C-O-M-B-O

Ollie off the top step to get the "C" while landing in a grind on the pipes leading out into the fountain. Ollie through the water spray to get the "O" and land in a grind on the other set of pipes for the **Grind of Faith** gap. Manual to the left and grind the ledge near the steps to get the "M".

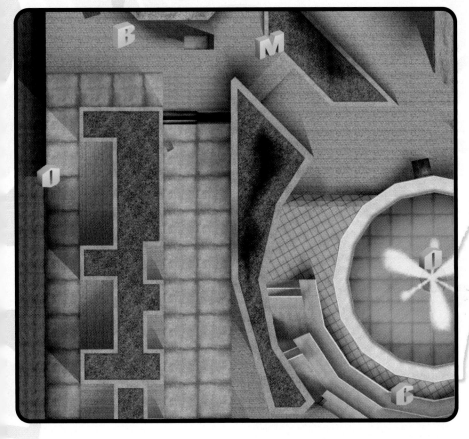

Maintain as much speed as possible, roll up the ramp to the observation platform and ollie into a grind on the electrical wire. Grind the wire over the top of the first utility pole and on towards the final letter.

Intro

Skater Basics

Trick Lists

Story Mode

Gaps

Classic Mode

Multiskater

Secrets

SMACK ALL THE BAGS

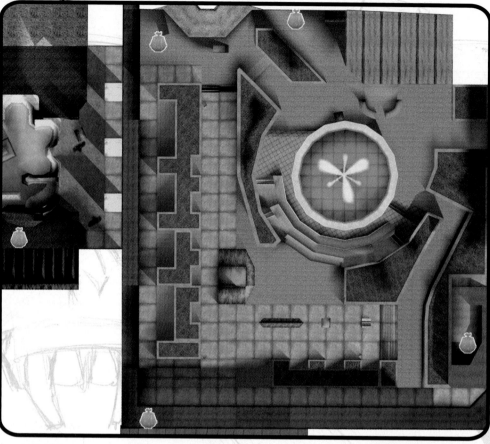

One of the bags is on the ground between the building with the blue awning and the one with the observation platform.

Another bag is sitting on the side of the street between the building with the observation platform and the fenced-off skatepark.

The third bag is at the opposite end of the street from the second one. Skate down the road, keeping the plaza on the left, and the bag is straight ahead.

Gain some speed by grinding down the railing of the staircase to the right of the starting point and launch off the angled curb onto the roof straight ahead. There is a bag on the lower rooftop.

The final bag is to the left of the skatepark across the street from the main plaza. Grind the electrical wire from the observation platform over the first utility pole to gain access to the area.

SMASH THE 5 HOAGIES

There is a hoagie on the ledge to the right of the fountain, as viewed from the starting point.

Air off the semi-circular curbs onto the blue awning across the fountain from the starting point.

Launch off the angled curb onto the rooftop to the right of the starting point. Climb onto the upper portion of the roof to smash the hoagie.

Climb onto the THPS sign to smash the next hoagie.

The final hoagie is on the low-lying ledge to the left of the fountain, as viewed from the starting point.

TRIPLE HEELFLIP OVER THE THPS SIGN

From the starting point, head to the right and launch off the kicker in front of the THPS Sign. Perform a Triple Heelflip in the air (Right + Flip, Flip, Flip) and land it cleanly.

GET THE SECRET TAPE

The Secret Tape is hovering high in the air, over the grass and tree between the fountain and the road. Skate along the sidewalk towards the Secret Tape and Wallride into a grind on the ledge to the left of the sidewalk. Ollie off the kinked end of the ledge to get popped into the air high enough to grab the Secret Tape.

LOS ANGELES

Complete 6 Goals at Canada or Philadelphia to unlock this location.

5 Stat Points available.

Grind curved ledge to open grates.

Grind 4 rails to trigger earthquake!

Grind 4 rails to trigger earthquake!

COURSE GOALS

High Score - 325,000 Points
Pro Score - 650,000 Points
Sick Score - 1,000,000 Points
High Combo - 250,000 Points
Collect S-K-A-T-E
Collect C-O-M-B-O
Blow Up the 5 Ice Lattes
Roll the Purple Gap
Crush 5 Low Carb Dishes
Get the Secret Tape

SCORING GOALS

The Los Angeles course is one of the most popular courses from *Tony Hawk's Pro Skater 3* and its notoriety is due in large part to the lengthy grind-combos available throughout the city. Although there are plenty of half pipes and quarter pipes in Los Angeles, the lengthy curbs, staircases, and electrical wires make the city a street-skater's paradise.

Knock off the scoring requirements with a lengthy combo that originates right at the starting point. Begin with a Triple Kickflip over the grass for the **Bunker** gap and land in a manual. Hop onto the rail near the sidewalk for the **Northern Tremor** gap and trick clear across the street into a grind on the semi-circular ledge for the **West Side** gap. Quickly hop into a Special Grind on the fountain and grind it lap after lap to build up an enormous base score. Use Focus to keep the grind going as long as possible. Trick into a Special Manual on the street and add some flip tricks to the combo to boost the multiplier.

Sick Mode: The High Score (750,000), Pro Score (150,000), Sick Score (2,000,000) and High Combo (550,000) goals can all be taken care of with the line described previously. And if that doesn't do it for you, use some Special Tricks when tackling the COMBO letters. Extend the combo past the library via the planters and across the street to the quarter pipes for added points.

COLLECT S-K-A-T-E

S From the starting point, skate along the wall to the right and Wallie off the end of it to snag the "S" out of the air.

K Transfer onto the rooftop near the circular fountain and air out of the ramp on the left-hand side to get the "K" hovering above.

A Hit the **Ridiculous Spine** behind the carwash to reach the "A" floating above it.

T Grind the concrete quarter pipes opposite the carwash and transfer to a grind on the far edge of the fire truck. Air off the cab into a Wallride on the side of the building and Wallie up to the "T" high above.

E The "E" hovers just under the freeway, near the support by the library. Grind up the wire to the roof of the library and Boneless onto the freeway (causing the earthquake isn't unnecessary). Hop off the board and drop into a hanging position from the side of the freeway over the yellow shack. Tap Down on the controls to begin to fall while pushing towards the "E" underneath the highway to get it.

COLLECT C-O-M-B-O

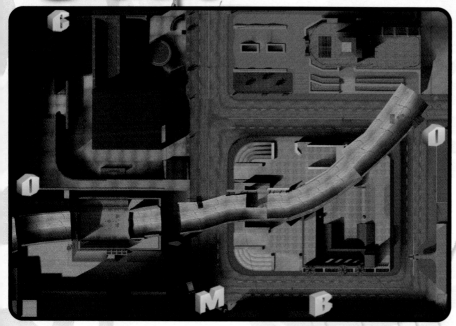

Skate to the rear of the office building with the circular fountain in front of it and air from the ground up to the "C" floating high above the ground. Land in a grind on the ledge for the **They're GRATE!** Gap and carry the grind across the ledges for the **Doorway Hop** gap towards the carwash.

Ollie out of the grind for the "O" and manual towards the fire tuck. Slide up the quarter pipe into a grind on the concrete quarter pipes to the right of the fire truck and trick into a grind on the edge of the truck for the "M". Pop off the cab of the truck into a grind on the building's ledge and Wallie into the air to snag the "B". Land in a grind on the steps below and carefully maintain the grind around the corner, past the theatre, and over to the bank where the final "O" is.

Use Special Grinds whenever possible during this combo as the line can be worth over 500,000 points with a bit of practice. Use some high speed Special Air Tricks to help increase the point tally.

BLOW UP THE 5 ICE LATTES

The first of the lattes sits on the quarter pipe directly behind the starting point. Turn around and grind across it.

Descend the steps from the starting point and turn to the right. Wallie into a grind on the edge of the office building near the corner where the trailers are blocking the road.

Enter the Morehead hotel entryway across from the plaza and air off the quarter pipe into a grind above the sign to smash the third latte.

One of the ice lattes is atop the roof of the carwash. Leap to the roof, then ride up into a lip trick on the sign to destroy the drink.

The final ice latte is difficult to spot if you don't know exactly where to look. Grind up the fire truck's ladder to the ledge and side jump over to the billboard across the street from the purple shack for the **Nice Move** gap. Get off the skateboard and climb onto the window ledge behind the billboard to find the final drink.

ROLL THE PURPLE GAP

The purple gap in question isn't the **Purple Transfer** that involves airing between the half pipe and the purple quarter pipe. Instead, air up and over the purple half pipe from one side to the other. Start near the stone spheres and ride up the back side of the purple half pipe. Ollie over the pipe while tapping into a Roll (Grab Button + Left, Left). Land it cleanly for the **Purple Skippin'** gap.

CRUSH 5 LOW CARB DISHES

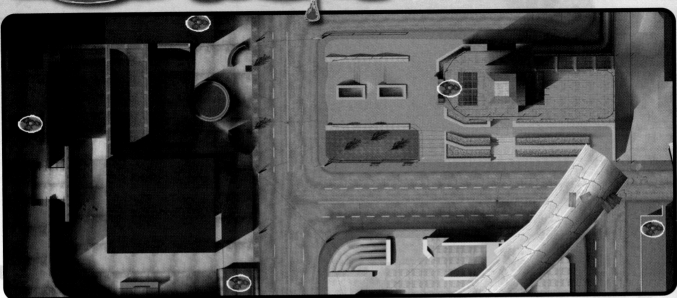

Grind the lengthy brown ledge behind the office building for the **They're GRATE!** gap bonus. This causes the grates on the floor to open. Drop inside to find the first low carb dish.

Grind up the cable to the roof of the library and roll around to the front. There is a low carb dish sitting out in the open on the roof, ready to be crushed.

The final low carb dish is atop the awning of the bank. It's directly across the street from the yellow stone shack. Double jump from the ledge and climb up.

Skate through the glass windows near the trailers on the street to crush the low carb dish on the bench in the building's lobby.

Climb onto the kiosk near the carwash and stomp the meal left sitting there.

GET THE SECRET TAPE

The Secret Tape is atop the library. Grind up the wire that stretches from the ground to the left of the starting point up to the lower roof. Skate around to the front of the library's roof and hop off the board. Leap and climb from ledge to ledge until at the top of the roof where the Secret Tape is.

Intro

Skater Basics

Trick Lists

Story Mode

Gaps

Classic Mode

Multiskater

Secrets

THE TRIANGLE

Complete 6 Goals at Los Angeles to unlock this location.

5 Stat Points available.

Grind the missiles to access the secret area!

COURSE GOALS

High Score - 500,000 Points

Pro Score - 1,000,000 Points

Sick Score - 1,500,000 Points

High Combo - 400,000 Points

Collect S-K-A-T-E

Collect C-O-M-B-O

Collect 5 Treasure Chests

Find the Secret Tape

Activate the Triangles!

Bust a Lip Trick on the UFO!

SCORING GOALS

As it has been with many of the courses in Classic Mode, the route outlined by the COMBO line on Triangle is definitely one of the best places to begin your assault on the scoring goals. Start with a couple of quick aerial tricks on the half pipes near the starting point, then side up the ramp and into a grind. Trick across to the rocks near the mountain for the **Cross Your Rock Fingers** gap and carefully trick back into a grind on the half pipe.

Transfer the grind to the rocks near the water and, from there, to the helicopter's propeller blade for the **Ledge 2 Blade** gap. Special Manual across to the wall in the distance and throw down a Special Trick off the base of the wall. Land in a Special Grind on the wall and build the base score up to over 35,000 points. Once satisfied with the base score, try tricking back and forth on the wall's ledges for the **Wall Crossing** gap.

Sick Mode: The High Score (1,000,000), Pro Score (2,000,000), Sick Score (3,000,000) and High Combo (750,000) requirements call for a bit more than the combo outlined above. Fortunately, the beaches of Triangle are perfect for improvisational skating. The majority of the ledges, ramps, and crashed ships and planes line up exceptionally well with one another, making it possible to combo numerous items in a single line. The wide open beaches are perfect for Special Manuals and the lengthy half pipes and the quarter pipes provide ample opportunity to bracket a lengthy combo with a couple of big air maneuvers.

COLLECT S-K-A-T-E

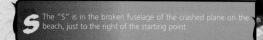
S The "S" is in the broken fuselage of the crashed plane on the beach, just to the right of the starting point.

K Grind the shipwreck to the left of the large cockpit where the Secret Tape was.

A Air off the ramp at the base of the structure under the helipad to get the "A"

T The "T" hovers above the structure beside the pirate ship. Transfer up and over the small wooden roof section to get it.

E Board the pirate ship and air up off the main deck along the mast near the bow. The "E" is just above the deck of the ship.

COLLECT C-O-M-B-O

Ride up the half pipe on the left and begin grinding on the coping. Trick across to the rocks straight ahead and land in a grind for the **Cross Your Rock Fingers** gap and to get the "O". Gap back across to the other side of the half pipe. Hold the grind off the riser onto the lower coping and continue the combo onto the rock finger near the water in the distance. Grind around to the left and ollie off the end of the rock formation into a grind on the helicopter's propeller to score the "M" and the **Ledge 2 Blade** gap.

Land in a manual and steer it straight ahead towards the "B" near the brick wall. Tap the Spine Transfer Button after nabbing the "B" to straighten out and land in a grind on the wall. Ollie across to the right-hand side of the wall for the **Wall Crossing** gap. Ollie into a manual on the platform to the right of the wall and air off the ramp at the back end of it to snag the "O" while boarding the pirate ship. Don't try to Spine Transfer into the ship, as you'll likely soar over the "O". Instead, push Up on the controls to board it the old fashioned way.

COLLECT 5 TREASURE CHESTS

The first of the treasure chests is on the structure to the left of the triangle nearest the water. Climb up onto it to get it.

Run around the beach clockwise towards the pirate ship. The next chest is on the beach near the ship's anchor.

Climb onto the rocky walkway to the left of the helipad and follow it in the opposite direction of the pirate ship to find another treasure chest.

Grind the outer ledge of the lengthy wall away from the pirate ship to find another treasure chest.

The final treasure chest is on the ground, in a rocky alcove near the water between a sunken ship and the large crashed airplane cockpit.

GET THE SECRET TAPE

The Secret Tape floats high above the cockpit of the crashed jumbo jet. Approach the vertical cockpit section from the left and Spine Transfer into it off the rocks. Once in the bowl-like cockpit, trick off the sides to get as much speed as possible and launch into the air to pluck the Secret Tape down from above.

ACTIVATE THE TRIANGLES!

There are three triangles on the beach that must be activated by grinding on them. The first is near the water, just beyond the half pipes. The other two are closer to the center of the island, near the large panels on the rock walls. Activate all three triangles and pop into a grind on the electrical current that runs between the three antennae that appears.

BUST A LIP TRICK ON THE UFO!

Skate across the helipad and Spine Transfer down onto the beach. Skate straight ahead towards the banked face of the wall and launch right up into the air to lip trick on the UFO above. Hold the lip trick long enough to claim the **Mother Ship Lip** gap to get credit for completing the goal.

Tony Hawk's Underground 2 introduces two new multiplayer games titled Scavenger Hunt and Elimi-Skate, the latter of which is only available online.

The online arena is a great place to test out your abilities with other top skaters from around the world. Before you go online, though, spend some time creating a Custom Skater with a unique look. Part of the fun in playing *Tony Hawk's Underground 2* online is seeing all of the crazy characters people create. Similarly, design a custom graphic so you can leave your mark across the course. Never head into competition without assigning a whole assortment of Special Tricks to your skater. Consider using the following setup: 3 Special Grinds, 3 Special Manuals, 2 Special Grabs, 2 Special Airs, and 1 Special Lip Trick.

TRICK ATTACK

This is a multiplayer version of the High Score mode. Here, skaters compete against one another to see who can earn the highest score within the allotted time limit (select between 30 seconds and 10 minutes). Put a lengthy scoring run together and set to the task of topping your opponent. The number of points you earn isn't what matters, only that you have more than the competition.

SCAVENGER HUNT

This addition is fun and it really rewards those who know the ins-and-outs of each of the various courses. Scavenger Hunt is a two-part game. Players spend the first portion of the game hiding their objects. Skate around the level and place an object by ollieing into the air and pressing Up + Flip Button. Since your competition must find your items, you want to place them in out of the way areas that are not only hard to reach, but also time-consuming to get to.

Once everyone has placed his or her items, the Scavenger Hunt can begin. Skate around the course with your eyes peeled for brightly colored objects floating in the air. Skate through the objects to collect them. The person who collects the most objects before time runs out is the winner.

SCORE CHALLENGE

This mode is similar to Trick Attack, but instead of playing for a specific duration, players choose a set score (choose from 100,000 to 100,000,000 points). The game continues until a skater or team reaches the chosen score. Take the players' abilities into account before choosing a point total. Save the 100,000,000-point goal for online team competitions, unless you're one of the few people who regularly drop 8-figure combos.

COMBO MAMBO

Combo Mambo is a timed game in which skaters compete to see who can score the highest combo. Select a time limit (30 seconds to 10 minutes) and get to laying down as big a combo as you can. The scores don't accumulate throughout the match. Rather, your highest combo remains as your score for the round until you beat it. Whoever had the highest combo at any point during the contest wins.

SLAP!

This is a great game to play when there is a vast difference in the abilities of the skaters present, as the object is simply to get enough speed and run into other skaters. Select a time limit (30 seconds to 10 minutes) and start grinding and tricking to build up your skater's momentum, then seek out other skaters and crash into them. Whoever has the most speed at the time of collision remains upright and gets a point for a Slap. Whoever has the most Slaps when time expires wins.

KING OF THE HILL

King of the Hill is another great game to play with a group of skaters of mixed abilities. The object is to see who can hold onto the Crown for the longest total time by avoiding the other skaters. Select a winning time of possession (30 seconds to 10 minutes) and take to the course in search of the Crown.

Whoever has the Crown suffers a dramatic decrease in speed the longer they hold onto it, making it easier for others to swipe it (collide with other skaters to steal the Crown). The key to victory is in maintaining lengthy combos. Additionally, it's also possible to hide on many of the levels. Consider hopping off the board and climbing to hard to reach areas in order to extend your time with the Crown.

GRAFFITI

Graffiti mode tests the player's ability to perform a variety of combos throughout an entire course. Each player is assigned a color and it is up to them to "paint" as many environmental objects as possible by tricking on them. Ramps, rails, ledges, etc. display the color of the person who incorporated that object into the higher scoring line. Players can steal tags from one another by scoring more points on a terrain than their opponent. Whoever has the most tags at the end of the time limit (30 seconds to 10 minutes) is the winner.

Graffiti is a very popular online game as it rewards those who know the course the best, as well as those who can link together lengthy combos. When playing online, concentrate on your own combo and not on stealing tags from opponents. It's always good to paint over another skater's object, but avoid fixating on a particular area as there is always the chance that the other skater incorporated it into a combo beyond your current ability. There are always areas off the beaten path that possess numerous ledges and rails; seek them out and make them your own!

HORSE

Horse is just like the old backyard basketball game of the same name. Here, players take turns trying to one-up each other with bigger and better scoring combos. Players have between 10 and 30 seconds to begin their combo and it ends when they either crash or touch down on all four wheels. The person who goes first sets the score with their first combo and play continues back and forth until someone is unable to beat the set score. That person then gets a letter. The first person to spell the entire word (up to 15 characters) is the loser.

FREE SKATE

The name says it all. Grab your board and skate to your heart's content without the hassle of timers and objectives. Free Skate is perfect for warming up or just hanging out online with your fellow skaters.

Intro

Skater Basics

Trick Lists

Story Mode

Gaps

Classic Mode

Multiskater

Secrets

firefight

Firefight is another great game to play when there is a wide variety of skill levels present. In Firefight, players shoot Fireballs at one another by ollieing into the air and tapping Up + Flip Button to shoot one from the front of the board or Down + Flip Button to shoot one behind them. Players begin the game with 100 health points and each hit by a Fireball costs a loss of 10 health points. One of the great things about the controls for Firefight is that it's possible to perform a Double or Triple Fireball attack by tapping the Flip Button repeatedly while airborne, just as if attempting a Triple Impossible. The Fireballs spread out like a fan, making it much easier to hit erratic skaters.

elimi-skate

Elimi-Skate is an online-only game that plays exactly like Trick Attack, with the key difference being the person with the lowest score is eliminated after each round. Play continues round after round until there is only one person left standing as the winner. Although the players who are eliminated don't have to leave the game server, they are forced to watch for the following rounds. It's important when playing Elimi-Skate to avoid always going for the big all-or-nothing combo as an untimely bail could cause you to be eliminated. Instead, keep an eye on the scores list in the corner of the screen and keep your name in the middle of the list at all times. Elimi-Skate is best played with at least four people.

SECRETS

Tony Hawk's Underground 2 has a wealth of unlockable skaters, videos, and levels for those who complete the various modes of play. Newcomers to the series will be happy to learn that some of the unlockables are earned through completion of Story Mode on the Easy and Normal difficulty settings, as well as the Sick setting. Similarly, veterans and completionists can take joy in knowing that completing both modes on the Sick setting also unlocks more skaters and that finding all of the gaps on all 15 levels unlocks the various cheat codes.

REWARDS TABLE

Goal Achieved	Level Unlocked	Skaters Unlocked	Movies Unlocked
Complete Story Mode on "Easy"	Pro Skater	Shrek, Phil Margera, Peds Group A	World Destruction Tour
Complete Story Mode on "Normal"	Pro Skater	The Hand, Paulie, Peds Group B	World Destruction Tour
Complete Story Mode on "Sick"	Pro Skater	Call of Duty Soldier, Nigel, Peds Group C	World Destruction Tour
Complete Story Mode with 100%	N/A	Peds Group F	Pro Bails 2
Complete Classic Mode on "Normal"	The Triangle	Steve-O, THPS1 Tony, Peds Group D	Pro Bails 1
Complete Classic Mode on "Sick"	The Triangle	Jesse James, Natas Kaupas, Peds Group E	Pro Bails 1
Complete Classic Mode with 100%	N/A	Peds Group G	Neversoft Skates
Get all gaps on all 15 levels	N/A	Peds Group H	*Cheat Codes*
Complete Boston in Story Mode	N/A	Ben Franklin	N/A
Complete Barcelona in Story Mode	N/A	Bull Fighter	N/A
Complete Berlin in Story Mode	N/A	Graffiti Tagger	N/A
Complete Australia in Story Mode	N/A	Shrimp Vendor	N/A
Complete New Orleans in Story Mode	N/A	Jester	N/A
Complete Skatopia in Story Mode	N/A	Ryan Sheckler	N/A

BRADYGAMES®

X
TENTH ANNIVERSARY

BradyGAMES published its first strategy guide in November of 1993, and every year since then, we've made great efforts to give you the best guides possible. Now celebrating our 10th anniversary, we'd like to take this opportunity to say a few things and extend a special invitation to you—our readers.

First of all, THANK YOU! Whether you're a long-time customer, or this is your first BradyGAMES guide, we appreciate your support. We hope that our guides have enhanced your overall experience when playing games. These days, completing a game isn't just about how quickly you finish. It's about uncovering absolutely everything a game has to offer: side quests, mini-games, secret characters, and multiple endings just to name a few. That's what the **TAKE YOUR GAME FURTHER**® banner at the top of our guides is all about.

Many games deserve more than just a standard strategy guide, and we recognize that. Our guides are produced with the highest quality standards and are tailored specifically for the games they cover. With the introduction of our Signature Series and Limited Edition guides, we raised the bar even higher.

Now for the "invitation" part. Although we constantly challenge ourselves to improve our guides, we'd like your help too. You're formally invited to tell us what you think about our guides. Like something we do? Let us know. Think something we've done is totally lame? Please let us know. We want your feedback no matter if it's good, bad, or just plain ugly. You can write or e-mail us at the addresses below, and we will read what you send. Your opinions are important to us, and may influence the direction for our guides in the future.

Write to:
BradyGAMES
800 E. 96th Street, 3rd Floor
Indianapolis, IN 46240

Send e-mail to:
feedback@bradygames.com

For now, we hope you enjoy this guide. Thanks again for choosing BradyGAMES.

www.thug2online.com

TONY HAWK'S UNDERGROUND 2
THUG 2 WIRELESS
Official Strategy Guide
Tips for ruling The World Destruction Tour anytime, anywhere.

Game Modes

STORY MODE: Join Tony Hawk and Bam Margera on a round-the-world, no-holds-barred, destruction tour through six international courses. Soar through the streets of Sydney, rip rails in New Orleans during Mardi Gras, and speed through the backwoods pipes of Skatopia! Pull off manuals, grinds, ollies and quarter-pipe air. Grab items like cash, spray paint and cell phones.

FREE SKATE: Hone your skills on any level. There's no time limit, items or goals. Just rack up the sickest combos and go for the high-score.

TUTORIAL: Learn the ropes to becoming a pro. Each tutorial provides the 411 on how to successfully pull off maneuvers like ground manuals, lip grabs and quarter-pipe flips.

Trick Lists

	Name	Command
Ground Tricks	Manual	RIGHT, then 1, LEFT, then 3
	Nose Manual	RIGHT, then 3, LEFT, then 1
	Ollie	5
Air Tricks	Indy Grab	RIGHT, 5, then 1 (IN THE AIR) LEFT, 5, then 3 (IN THE AIR)
	Kick Flip	RIGHT, 5, then 3 (IN THE AIR) LEFT, 5, then 1 (IN THE AIR)
Grinds	50-50 Grind	MOVE OR JUMP ONTO RAIL
	Nose Grind	GRIND RIGHT, 5, then 3 (IN THE AIR) GRIND LEFT, 5, then 1 (IN THE AIR)
	Tail Grind	GRIND RIGHT, 5, then 1 (IN THE AIR) GRIND LEFT, 5, then 3 (IN THE AIR)
Quarter Pipe Air Tricks	Grab	RIGHT OFF A PIPE, then 1 LEFT OFF A PIPE, then 3
	Spin	RIGHT OFF A PIPE, then 3 LEFT OFF A PIPE, then 1
Quarter Pipe Lip Tricks	Tail Plant	RIGHT INTO PIPE, HOLD 1 LEFT INTO PIPE, HOLD 3
	Hand Plant	RIGHT INTO PIPE, HOLD 3 LEFT INTO PIPE, HOLD 1
	Lip Grind	2 or 8 WHILE HOLDING A PLANT

Boston

COURSE OVERVIEW: Boston may be the first destination in story mode, but this huge outdoor park still has plenty of opportunities for pulling off dope combos. Rail the planters, benches, and cannons to link big air combos between the quarter pipes on either end of the course.
COURSE GOAL: Knock the heads off of five American patriot statues. Air off the ramps on either side of the statues by hitting 5 to give them a skateboard haircut. Try pressing Trick A (1) or Trick B (3) in the air to pull of an indy grab or kick flip for extra style.
MYSTERY GOAL: Grind all of the cannons on the map to get an explosive reaction.
ILL SCORING: Snatching the bonus items takes some airborne maneuvering. T.H.U.G. 2 Wireless may be old-school 2D, but you can still move horizontally in the air by holding 2 and 8.

Barcelona

COURSE OVERVIEW: The sick rails in Parc Guell are ripe for grinding. Use the trick opportunities on this map to pull off multilevel combos or take the high road across a gap.
COURSE GOAL: Rail the salamander sculptures. There are 5 salamanders and all are positioned on staircase railings. Take out the three salamanders on the left side of the map first, then go for the remaining two on the right. If you start trippin', the salamanders without the spine scales are the ones you've already railed!
MYSTERY GOAL: Skate past the toreadors with some Toro, Toro-action to impress them.
ILL SCORING: You don't have to wait for a half pipe to rack up the high-points. Ride up a quarter pipe and hit Trick A (1) then turn around, ride up the same quarter pipe again and hit Trick B (3). You'll get an additional multiplier each time you repeat.

Berlin

COURSE OVERVIEW: This industrial train yard in Berlin holds a few wicked surprises. Use the chain link fence at the bottom of the map to rail from one end of the map to the other while activating the crossing gates to clear the gaps in between.
COURSE GOAL: Flip the 5 switches to derail the cargo train full of wieners. The cargo trains that pass by must be ridden if you want to reach the 3rd, 4th and 5th switch locations. Reach the top of the tunnel by hitting (5) while airing out of the quarter-pipes on either side of the overhang, then take out Switch 3 on the left side of the platform. Hit stop (0) near the platform edge, wait for a train to pass underneath, then skate onto it and press up (2) to reach the area at the top of the map and take out Switches 4 and 5!
MYSTERY GOAL: Punk the nihilists' boom boxes to see them rock out.
ILL SCORING: There's a pattern to the balance meter used for manuals, grinds and lip tricks. Pressing right (6) and left (4) in quick succession can keep your skater hanging onto combos for days.

Sydney

COURSE OVERVIEW: The heat is definitely on in this tricky Aussie beach course. Stopping (0) in front of the pipes, then airing out of them slowly while pressing 5 in the air will help you land on top of the hard to reach graffiti structures.
COURSE GOAL: Knock down Nigel's cameramen, then take out Nigel himself. To reach all of the camera man and Nigel, you'll need to activate the two cranes on this map and skate over the construction areas. Ollie (5) into the crane cabs to drop the metal girders, then air off the wooden ramp to land on the girder to clear the last part of the gap. All 5 camera men must be thrashed before you can go for Nigel.
MYSTERY GOAL: Pull off a 50 point combo near the kangaroos to prevent them from boxing you.
ILL SCORING: Not all items can be attained in the most obvious ways. Sometimes leaping off pipes at odd angles or tweaking jumps off ledges can score the uber tricky items.

New Orleans

COURSE OVERVIEW: It's off to the Big Easy for some crazy rails and death defying leaps. The key to besting this course is to make it to the roof by grinding the multiple balconies and airing over the gaps between the buildings.
COURSE GOAL: Grab 5 sets of beads and deliver them to the hotties on the balcony. A beaded necklace must be snatched before the babes will go wild for you. If you have trouble reaching the beads floating over the balconies, ollie while railing (5) to snag them. Once you have obtained a beaded necklace, skate past a babe to give it to her and receive your... reward.
MYSTERY GOAL: Snake all the voodoo dolls to prove you're a rail legend.
ILL SCORING: The best way to score huge combo multipliers is to air trick a few times (5 then 3, or 5 then 1), turn around, and perform a different air trick on the way back. Repeat as many times as you can, until you bail or your fingers cramp.

Skatopia

COURSE OVERVIEW: Skatopia is the final course in Story Mode -- a dense freestyle park with mad trick opportunities. Transfer from the wooden bowls to the suspended clotheslines to achieve maximum combo points.
COURSE GOAL: Find all the video tapes and take them to Bam before your time is up. You must use the two pipe tunnels that run underneath the compound to make it through each section, score all 4 the tapes and finish this course within the 5 minute time limit. Once you've snagged all the tapes, you can find Bam hanging out near the two porta-potties on the right side of the course.
MYSTERY GOAL: Clear the trashed car gaps to set them on fuego.
ILL SCORING: To get big air and distance, hit 5 when you're in the cradle of a pipe. Your skater will shoot into the stratosphere and hitting 5 again will send him soaring over hard to pass obstacles.

Cheat!

Having trouble dealing? No worries. Enter the keys that spell out "n00b" in the Level Selection Menu to unlock all levels.

Co-Published by **JAMDAT** mobile **ACTIVISION**

Find out about a free download to optimize Intel motherboards for faster game play at www.intel.com/go/gaming